# America's Quest for Supremacy and the Third World

## A Gramscian Analysis

Enrico Augelli and Craig Murphy

Pinter Publishers, London

This book was written under the auspices of the Center for International Affairs, Harvard University.



First published in Great Britain in 1988 by
Pinter Publishers Limited
25 Floral Street, London WC2E 9DS



**British Library Cataloguing in Publication Data**
A CIP catalogue record for this book is available from the British Library

**Library of Congress Cataloging-in-Publication Data**
Augelli, Enrico.
America's quest for supremacy and the Third World.
Bibliography: p.
Includes index.
1. United States—Foreign relations—1945– —Philosophy. 2. United States—Foreign relations—Developing countries—Philosophy.
3. Developing countries—Foreign relations—United States—Philosophy. 4. Gramsci, Antonio, 1891–1937.
I. Murphy, Craig. II. Title.
E840.A93 1988 327.730172'4 88-17853
ISBN 0-86187-930-9



Typeset in 10/12 Plantin Light
by Joshua Associates Ltd, Oxford
Printed by Biddles Ltd, Guildford and King's Lynn

# Contents

# Acknowledgements

We want to thank the institution that brought us together, Harvard University's Center for International Affairs, where Augelli was a European Fellow and Murphy a Visiting Scholar throughout the 1984–85 academic year. This book began as papers for panels organized by Dimitris Stevis for the 1986 and 1987 annual meetings of the International Studies Association. We are grateful to him and to all of those who commented at those sessions.

We also want to thank Susan Strange, who heard our first paper and suggested that we expand it into a book, and the editor she contacted, Heather Bliss, for convincing us to continue our collaboration.

We are grateful to Peter Glendening, who translated those passages from Gramsci we quote that had not previously been translated into English; Marina Aldrovandi, who provided bibliographic, translation, and editorial help as Augelli's research assistant; and Heather Stone, who helped type the manuscript.

Finally, our deepest thanks to JoAnne Yates (who put up with smoke, Craig's absences, and even charter flights) and Gabriella Carbonelli (without whom at least Enrico's part of the book never would have seen the light of day).

# Introduction

This has not been a good century for those with imperial ambitions. The defeat of Hitler's 'thousand-year' *Reich* also meant the defeat of the much older empires of modern Europe; decolonization of British, French, Dutch, and Belgian dependencies followed from the second world war. By 1975 the mutually reinforcing revolutions in the Portuguese metropole and the colonies brought the last and oldest of the modern European empires to an end as well.

Even more striking in 1975 was the fate of the global ambitions of one great victor of the world wars; America's post-war empire appeared ready to disappear with the rest. The US had lost its paramount role in the world economy that it had helped shape. American firms in the sectors that had led the unprecedented global industrial expansion after the war were losing their competitive edge; even many Americans preferred Japanese or German cars to ones built at home. American initiative in the new industries of the next industrial wave—consumer electronics and even microprocessors—appeared to be no match for that of its major allies. The American dollar was no longer good as gold; monetary maneuvers on the part of a US government desperate to make its industrial partners bear some of the costs of managing the world economy assured that. Even the comfortable assumption that American gains in productivity would always outstrip those of other industrial nations had been replaced with the uneasy realization that other industrial economies would soon outpace the United States.

The signs of the downfall of the American global system appeared clearest in its relations to its weakest partners, the less-industrialized nations of the Third World, many of them recently independent, and most of them with relatively weak governments that could not exact significant resources from their own populations. Even so, these governments had been able to make successful demands on the world economy that the United States had helped establish and still protected. Oil producing nations had doubled and redoubled the price of the leading commodity in world trade. In 1974, standing behind the oil producers, the Third World defiantly demanded a change in the world economy's rules, a 'New International Economic Order,' that would further divide the power to govern international economic affairs, strengthening the non-oil producing Third World nations enough to make their alliance as much of a potential challenger to US supremacy as America's industrial partners and the oil-rich nations had become.

It was not only on economic grounds that the American empire was challenged. The US military suffered its first modern defeat, and that by a Third World army. Later, as the 1970s wore on, the United States suffered other 'defeats' in the Third World. It failed to prevent the rise of revolutionary regimes in Ethiopia, Lusophone Africa, and Afghanistan and suffered the humiliation of lacking the equipment or foresight to mount a successful attempt to rescue the American hostages held in Iran throughout the 1980 presidential campaign year.

By then the confidence of the American public in the traditional symbols of American power had been shaken for a decade. In the early 1970s, within the space of four years, Americans had to accept a half-a-dozen events they long-assumed to be impossible: the dollar became just another promise. The US lost a war. A vice-president and president were forced to resign. And even before those agonies were completed Americans suffered what was even a greater shock for the generation that had grown up in the prosperous and mobile era after the war: the oil crisis.

In the cold winter of 1973–74 the American habit of frequent, low-cost travel over the vast distances of the continent had to end. An entire *Gestalt* of freedom, ease, mobility, and plenty was broken. The cover of the radical magazine *Ramparts*, one of the voices that had helped unify the national leftist political movements of the 1960s, told the story: 'The Last Christmas in America.'

*Ramparts* looked forward to the new realism that hard times would foster, but the Christmas after the first oil crisis was also the magazine's last; there was no longer a market for its progressive vision in the bleaker nation it had foretold. Before the decade was out the US entered the deepest and most persistent economic downturn since the Great Depression of the 1930s. New graduates faced levels of unemployment that their teachers had confidently told them were unimaginable in the Keynesian world of the American post-war economy.

It was not only the American public that perceived a great change in the 1970s; the best scholarly analysis pointed to the same thing. The American community of international relations scholars alternatively lamented the end of American dominance, forecasting global calamity as a result,[1] or looked for the peaceful and productive opportunities associated with the United States becoming an 'ordinary country,' more like other industrialized nations.[2] Overseas, Fernand Braudel, perhaps the greatest authority on the modern world-economy, went even further to speculate that the global social changes of the early 1970s reflected a major global turning point, not just a major cyclical downturn in the business cycle, like the Great Depression of the 1930s, or even the beginning of the end of America's supremacy, but the beginning of the end of a cycle of European dominance of the world which began four centuries ago.

Yet, by the time Braudel's words were published in the United States, in the 1984 translation of volume three of *Civilization and Capitalism*, they already appeared *passé*. As Ronald Reagan's partisans were fond of proclaiming,

'America' was 'back.' Although some Third World economies suffered through the worst depression in their modern history, and most industrial nations experienced a decade of slow growth, the Reagan years appeared to many in the United States as ones of unprecedented prosperity. The job outlook for university graduates brightened. (Although overall unemployment generally remained higher than it had been throughout the 1970s.) Inflation moderated. Many Americans had money to spend on the new consumer products: video games, home computers, sportier cars. Americans felt confident again.

The key to that confidence, the one real change that had taken place in the Reagan years, was the reassertion of the United States's international role. After his re-election in 1984 (a year that turned out to be not quite as bad as many Americans, weaned on Orwell's vision, had spent much of their lives expecting) Reagan presided over a nation that was, once again, the world's acknowledged leader. It is true, Reagan had made no dramatic proposals to organize world opinion or transform world politics and it is doubtful that he would have had the power to do so. It is true that in Lebanon the American armed forces, enriched by Reagan's unprecedented peacetime rearmament budget, demonstrated no more competence than they had in Jimmy Carter's botched attempt to rescue the Iran hostages. And it is true that economists now worry about problems that became acute under Reagan: the growing Third World debt, the growing official US debt, and America's continuing lack of competitiveness implied by its growing trade deficit. Nevertheless, the US had won a war (albeit a small one) in Grenada, proving that the aging superpower was not yet a completely toothless tiger. And Reagan demonstrated American willingness to use force anywhere that American interests were compromised or 'American values' threatened.

We find two aspects of this new American attitude and role in the world fascinating and difficult to explain. First is the fact that the American people, who scholars often present as remarkably sophisticated politically,[3] appear to have been mobilized by an undistinguished, aging actor who tells corny jokes and rambling stories and who rarely worries about logical consistency. Second, and perhaps even more puzzling, is the fact that both America's allies and adversaries, who had objected to American leadership under Carter, despite his more caring attitude toward the world outside the US, accepted a substantial reconstruction and concentration of international power in Reagan's hands.

Both Reagan's reputation as the 'Great Communicator' and the apparent lack of any substantive change in the economic base of American power as well as the country's basically unchanged military competence suggest that explanations of both the Reagan phenomenon and the reconstruction of American supremacy will have to emphasize ideology and changes in political–economic strategy as much as the dynamics of traditional power politics. That is why we turned to Antonio Gramsci, one of the most perceptive modern students of ideology and political power, to help us explain these puzzling developments and analyze their effect on the Third World.

For those who have not yet had the chance to meet Gramsci on their intellectual journeys it may be useful to recall that this once obscure Sardinian Marxist was a man of thought and action who became the leader of the Italian Communist Party in the 1920s and died in 1937 after ten years in fascist prisons. There he wrote one of the most thoughtful modern studies of politics and society, his *Prison Notebooks*, the basis for our analysis.

In the half-century since his death scholars and politicians have studied Gramsci's writings, arguing about what he really meant, assessing the value of his ideas, and applying them to practical problems. From Italy, where his theories have become a source of inspiration for scholars across the political spectrum as well as the orthodoxy of the Italian Communist Party, analysis of Gramsci's work spread to France, and, from there, more recently, to the English-speaking world. The resulting body of research—large, although often contradictory and uneven—assures the position of Gramsci's work among the Marxist classics. Commentators on Gramsci generally agree that he made an important contribution to the renewal of Marxist theory by fighting against the economic determinism prevalent at the beginning of the century.[4] Gramsci felt that such 'economism' not only simplified a much more complex reality, but also reflected a fatalist attitude towards history and social change. He realized, as experience has shown, that capitalism would not fall nor would socialism arise in the absence of political action by an organized working class. To overcome this shortcoming of conventional Marxist interpretations, Gramsci re-evaluated the importance of society's 'superstructures' (law, religion, culture, etc.) and he attributed a new importance to politics and to political activity.

His work remains important to Marxists today. It has been used to critique the fatalism inherent in Louis Althusser's attempt to create a purely 'scientific' Marxism. (In Althusser's structural model people are forced to act out a script written by social forces over which they have little control.) Gramsci's theory recognizes the role of human will without accepting the radically voluntarist assumptions of Sartre's existentialism or those versions of the Frankfurt School's critical theory that attribute the human capacity to change the world to consciousness alone.[5]

More significantly, to us, Gramsci's ideas help bridge the gap between Marxist and liberal social science. They allow scholars from both camps to begin to understand each other by providing a common ground for communicating about their different interpretations of history and society. Gramsci ignores the strict opposition between 'Marxist' and 'bourgeois' thought that so many scholars accept, a view that makes it impossible for either camp to enrich the other. The attempt to maintain the strict opposition between camps leads both Marxist and bourgeois scholars to emphasize some of the least-realistic assumptions of their own theories. Marxist scholars fall back on economic determinism and explain every social change as the result of class struggle even when facts have to be stretched to fit the theory. Liberal scholars see self-interest underlying even the most altruistic action or else, when they have decided to reject such single-factor explanations, they fail to differentiate between fundamental forces and marginal, episodic factors.

Our research builds on the common ground for Marxist and liberal social science that Gramsci provides. This is not a book on Gramsci's thought, but a book which uses Gramsci's ideas to help understand contemporary international relations. Gramsci gives us a method of analysis which we apply to a problem which interests us, even though it may not have interested him.

This is a perfectly reasonable thing to do because even though Gramsci's theory as a whole must be considered part of what he calls the 'philosophy of praxis,' the Marxist philosophy aimed at a particular type of social transformation, his worldview can be distinguished from his analytical method and its new conceptual instruments, and either can be separated from the revolutionary strategy he recommended. We use Gramsci's analytical methods and conceptual tools, isolating them from his view of the world and leaving aside his political program. Gramsci would not have objected to this approach. He himself derived hypotheses about society from the broader philosophical analyses of perceptive thinkers whose worldviews he did not always accept, considering it, 'a process of abstraction which is inherent in the scientific method itself.'[6] Although some orthodox Marxists may see this approach as a distortion of Gramsci's thought, we would hope that instead they might consider our attempt to abstract social science theory from Gramsci's more complex philosophy of praxis as an aid in understanding his overall message. Certainly most Marxists would agree that Gramsci really did further political analysis by devising new conceptual tools. Demonstrating the usefulness of those tools is, to our minds, one way to illustrate the importance of his thought. But this means making Gramsci's work more than a mere inspiration for revolutionary strategies; it means placing Gramsci among the great social theorists, both Marxist and bourgeois, who have made significant and lasting contributions to our understanding of social reality.

Nevertheless, we accept, as Gramsci did, that totally detached, impartial social scientific analysis is not possible. As Gramsci says, in politics and sociology there are no neutral ideas, no views unaffected by the past experience, value-systems, class position, and social status of the analyst.[7] We wrote this book because we share a point of view influenced by our study and work in the development field. We believe that the aspirations and expectations of the Third World as expressed in the 1970s program for a New International Economic Order are legitimate. Moreover, we consider what might be called the 'north–south Keynesian compromise' suggested in the two major reports of the Brandt Commission[8] to be a sensible basis for ethical north–south relations and we regret that this view is not shared by more of the international community. In fact, we are convinced that only on the basis of the implementation of such a program will it be possible to build a more just international community concerned with meeting human needs and expanding human aspirations. We hope that this book will have a role in encouraging the ends we seek. By helping to expose the means through which the current system of international domination has been reinforced and the greater part of the Third World marginalized, we may be able to contribute to change by helping, as Gramsci said, 'educate politically ... those who are not in the know.'[9]

Even though we have limited ourselves to applying Gramsci's work as a method of social science analysis we still must choose among various interpretations of his work. Gramsci did not have the time to prepare his *Notebooks* for publication nor would the psychological and physical conditions in prison have allowed it. This is the first and most obvious reason why scholars disagree about what he really meant. The second stems from Gramsci's life as a political activist and writer before his imprisonment. Some see his *Notebooks* as simply a more mature development of what he believed and said previously. Others see a major 'epistemological' break between what he said as a free man and what he wrote in prison. Non-Italian-speaking readers confront a third difficulty, the lack of complete translations. The Istituto Gramsci's unabridged critical edition of the *Notebooks*, published in 1975, has yet to appear in English.[10] The much-shorter English *Selections from Prison Notebooks*,[11] inevitably leaves out important parts of the text and reorders the material in a way that necessarily reflects the editors' own concerns. Moreover, as every translator knows, translation itself always involves interpretation.

Although we were able consult the original source in the unabridged Italian edition, we were still confronted with all the other problems of interpretation and want to state our positions at the outset. For us, Gramsci's *Notebooks* do not represent a major break with his previous work. His primary goals remain constant: to dismantle capitalism and construct socialist society. Yet, his understanding of contemporary society changed as a result of his prison studies.

In prison Gramsci concentrated on three questions:

Why, contrary to Marxist theory, had a revolution taken place in underdeveloped Russia rather than in the industrialized West?

Why had fascism taken hold in Italy despite the existence of a strong and organized working class?

And, finally, why was the news about Soviet socialism under Stalin so contradictory?

In answering the first question Gramsci came to reject simplistic economic determinism. In answering the second, he abandoned the voluntarism of his youth, his belief that organized workers could do anything that they set their minds to. In answering the third, Gramsci deduced that a successful revolution did not necessarily imply the construction of a socialist and democratic society. All three questions led him to carry out a general analysis of society and develop a nuanced theory of political change. It is this analysis and theory that guides our study.

In view of our interest in applying Gramsci's insights it is irrelevant for us to enter into the debate about the 'epistemological break' or to attempt to found our interpretation on Gramsci's pre-prison writings. We believe that the *Notebooks*, though often difficult to interpret, make up a coherent whole, a work that rewards patient reading with careful attention to semantics.[12] This position also reflects the way we approach the first problem mentioned: We believe that although Gramsci was not able to provide a final, formal, order for his thoughts, his *Notebooks* are internally consistent.

Given the many problems of interpretation, we do not use Gramsci's theory of society in its entirety. To do so would require in-depth study of the dynamics of what Gramsci calls the 'historical bloc,' the dialectical unity between economic structure and superstructure, and we would have to explore all of Gramsci's various improvements upon Engels's overall model of social change, the transition from one historical social epoch to the next. This would be difficult to do now; although some interesting studies of the Gramscian historical bloc exist,[13] the body of research using this, Gramsci's 'ultimate' social concept, is too small to allow its straightforward application to international relations. Nonetheless, we recognize that a more global approach has met with some success in Robert W. Cox's application of a structuralist model inspired by Gramsci to the study of successive world orders.[14] Cox takes into account three interrelated forces—material abilities, ideas, and institutions—and identifies the dynamics of social change with the shaping of social forces by relations of production.

Our aim is at the same time more modest and more ambitious than Cox's. More modest, in that we only want to understand a limited set of problems: the Reagan phenomenon in the context of the history of American foreign policy and the way in which a new concentration of international power occurred in the United States in the 1980s.[15] More ambitious, because we believe that simply a more detailed elaboration of a few Gramscian concepts will prove more valuable for explaining international relations than the ones scholars currently have at their disposal.

Among the many concepts that Gramsci advanced—'passive revolution,' 'war of movement' versus 'war of position,' 'traditional' and 'organic intellectuals,' 'popular-national' sentiments, 'Cesarism,' 'intellectual and moral reform,' etc.—we have chosen his understanding of 'ideology' and 'supremacy' as the core of our analysis of the change in the American relationship with the Third World over the last decade. The book consists of two parts, corresponding to these two concepts. Both parts begin with an outline of one of Gramsci's concepts followed by applications.

The first part leads up to an explanation of the Reagan phenomenon. We demonstrate that Reagan reflects what Gramsci calls 'common sense' (ideology without critical reflection) and show the support for his program that can be found in what really is common sense to most Americans. To do that we first deconstruct American ideology using Gramsci's method. Then we apply the reconstructed model to analyses of the general orientations of American foreign policy and foreign assistance policy in order to verify the significance of the ideological themes we have isolated and provide the necessary historical background for understanding the changes in the 1980s. Finally, we use this substantiated model of American ideology to discuss Reagan's rise to power.

A Gramscian explanation of Reagan's success proves more powerful than the more traditional explanations offered by either 'pluralist' or 'elite' theory. According to pluralist theory, American presidents gain popular support for a political program in a national competition of ideas. In the more elaborate version, the democratic process in the United States takes place through competition among different interest groups until a coalition prevails and imposes its political orientation on the country. According to elite theory a kind of permanent conspiracy exists: American businessmen look for an instrument, a person they can trust, to control the government and dominate the country. In general, Gramscian analysis rejects both the assumption of widespread competition in parliamentary states and that of conspiracy as unrealistic. Moreover, Gramsci's emphasis on the role of cultural factors in politics makes it possible for us to derive a single explanation of the Reagan phenomenon, the long-term orientation of American foreign policy, and the unique American approach to relations with the less-industrialized world, three factors which combine in the reconstruction of American supremacy in the 1980s.

The second part of the book analyzes how the United States succeeded in reconcentrating international power in the 1980s and looks at the consequences of that development for the Third World. At the center of our analysis is Gramsci's concept of 'supremacy,' a broader concept than his more widely-known notion of 'hegemony.' We transpose the use Gramsci makes of Machiavelli's distinction between concentrating power either by force or through consensus at different levels of society (the economy, civil society, and political society) to international society. This presents no insurmountable difficulties due to the unusually central role the United States government has played in the capitalist world-economy since the second world war. Gramsci's concepts are particularly appropriate for interpreting American foreign policy during the years when this role was challenged and then reestablished. Reagan's global 'counterrevolution' can be described in the same terms Gramsci used to propose a strategy for a successful revolution. Of course, we are not suggesting that Reagan or his advisors consciously followed Gramsci's injunctions, but that they have been successful in so far as they have followed—at times by chance, at times because no alternative was available—the methods Gramsci proposed. We hope that our demonstration that Reagan's success has been a function of the degree to which he has been an unwitting 'Gramscian' will serve as a convincing confirmation of the significance of Gramsci's thought even to anti-Marxist scholars.

## Notes

1. An early theme of much of the neorealist scholarship and studies of international regimes that has filled the pages of prestigious American international relations journals for fifteen years. See Susan Strange's analysis of the ethnocentric motivation of this, nonetheless, useful literature, '*Cave, hic dragones*: A Critique of Regime Analysis,' *International Organization*, 36 (1982): 479–96.
2. Richard Rosecrance, ed., *America as an Ordinary Country* (Ithaca: Cornell University Press, 1976).
3. E.g., Samuel P. Huntington, *American Politics: The Promise of Disharmony* (Cambridge, MA: Harvard University Press, 1981).
4. Introductions to Gramsci in English include: Joseph V. Femia, *Gramsci's Political Thought* (Oxford: Clarendon Press, 1977); John Hoffman, *The Gramscian Challenge* (Oxford: Basil Blackwell, 1984); James Joll, *Gramsci* (Glasgow: Fontana, 1977); Anne Showstack Sassoon, *Gramsci's Politics*, 2nd ed. (London: Hutchinson, 1987); and Roger Simon, *Gramsci's Political Thought: An Introduction* (London: Lawrence and Wishart, 1982), which has a useful short annotated bibliography.
5. See Robert Bocock, *Hegemony* (London: Tavistock, 1986).
6. Antonio Gramsci, *Quaderni del Carcere* (Torino: Einaudi, 1975), II, 1458.
7. See pp. 15–16, below.
8. Independent Commission on International Development Issues, *North-South: A Programme for Survival* (Cambridge, MA: MIT Press, 1980) and The Brandt Commission, *Common Crisis North-South: Cooperation for World Recovery* (Cambridge, MA: MIT Press, 1983).
9. This is a comment on Machiavelli's doctrine. Antonio Gramsci, *Selections from Prison Notebooks*, Quentin Hoare and Geoffrey Nowell Smith, ed. and trans. (London: Lawrence and Wishart, 1971), 135.
10. Antonio Gramsci, *Quaderni del Carcere*, Istituto Gramsci critical edition, Valentino Gerratana, ed. (Torino: Einaudi, 1975). This work is based on ten years of research with Gramsci's original manuscripts and consists of four volumes. Volume I: Quaderni (Notebooks) 1–5 (1929–32). Volume II: Quaderni 6–11 (1930–33). Volume III: Quaderni 12–29 (1932–35). Volume IV contains an extremely useful and extensive (nearly 1000–page) critical appendix, which includes, among other things, an index of works quoted in the *Notebooks*, several critical notes, a subject index, and a valuable concordance which allows the reader to trace Gramsci's original passages in the previous editions of the *Notebooks*, the first Einaudi edition, published between 1948 and 1951, and the Editori Riuniti reprint of 1971.
11. Quentin Hoare and Geoffrey Nowell Smith, ed. and trans. (London: Lawrence and Wishart, 1971). This selection is based on the first Einaudi edition and is accompanied by an 80–page introduction on Gramsci's life and works in their historical context. The book has a short, 10–page, name and subject index.
12. A great deal of the existing confusion about what Gramsci really said is a function of a lack of widespread understanding of his terminology. It is worth emulating

Norberto Bobbio's path-breaking paper presented at the 'Convegno di studi gramsciani' held in Rome in 1958, in which he explained the three different meanings of 'dialettica' as used by Gramsci. See Norberto Bobbio, 'Nota sulla dialettica in Gramsci,' *Studi gramsciani* (Roma: Editori Riuniti, 1973), 73–86.

13. See in particular, Hughes Portelli, *Gramsci e il blocco storico* (Bari: Laterza, 1973).
14. Especially, 'Gramsci, Hegemony, and International Relations: An Essay in Method,' *Millennium*, 12 (1983): 162–75.
15. Our questions differ from Stephen Gill's in, 'US Hegemony: Its Limits and Prospects in the Reagan Era,' *Millennium* 15 (1986): 311–36. Gill treats the domestic sources of Reagan's rise as less problematic and his more structural interpretation, which resembles Cox's, leads him to treat the 1970s as a 'crisis of authority' for the US but not as a real challenge to US supremacy.

# PART I
# IDEOLOGY

# 1 Gramsci's understanding of ideology

'Ideology' can mean so many different things that when lay people discuss it they often misunderstand one another and when scholars try to clarify things they often leave us in more of a muddle. The least-confusing and most-thorough way of examining the concept would be to begin with the history of the term, starting with its first use by Destutt de Tracy, then looking at what Marx and Engels said, and finally tracing the reaction of various schools, both Marxist and non-Marxist, right up to the most recent structuralist and semiological interpretations.[1] Gramsci's thoughts on ideology would be only a small part of such a study, even though the study of ideology makes up a significant part of his life work. Because he criticized the Marxist economism prevailing at his time and held that it was necessary to reassess the importance of society's superstructure, ideology, an essential element of the superstructure, came to assume a central role in Gramsci's work. Gramsci developed an unusually clear understanding of the subject through his own historical investigation. Repeating his analysis of the scholarly debates about ideology would take us far from our purpose, but we will mention those debates as we clear the field of interpretations that Gramsci considered inadequate.

## Gramsci's critique

First of all, Gramsci denies that ideologies are mere illusions. He asserts their real existence and points to the evidence of their vitality and their influence over historical events. This represents a break with a great deal of earlier Marxist thinking. The view that ideologies are illusions is central to the only work Marx and Engels devoted to the topic, *The German Ideology*,[2] which lays the foundation for a materialist interpretation of history in opposition to German idealism, their target. Their analysis exemplifies the very simple materialist concept of ideology that Gramsci rejects:

> Morality, religion, metaphysics, all the rest of ideology and their corresponding forms of consciousness, thus no longer retain the semblance of independence. They have no history, no development; but men, developing their material production and their material intercourse, alter, along with this, their real existence, their thinking, and the products of their thinking. Life is not determined by consciousness, but consciousness by life.[3]

and again

It follows from this that all struggles within the state, the struggle between democracy, aristocracy and monarchy, the struggle for the franchise, etc., etc., are merely the illusory forms in which the real struggles of the different classes are fought out among one another.[4]

In his later work Marx disparaged much of the language and analysis of *The German Ideology* and he retreated from its naive materialism. But this ideology, too, had its own power. It was diffused in the official doctrine of the early Second International.

Gramsci tries to correct this narrow interpretation of Marxism by recalling, 'Another proposition of Marx is that a popular conviction often has the same energy as a material force.'[5] When ideas become widely-held convictions they play a prominent role in social history although they are not eternal forces of history that philosophical idealists posited and that cruder materialists, rightly, criticize. Nevertheless, as Gramsci contends, ideology cannot be relegated to an illusory, fantastic world devoid of any significance and of any real consequences.

Gramsci also opposes a common view that the force of ideology must always be a negative one, a position that has long been held both by many Marxists and by most positivists. The negative connotation of 'ideology,' as prejudice and source of error, even predates both Marxism and positivism, as Karl Mannheim documents in *Ideology and Utopia*.[6] Mannheim denounces what were in his time (the 1930s) the most recent, totalizing developments of this interpretation, referring in particular to the idea of 'false consciousness,' a concept implicit in the passages quoted from *The German Ideology*. Engels explained the connection this way:

Ideology is a process accomplished by the so-called thinker consciously, it is true, but with a false consciousness. The real motive forces impelling him remain unknown to him; otherwise it simply would not be an ideological process. Hence he imagines false or seeming motive forces. Because it [ideology] is a process of thought he derives its form as well as its content from pure thought, either his own or that of his predecessors.[7]

Gramsci completely rejects this purely negative conception of ideology:

The bad sense of the word has become widespread, with the effect that the theoretical analysis of the concept of ideology has been modified and denatured. The process leading up to this error [the equation of 'ideology' with 'error'] can be easily reconstructed: 1) ideology is identified as distinct from the structure, and it is asserted that it is not ideology that changes the structures but vice versa; 2) it is asserted that a given political solution is 'ideological'—i.e. that it is not sufficient to change the structure although it thinks that it can do so; [therefore] it is asserted that it [the proposed political solution] is useless, stupid, etc.; 3) one then passes to the assertion that every ideology is 'pure' appearance, useless, stupid, etc.[8]

Gramsci followed Lenin who had previously rejected a purely negative view in *What Is to be Done?*, where he contrasted 'bourgeois and socialist ideology.'[9] For Gramsci, as much as for Lenin, 'ideologies' are, first and foremost, political and social programs and the concepts on which they are based. Errors can be found in actual, historical ideologies, but 'ideology' is in no way the special abode of error.

Gramsci never confronts the negative connotations of 'ideology' in non-Marxist thought as directly as he confronts the conflation of 'ideology' and 'error' in the Marxist tradition. Nevertheless, he does not spare the positivist and empiricist illusion of a realm of social science free from ideological influence and able to reveal eternal truths, truths not bounded by history and culture. Gramsci reduces 'bourgeois' sciences to the same level as the 'ideologies' that positivists and empiricists see as major sources of error, making bourgeois and Marxist thought subject to the same criteria of truth.

Gramsci believes that neither matter-of-fact experience nor the investigation of concepts by common sense provides any special avenue to the truth. As far as the vast majority of people are concerned, Gramsci warns, '. . . to refer to common sense as a confirmation of truth is a nonsense.'[10] Common men or women are too much taken up with practical life, with the contradictions of the society of which they are a part, and with their culture to be able to find the source of truth in their immediate experience or in the concepts they live by.

Against the claims of positivist and empiricist social research Gramsci also objects that, '. . . any sociology presupposes a philosophy, a conception of the world, of which it is but a subordinate part.'[11] He adds more specifically with regard to empiricism in the social sciences:

> An enquiry into a series of facts to discover the relations between them presupposes a 'concept' that permits one to distinguish that series from other possible series of facts. How can there take place a choice of facts to be adduced as proof of the truth of one's own assumption if one does not have a pre-existing criterion of choice? But what is this criterion of choice to be, if not something superior to each single fact under enquiry? An intuition, a conception, which must be regarded as having a complex history, a process that is to be connected with the whole process of the development of culture (etc.).[12]

Gramsci believes that we should recognize and distinguish the inner logic and methodology we follow in social inquiry from our initial assumptions and the aims that we pursue. 'Even theology,' he says, 'is based on a certain series of assumptions and then builds on these a whole massive edifice of solidly coherent and rigorously deduced doctrine. But is theology therefore a science?'[13] Not, we conclude from Gramsci, if it makes claims to eternal truth and provides no method to challenge those 'truths' it does presents. Even the truths discovered by natural science using the experimental method are not static truths. They can be amplified by subsequent discoveries. And they are not eternal truths. They can be rejected after the discovery of fresh, contradictory, truths.[14] 'Scientific truth' is a historical, limited, category for Gramsci.

Further, Gramsci does not believe that adherence to any 'scientific' method can assure 'objectivity.' As far as he is concerned, real science always involves the viewpoint of human beings in specific cultural contexts. Without reference to real men and women, the creators of all values (the classical 'measure of all things'), 'objectivity' becomes a purely abstract and metaphysical concept. But people *do* define their aims and objectives (and, hence, the point of view from which they consider themselves, and others can consider them, 'objective') as much as they use 'science' to pursue their ends. To be 'scientific,' for Gramsci, means to gather knowledge, 'in conformity with the end.' According to Gramsci, the 'scientific method' of those whose objective is to change things (whether those people are engineers or revolutionaries) is likely to be, not surprisingly, that of experimentation and rational argument, experiment to see if proposed changes work, rational argument to encourage the cooperation of others when change can only be accomplished by acting collectively. An inquirer's real desire to change something is the guarantee of her honest search for truth, the source of her 'objectivity.' Unfortunately, the very technical success of the engineering-oriented natural sciences has helped produce an ideology of 'unlimited progress' that makes it easy for us to be lazy about conceptualizing and specifying the ends we wish to pursue. The science that influenced the engineering changes of the industrial era, Gramsci argues, has yielded to a scientific superstition that makes the older, religious, superstition, which is more conscious of the ends it pursues, look positively noble, and, in a strange way, more 'objective.'[15]

To summarize Gramsci's critique: ideology is not mere appearance but a dynamic, material, and on-going force. Purely negative conceptions of ideology appear to him as reductionist and misleading either because they tend to obscure the actual importance of existing convictions or because they separate 'ideology' from 'science.' Gramsci sees little basis for this absolute dichotomy.

## Ideology as worldview and political force

Gramsci's critique of other's views of ideology began as a search for a concept to use in his own analysis. He eventually developed two interrelated concepts: Ideologies can be treated philosophically as different worldviews; at the same time they can be treated from the point of view of a functional sociology as forces of domination or liberation.[16]

### *Ideology as worldview*

As a conception of the world, ideology can appear either as lofty theory, identical to 'philosophy,' or it can appear in the most degraded form as 'folklore.' Between these two poles, ideology appears in the guise of 'common sense,' which combines elements of philosophy or 'good sense' with elements of folklore.[17] Gramsci writes:

Perhaps it is useful to make a 'practical' distinction between philosophy and common sense in order to indicate more clearly the passage from one moment to the other. In philosophy the features of individual elaboration of thought are the most salient; in common sense on the other hand it is the diffuse, uncoordinated features of a generic form of thought common to a particular period and a particular popular environment.[18]

Philosophy, says Gramsci, is an 'intellectual order,' structured and coherent. As philosophy, ideology can appear 'implicit' in the highest realms of human thought and activity, in art, religion, and ethics as much as in production or high finance. Of course, many philosophies coexist at any one time, as do many worldviews. Not all philosophies appear woven in the very fabric of a society. Gramsci distinguishes between those that are, 'historical' philosophies, and all others. 'A philosophy is "historical" insofar as it spreads, insofar as it becomes a conception of the reality of a social mass (with a conforming ethic).'[19] Other philosophies may be just as sophisticated, coherent, and elaborated, but they remain the products of individuals and of little historical consequence.

'Common sense' lacks the organic elaboration and coherence of philosophy. Common sense, '. . . is the "folklore" of philosophy, and, like folklore, it takes countless different forms. Its most fundamental characteristic is that it is a conception which, even in the brain of one individual, is fragmentary, incoherent and inconsequential, in conformity with the social and cultural position of those masses whose philosophy it is.'[20] Common sense is therefore the 'philosophy of the multitude,' it is the philosophy of the non-philosophers, or in other words the conception of the world which is uncritically absorbed by the various social and cultural environments in which the moral individuality of the average man and woman are developed.'[21] Common sense is not, therefore, an abstract philosophy produced by the mind of one or more intellectuals, but the philosophy of,

. . . real men, formed in specific historical relations, with specific feelings, outlooks, fragmentary conceptions of the world, etc., which were the result of 'spontaneous' combinations of a given situation of material production with the 'fortuitous' agglomeration within it of disparate social elements.[22]

But even in its incoherence, with all its lack of organization, and with all its contradictory features, common sense is still, nevertheless, a conception of the world. As such it is a species of philosophy and ideology, the people's philosophy, the people's ideology. It may be regarded as 'lay religion.'[23] All men and women are, therefore, in some way philosophers and ideologists:

It must first be shown that all men are 'philosophers,' by defining the limits and characteristics of the 'spontaneous philosophy' which is proper to everybody. This philosophy is contained in: 1) language itself, which is a totality of determined notions and concepts and not just of words grammatically devoid of content; 2) 'common sense' and 'good sense;' 3) popular religion and, therefore, also in the entire system of beliefs, superstitions, opinions, ways of seeing things and of acting, which are collectively bundled together under the name of 'folklore.' . . . everyone is a philosopher, though in his own way and unconsciously, since even in the slightest manifestation of any intellectual activity, in 'language,' there is contained a specific conception of the world.[24]

Now the positive reasons for Gramsci's denial that ideologies are mere appearance becomes clear. What indeed would people be without some conception of the world? We would be unable to reason, unable to make choices. We would be unable to speak and to communicate with one another and unable to act. Why, then, do most people deny being inspired by ideology as often as scholars say that common people lack reason? Gramsci answers that our ideologies are often unconscious, '. . . ways of life appear to those who live them as absolute, "as natural."'[25] In short, we rarely question why we think and act in a certain way, but, rather, regard our ways of thinking and acting as absolutely objective and eternal and, as such, as needing no deep study into their origins or consequences.

The positive reason for Gramsci's refusal to equate ideology with error also becomes clear: because there is no eternal, pure, 'purely scientific' criteria that we can use to choose one concept of the world over another. For Gramsci, no extra-political or extra-social rationality exists, and, therefore, if we wish to judge a worldview we can only do so relative to its social and political context and relative to the aims that define our own 'objectivity.'

*Ideology as an instrument of liberation*

If Gramsci's concept of ideology were limited to this notion of 'ideology as worldview' critics could easily charge that he escaped the materialist trap of economism only to fall into the pit of philosophical idealism. But, even though Gramsci may be remembered best as the theoretician of superstructures, he remains an historical materialist; the originality of his thought consists in his synthesis of the idealism of the celebrated Italian historian and philosopher, Benedetto Croce, and Marx's materialism. To correct the impression of Gramsci as a mere philosophical idealist we must turn to the second concept of ideology contained in his work, the one developed as a functional sociology of ideology's role in domination and liberation, and we must look at the relationship of ideology as worldview to ideology as political force.

Why do people produce ideologies? What makes ideologies grow and spread to become the worldview of large parts of a society, lay religions of the masses? For Gramsci, one part of the answer to these questions lies in the relations of production and in the interests expressed in a society full of contradictions by different social classes in their mutual struggle. While Gramsci did not accept *The German Ideology*'s view that ideologies are merely an illusory reflection of real social struggles, he affirmed that ideologies are one expression of social struggles and one of the tools used in them. He says, 'All hitherto existing philosophies (philosophical systems) have been manifestations of the intimate contradictions by which society is lacerated,'[26] and adds:

... it is understood that the philosophy of praxis, despite Croce's 'surprise' and 'scandal,' studies, 'in the philosophers precisely (!) that which is not philosophical: the practical tendencies, and the social and class affections which they represent. Therefore in the materialism of the eighteenth century they glimpsed the French life of the time, wholly intent upon the immediate present, the convenient, the useful; in Hegel, the Prussian state; in Feuerbach, the ideals of modern life, to which German society had not yet raised itself; in Stirner, the soul of haberdashers; in Schopenhauer, that of the petite bourgeoisie and so forth.'[27]

He sets out his thoughts on the degree of distinctiveness of the functional role of ideology even more explicitly when he charges Croce and the bourgeois thinkers who follow him with making the same 'error' that they claim Marxists make:

... the error of practical origin is committed by their historian, Croce, who, after having distinguished between philosophy and ideology, ends up confusing a political ideology with a worldview, demonstrating in practice that such a distinction is impossible, that it is not a question of two categories, but of one and the same historical category, and that the distinction drawn is one of degree only; the worldview that represents intellectual and moral life (catharsis of a given practical life) of an entire social group ... is philosophy; every particular conception of the groups within a class who propose to help in resolving immediate, circumscribed problems, is ideology.[28]

In Gramsci's affirmation of the accuracy (but not the implications) of Croce's critique of traditional Marxist treatments of philosophy, we see Gramsci not only explicating the concept of ideology as political force, but also demonstrating the tendential coincidence between 'ideology as political force' and 'ideology as worldview.' In fact, the distinction between the two roles of ideology, between Gramsci's two concepts, can only be drawn for didactic purposes, just as, Gramsci argued, the distinction between structure and superstructure is 'merely didactic.'[29]

Gramsci's concept of ideology, and many of his other important concepts, can be thought of as having two sides, one more 'materialistic,' side and another, more 'idealistic' one. For example, another way that Gramsci expresses both the distinction between, and (ultimately) the unity of, his two concepts of ideology is through his parallel distinction between 'historical philosophies' and 'historically organic ideologies.' 'Historical philosophies' are those which create a world outlook that spreads. But these worldview spread only insofar as they are 'organic ideologies' in the material structure of production, that is, insofar as they correspond to existing contradictions and social struggles. Historical philosophies have to make sense to the groups that espouse them.

Nevertheless, Gramsci does not see philosophies espoused by the intellectuals of the dominant class becoming the common sense of the popular masses (the workers and peasants). That is not how ideology is 'used' in political struggles. In fact Gramsci states that, allowing for the low cultural level and scanty realization of the critical capacity of the masses, 'philosophy can only be experienced [by them] as faith,'[30] and that they, 'are slower to change their conceptions, or ... never change them in the sense of accepting them [newer world outlooks] in their "pure" form, but always and only as a more or less heterogeneous and bizarre combination.'[31] According to Gramsci, the philosophy-common sense connection occurs across time. While the current philosophy of the dominant class is never transformed wholly into common sense, all the same, every, 'previous philosophy ... has left stratified deposits in popular philosophy,'[32] and, '... several elements survive of an ideology that has emerged to guide the popular masses,'[33] even after a change in the structure, a change in the economic limits on the range of possible social relations.

Common sense, to Gramsci, is therefore not only the product of the competing philosophies of the moment, but also the result of the fragmentary, incoherent sedimentation of the historical philosophies which follow each other in succession within the specific cultural environment of the social group considered. On the other hand, considering that historical philosophies have been the intellectual expression of the various economic structures that followed one another throughout history, common sense reflects a synthesis of all the prior social relationships that have bound people together. At the same time, common sense reflects a synthesis of all the prior relationships between the human species and the rest of nature. Gramsci says, '... our present method of thought ... has subsumed and absorbed all this past history, including all its follies and mistakes.'[34] According to Gramsci, this ideological sedimentation of common sense has grave effects on the consciousness of the general public. The clutter of common sense makes critical reflection difficult. Removing that clutter is a revolutionary political task that must involve 'intellectuals' as well as common people. It is in this relationship that ideology finds its liberating role in political struggles. Intellectuals are influenced by common sense in their philosophical or scientific elaborations, but they possess a capacity of critical analysis that can permit them to rid themselves of the influences of the past.[35]

Of course, given this special capacity of intellectuals, their misunderstanding of the world may be more damaging than that of the average man or woman. Even though Gramsci does not posit a concept of 'false consciousness,' within the framework of his analysis one could speak of something related: the typical intellectual's *lack of* consciousness of his or her dependence on the dominant class and a lack of consciousness of the historical and cultural factors which condition his or her work. The intellectual's lack of consciousness may be greater than that of the common person even though the intellectual has developed skills to overcome it.

In contrast, Gramsci identifies the typical problem of the common person as one of 'contradictory consciousness.' The popular masses are likely to be more dependent on the psychological leavings of the past than the intellectual because the masses live their own ideology as 'natural' or even more as a 'faith' from which they have little critical, analytical capacity to free themselves. The contradictions in the common sense of the masses, their naturally lived ideology, together with the contradictions present in society create in the common person the 'contradictory consciousness' identified by Gramsci. He says:

> Having observed that, since the ensemble of social relations is contradictory, man's consciousness cannot fail to be contradictory, the problem arises of how this contradiction manifests itself and how unification can progressively be achieved. It is manifest in the entire social corpus, with the existence of historical group consciousness (with the existence of stratifications corresponding to various phases of the historical development of civilization, and with the antitheses in the groups which correspond to one and the same historical level) and it is manifest in single individuals as a reflection of such a 'vertical and horizontal' separation.[36]

It is above all relative to this problem of contradictory consciousness that the 'philosophy of praxis,' i.e. Marxism, is, in Gramsci's view, superior to all other ideologies; this is what makes Marxism liberating. To Gramsci, liberation is not merely eliminating the economic exploitation of the working class and making it politically dominant. Liberation involves freeing common sense from contradictory consciousness and developing and extending its sound core of 'good sense.' The philosophy of praxis must therefore, according to Gramsci, criticize all past philosophies so as to remove the incrustations they have left, and demonstrate that ideologies are always instruments of power, because it is only with a merging of thought and action that the historical role of humanity (our species being) can be regained. In this sense, for Gramsci, the philosophy of praxis is the ideology *par excellence*, the one that best exemplifies his functional concept of ideology:

> To the extent that ideologies are historically necessary they have a validity which is 'psychological;' they 'organize' human masses, and create the terrain on which men move, acquire consciousness of their position, struggle, etc.[37]

According to Gramsci, it is only by raising the cultural level of a population, which must be achieved by means of a constant dialogue between intellectuals and masses, that the process of unifying ideology and philosophy and philosophy and history can be accomplished. The two concepts of ideology we have described here will then no longer differ because common sense will have been raised to the level of philosophy at the same time that ideology will lose its characteristic of being an instrument of domination, becoming, instead, the philosophy and worldview of society. Gramsci saw his revolutionary struggle as one of creating social consensus around coherent 'good sense,' creating a world very different from the world of contradictory consciousness in which we actually live.

*Ideology as an instrument of domination*

Here we are less concerned with Gramsci's revolutionary aims than with how his concepts can help us understand the imperfect world as it is. Gramsci's ideas concerning the functional role of ideology for the class in power and the tasks of intellectuals in this context are already familiar to many students of international relations. But one aspect of his thoughts on this subject needs to be addressed because it has frequently been misrepresented. This is the problem of the relationship between the ideology of the classes in power and common sense. In fact, it is precisely within this relationship that Gramsci locates much of the problem of domination. As we have said, the dominant class does not gain 'ideological hegemony' by spreading its ideology throughout society until it permeates even the most recondite places. For Gramsci, the degree of ideological hegemony of the dominant class is not equivalent to the capacity of its philosophy to transform common sense and to be transformed into common sense.[38] His analysis is much more subtle.

Rather than becoming the ideology of the masses, the philosophy articulated by the dominant class's intellectuals operates by helping to thwart the development of common sense into good sense. Ideologists allied with the dominant class help assure that potential taproots of critical reason do not develop in the consciousness of the masses, even though those ideologists are unable to, or uninterested in, shaping common sense to conform with the views of the dominant class. Gramsci expresses this concept clearly in one passage in which he criticizes Bukharin's 'Popular Manual of Marxist Sociology.' Gramsci says:

> These systems influence the popular masses as an external political force, an element of cohesive force of the ruling classes and therefore an element of subordination to an external hegemony. This limits the original thought of the popular masses in a negative direction, without having the positive effect of a vital ferment of interior transformation of what the masses think in an embryonic and chaotic form about the world and life. The principal elements of common sense are provided by religion, and consequently the relationship between common sense and religion is much more intimate than that between common sense and the philosophical systems of the intellectuals.[39]

Gramsci neither believes that the whole population of any country shares the same culture nor that it shares the same values. He often writes about the wide cultural differences between upper and lower classes and between different regions. Moreover, what he calls 'passive consensus,' or, 'passive consent,' is not the social consensus identified by structural-functionalist sociology. It comes from Machiavelli's dual model of 'force' and 'consensus' as the two fundamental modes of developing political order.[40] Gramsci uses the term 'passive consent' to cover a wide range from 'tacit agreement,' to 'passive acceptance,' to 'indifference,' and perhaps even, 'unexpressed dissent.'

Gramsci wanted to understand the passivity of the working class and, even more, the peasantry. He wanted to know why they did not rebel despite their marginalization. He realized that the cultural past (sedimentations of archaic historical philosophies) prevent not only popular rebellion but even, in certain circumstances, class struggle. The contradictory consciousness of working class and peasant activists can explain such passivity:

His theoretical consciousness can indeed be historically in opposition to his activity. One might almost say that he has two theoretical consciousnesses (or one contradictory consciousness): one which is implicit in his activity and which in reality unites him with all his fellow-workers in the practical transformation of the real world; and one, superficially explicit or verbal, which he has inherited from the past and uncritically absorbed. But this verbal conception is not without consequences. It holds together a specific social group, it influences moral conduct and the direction of will, with varying efficacity but often powerfully enough to produce a situation in which the contradictory state of consciousness does not permit of any action, any decision or any choice, and produces a condition of moral and political passivity.[41]

Gramsci believed that the passivity of the masses could be overcome by the catalytic role of intellectuals helping the popular masses acquire consciousness of the their position in society and by offering workers and peasants alternatives to the present state of affairs that they would not be able to elaborate on their own.

Of course, it is of at least minor importance that ideology can legitimate ('justify') the interests of the dominant class to allied groups; those interests would appear in all their crude brutality without the philosophical garb that gives them moral dignity. From this standpoint ideology, expressed in philosophical form, has the function of increasing the prestige of the dominant class, even though this position is already implicit in the relations of production. At the same time the dominant ideology affirms the rules of the game which the state must see are respected, even if this requires the use of force. Still, the greatest power of ideology come from the way the development of the critical consciousness of the oppressed can be thwarted when the intellectuals who would normally be allied with them are wooed away by the intellectuals of the dominant classes. This, and not the production of some unlikely society-wide consensus, is the essence of Gramsci's notion of domination through ideology.

Gramsci provides a concrete example of this negative function in his systematic criticism of Croce's role in Italian society. Gramsci reproaches Croce for having linked southern intellectuals with the bourgeoisie.[42] The negative role that Gramsci attributes to Croce in this context did not consist in his getting the peasant masses to accept his idealist philosophy. If that had happened Gramsci would have been less critical because then, at least, Croce would have raised the intellectual level of the southern peasantry. Gramsci criticizes Croce for having co-opted the intellectuals produced by the peasantry, thus preventing them from elaborating a philosophy in keeping with the peasants' interests that would help them increase their own moral dignity and cultural prestige. 'Ideological hegemony' as 'consensus on the ideology of the ruling classes' may be a force that affects intellectuals, according to Gramsci, but it is unlikely to affect whole societies.

Gramsci draws attention to a final way in which the ideology of the dominant class diminishes the powers of the dominated. The ideologists of the dominant class help divide dominated groups with fundamentally similar interests by providing new justifications for old antagonisms. For example, Gramsci denounces the role of the Italian bourgeoisie in helping divide the northern working class from southern peasants by promulgating 'scientific' racism.[43]

In addition, the ideology of the class in power can seep into common sense just enough to help block the taproots of critical reason. In this context Gramsci explicitly mentions the 'material structure of ideology,' that is, that complex of institutions and organizations whose task it is to influence common sense. Such action takes place through forms of popularization which hide the conceptual debate over the fundamental principles of the dominant class's ideology. That is to say: the schools, the private media, the press offices of government, and other institutions spread simplified versions of the dominant class's ideology which obscure the critical philosophical debates in which that ideology originated, making the ideology appear to be just 'the way it is.' The material structure of ideology disseminates prejudices instead of the material of critical thinking. This not only prevents the cultural enhancement of the popular masses (who might, for example, be empowered by the same institutions if they exposed the critical differences between the ideology of the dominant class and the common sense and by challenging people to confront, understand, and choose between alternative premises), it also helps prevent common people from acquiring a capacity of critical analysis that would enable them to distinguish between ideologies in keeping with their interests and those that are not. Gramsci considered the role of the Catholic Church in Italy to be a perfect example: Priests endlessly repeating simplified concepts until they become part of a common understanding that no one will analyze or question. Thus, while, according to Gramsci, the primary link between historical philosophies and common sense is found in the past, in the history of attempts by the dominant classes to have their ideologies influence common sense and the resulting residue of historical philosophies in the lived ideology of common people, a social and functional relationship between philosophy and common sense occurs in the immediate present, in today's activities of the ruling class.

Gramsci sums up what we have said so far in a unitary concept when he says: 'The relation between common sense and the upper level of philosophy is assured by "politics," just as it is politics that assures the relationship between the Catholicism of the intellectuals and that of the simple.'[44] It is therefore within the framework of concrete political activity that ideology constitutes, according to Gramsci, an instrument of domination. This domination, as we have seen, manifests itself in preventing the development of existing cultural potentialities and creating disarray in the ranks of the adversaries to the *status quo* and in strengthening a contradictory consciousness in the common sense which prevents common people from defending their most immediate interests, let alone undertaking coherent, collective action aimed at transforming the world as it is.

While what we have said so far should be enough to explain why 'social harmony' can exist in societies wracked by inherent conflicts of interest, Gramsci goes further to explain how concepts of social identity, popular views of race and territory, of 'us' and 'them,' preserve domination. In reality:

> ... in history and in the production of history, the 'individualized' representation of States and Nations is a mere metaphor, ... they exist as 'vertical' group distinctions and as 'horizontal' stratifications, i.e. as the coexistence and juxtaposition of different civilizations and cultures, linked by State coercion and organized culturally into a 'moral conscience' that is both contradictory and at the same time 'syncretistic.'[45]

Gramsci explains a 'moral conscience, contradictory but syncretistic' by showing that in European history there has been an 'ethical principle' which has bound together ruler and ruled. In the nineteenth century this was that of 'imperial authority,' which explains why peasants of Croatia or Venice fought, respectively, against the Milanese and Viennese liberals who wanted to liberate them from the oppressive political systems to which they were subject. Gramsci says that in his own time this ethico-political principle has become identified with nationalism:

> The combination in which the hegemonic ethical-political element presents itself in State and national life is 'patriotism' and 'nationalism,' which is the 'people's religion,' i.e., the nexus through which the unity of the rulers and of the ruled takes place.[46]

Reading Gramsci's writings today we could think that he simply alludes to the nationalist outburst which provoked the first world war. But his analysis shows that nationalism became a more lasting principle in many countries by fusing in itself the core elements of religion and liberalism. Patriotism became a 'civil religion' of the masses, justifying persecution in the name of 'liberty' and 'country' to match that conducted by the Inquisition in the name of God.[47]

## Liberalism as ideology

To further clarify Gramsci's views it is useful to apply the conceptual tools he elaborated to the analysis of a specific ideology. The power of liberalism as a part of America's civil religion, the importance of liberalism to those who dominate the United States and other industrialized, capitalist nations, and the unusual faith in liberalism demonstrated by many American intellectuals make it the logical choice. We will limit our analysis to the political philosophy of liberalism, placing special emphasis on the liberal theory of human motivation, but leaving most of liberal economic theory aside.

The significance of liberal political theory in the dominant social order before Fascism made it a major topic for Gramsci; his own analysis included both observations on liberalism in general and a more specific critique of Croce's liberal philosophy. Although Gramsci understood liberalism as an instrument of power as much as a conception of the world he considered it historically more advanced than the common sense of the Italian public of his day; in common sense archaic religious notions, including ideas of 'community,' made obsolete by socio-economic development, still survived.

In contrast, since Hobbes and Locke, liberal theorists, have conceived of society as a sum of atomic individuals who establish relations with each other of their own free will on the basis of considerations of individual utility. Individuals making up the whole pursue their own personal 'interests.' Liberal theorists posit free will in the choice of interests, but they single-out the pursuit of wealth and power as recurrent motives for human action. Often liberals will say that actions that cannot be related to these two objectives are the result of 'passions,' which is to say that what motivates them is something irrational or insufficiently specific as compared to the human interests in wealth and power.[48]

Gramsci criticizes the concept of an atomized society. He sees individuals as born in specific historical and cultural contexts which initially form their common sense, instilling values and norms of behavior[49] and making them internalize rules by applying social pressure.[50] Nonetheless, Gramsci does not accept this state of affairs as eternal. He notes that, 'the environment . . . does not justify but only "explains" the behavior of individuals.' Clearly, it is:

> . . . better to work out consciously and critically one's own conception of the world, and thus, in connection with the labours of one's own brain, choose one's sphere of activity, take an active part in the creation of the history of the world, be one's own guide, refusing to accept passively and supinely from outside the moulding of one's personality.[51]

Liberal political theory does not recognize the importance of such critical self-understanding in developing truly 'individual' motivations. It portrays an abstracted individual, in isolation from his social context and presupposes a generalized individual ability to exercise free will which, on the contrary, Gramsci argues, can only be the result of the personal attainment of consciousness, or the outcome of the movement of society as a whole from the domain of 'necessity' to that of 'freedom,' taken in its Hegelian sense as 'consciousness of necessity.'

Unlike the liberals, Gramsci believed, 'each individual is the synthesis not only of existing [social] relations, but of the history of these relations. He is a *précis* of all the past.'[52] Our goals and characteristic actions are shaped by our common sense which, in turn, accumulates the historical experience of our society. It is only in this context that the motivations and norms which define individual interests can be determined. To claim that 'wealth' and 'power' are the main goals to which humans tend can, at best, be an adequate representation of those societies which have long-supported these objectives. More likely, the claim will be part of a particular political–ideological project aimed at disseminating these motivations, a project aimed at convincing people to pursue only wealth and power, or, even more likely, to justify the actions of those who pursue only those goals.

The other type of motivation posited by liberalism, 'passion,' demands separate analysis. Gramsci does not exclude passions from his political theory. He emphasizes the need to, 'overcome bestial and elemental passions,' by developing the, 'healthy nucleus, that exists in "common sense," the part of it which can be called "good sense,"'[53] and Gramsci highlights how the search for more efficient forms of production and of economic development, 'industrialism,' was, '... a continuing struggle ... against the element of "animality" in man.'[54] Like the liberal political theorists, Gramsci is not fond of 'passions.'

But what Gramsci identifies as 'passions' and the actions motivated by them and what liberal theorists identify as such are often quite different. Gramsci explicitly criticizes Croce's attempt to reduce political activity to the domain of passion. Croce's concept, Gramsci notes, does not explain how 'organized and permanent passions,' such as those of political parties, or armies, or nation states, can exist.[55] Furthermore, referring to the worldview contained in common sense he states, 'It is necessary therefore to explain how passion can become moral "duty"—duty in terms not of political morality but of ethics.'[56] One could add, taking examples used by Gramsci, that moral duty can drive individuals to kill other people without hating them in the course of war or make a ship's captain go down with his ship against the most basic interest in survival; duty can be 'dispassionate,' yet lead to actions that contradict individual or collective interests. Gramsci fears that the liberal understanding of 'passions' blurs important distinctions. By equating all 'archaic' common sense motivations with 'passions,' liberal theorists devalue all motivations except the ones their theory highlights, the 'interests' in wealth and power. The failure of liberalism is analogous to that of dogmatic Marxism: it attempts to account for human actions solely in terms of economic or utilitarian motivation, implicitly claiming that humans act rationally only when pursuing base, selfish interests. To Gramsci, humans cannot be reduced to the simplistic categories of interest and passion: people are historical realities, the synthesis of their past and present social relations with which their consciousness interacts.

The discrepancies between the political philosophy of liberalism and social reality would not have worried Gramsci had he not detected in them the consequences of the other aspect of ideology, its functional role in maintaining social domination. Analyzing the situation in the Italy of his time, he states:

But a current and a party, specifically calling itself liberal, became established which has transformed the speculative and contemplative position of Hegelian philosophy into an immediate political ideology, a practical instrument of domination and social hegemony.[57]

To understand why Gramsci considered this a cause for concern we must say a bit about his analysis of the process of aggregation of interests and the political dynamics of social change. He writes:

The first and most elementary of these [moments] is the economic-corporate level: a tradesman feels *obliged* to stand by another tradesman, a manufacturer by another manufacturer, etc., but the tradesman does not yet feel solidarity with the manufacturer; in other words, the members of the professional group are conscious of its unity and homogeneity, and of the need to organize it, but in the case of the wider social group this is not yet so. A second moment is that in which consciousness is reached of the solidarity of interests among all the members of a social class—but still in the purely economic field. . . . A third moment is that in which one becomes aware that one's own corporate interests, in their present and future development, transcend the corporate limits of the purely economic class, and can and must become the interests of other subordinate groups too.[58]

The aggregation of interests and the growth of social groups initially may be spontaneous; people easily share the concerns with those with whom they work and with others in similar social roles. Yet, even in the initial stages this process of building social solidarity may be impeded by common sense. It is in this political context that the role of the intellectuals and the ideologies that they produce becomes significant. The processes of aggregating interests may be promoted or hindered by intellectuals whose ideas can help people see common interests and find new ways to pursue them. The fact that social groups create their own ideologies by supporting intellectuals allied to them is thus not coincidental. Gramsci writes:

Every social group, coming into existence on the original terrain of an essential function in the world of economic production, creates together with itself, organically, one or more strata of intellectuals which give it homogeneity and an awareness of its own function not only in the economic but also in the social and political fields. The capitalist entrepreneur creates alongside himself the industrial technician, the specialist in political economy, the organizers of a new culture, of a new legal system, etc.[59]

Each social group will not only try to energize its own intellectuals, it also can try to co-opt the intellectuals of other classes as well as the 'traditional intellectuals,' the intellectuals who are the expression of archaic social relations. Traditional intellectuals tend to believe that they are an independent social force, unbeholden to any other class, and, as a result, they (along with other intellectuals who have come to share their self-understanding as intellectuals) may be relatively unaware of their own assimilation. In reality, they generally put themselves at the service of the class in power and become, 'the clerks of the dominant group' and, 'the officials of the [existing] superstructures.'[60]

This is exactly what happened in industrial societies when liberalism became the ubiquitous ideology of traditional intellectual centers as well as the doctrine of organized political parties. Schools and parties began to disseminate an atomistic conception of society and glorify the individual pursuit of wealth and power. These liberal ideas, which Gramsci considers progressive compared to the more archaic elements of common sense, start to leave their residue in the minds of women and men. Yet, liberalism does not encourage critical reflection or lead to the identification of new common interests or to new forms of collective action. Its atomism proscribes most collective action, and, in its most pernicious forms, liberalism treats the archaic bases for collective action (of which we have a common sense knowledge) as passions, as negative motivations that we should repress. Liberalism actually helps make the people who accept it social atoms incapable of most collective action.

If, as Gramsci maintains, 'in modern history the historical-political "individual" is not the "biological" individual, but the social group,'[61] isolated individuals are not in a position to defend their economic interests or see their vision of the world realized, as far more powerful and determining organized forces are within society.[62] Liberalism falsifies perceptions of social relations, exalting individual autonomy while obfuscating the fact that in society wealth and power objectives are pursued by organized groups. Liberalism, therefore, impedes the aggregation of the dominated groups, whose members will continue to be bound by the rules of the game and to the objectives set by the dominant group. In this way liberalism is one of the instruments of the dominant classes and proof that ideologies are more than just expressions of social struggle, they are tools used in such struggles.

## Toward applying Gramsci's concepts

At the beginning of this section we stated our intention to explore Gramsci's concept of ideology in order to stress those aspects that are the most useful for interpreting contemporary American politics and foreign policy. Although we have attempted to give a synthetic picture of Gramsci's views, we have not extended our analysis to all of Gramsci's ideas that relate to the common sense notion of 'ideology.' Nevertheless, we believe that a number of critically useful distinctions can be clarified by even this brief account. We believe that the concept of 'contradictory consciousness' helps us understand contemporary society in the United States, or any other modern nation.[63] In order to understand American politics, in particular the relationships of domination, it is important to understand the contradictory consciousness of common people, what the common sense of most Americans is, and how what is common sense relates to the ideology of the governing classes.

To avoid prejudicing the case about the historical constitution of the American social system as a whole our immediate aim must be to define an important part of the American common sense and identify how elements within it are associated, more closely or more distantly, with different social strata, ethnic groups, and cultures. Our goal is to develop a clearer distinction—as Gramsci would—between the views of the masses and those of the people in power and of the intellectuals which are their expression. Unfortunately, we will not be able to do so by compiling the results of the primary research on American society which has adopted Gramsci's concepts. That body of research is too small.[64] The materials we have available to us, other scholars' analyses of contemporary American politics and American cultural history that begin with concepts which differ from Gramsci's, require us to come to that fundamental distinction gradually, beginning with an 'idealistic' reconnaissance, so to speak, of historical philosophies that have followed each other in America and of the degree and nature of their sedimentation in the consciousness of Americans in different social positions. We will then verify that analysis by looking at the apparent motivations underlying American foreign policy in general and American foreign aid policy in particular, governmental policies that scholars generally recognize as influenced in different ways by different parts of American society, with elites in business and government setting policy and the mass public only providing legitimation when policy changes or in rare cases, such as war, when active public support is essential. Finally we will use the same analysis to explain Reagan's rise to power and the apparent ideological shift of the American political system at the beginning of the 1980s, social phenomena that required more widespread public involvement.

## Notes

1. Jorge Larrain, *The Concept of Ideology* (London: Hutchinson, 1979) and David McLellan, *Ideology* (Milton Keynes: Open University Press, 1986) are both clear, concise works on the subject.
2. Karl Marx and Fredrich Engels, *The German Ideology* in *Marx and Engels: Basic Writings on Politics and Philosophy* (London: Fontana, 1984).
3. Ibid., 288.
4. Ibid., 296.
5. Antonio Gramsci, *Selections from Prison Notebooks (PN)*, Quentin Hoare and Geoffrey Nowell Smith, ed. and trans. (London: Lawrence and Wishart, 1971), 377.
6. Karl Mannheim, *Ideology and Utopia* (London: Routledge and Kegan Paul, 1979. The first edition was published in 1936). After having identified Bacon's 'idola' as the precursor of this concept, and after having shown that a negative interpretation of ideology is implicit in the psychology of interest that started with Machiavelli and reached its crowning moment in the Enlightenment, Mannheim states that in the twentieth century scholars no longer limit themselves to questioning the psychological motivations underlying the formulation of opponents' positions (the

'interests' underlying 'ideology'), they often criticize them on the ontological or noological level as well. Whereas earlier, Mannheim says, critics sought the source of error in individual intellectual prejudices (that is, at the psychological level), they now are apt to suppose their adversaries to be unable to reason correctly: '... antagonists will seek to annihilate not merely the specific beliefs and attitudes of one another, but also the intellectual foundations upon which these beliefs and attitudes rest' (p. 57). Early in the career of 'ideology' Napoleon made this type of accusation when he dubbed the group of philosophers who opposed his imperial ambitions (including Destutt de Tracy who had coined the term 'ideology'), 'ideologists' at the same time that he called their theoretical elaborations unrealistic. Today, says Mannheim, 'The word ideology is used by the proletariat [or, at least, by some of those who claim to speak for them] as a weapon against the dominant group,' with the same negative connotations (p. 66). This accusation is not valid for Gramsci. While Gramsci was quite willing to assert that many people (workers as well as capitalists) were often mistaken, and while he was quite willing to assert that it might often be in one group's interest for others (or even themselves) to remain mistaken, he was unwilling to say that any human beings were incapable of reason or that fundamental presuppositions of any group condemned them to ignorance.

7. Quoted in McLellan, p. 18. Mannheim recognizes that this type of argument, used by Marxists to discredit bourgeois thought since the mid-nineteenth century, is no longer just their own. Bourgeois thinkers (starting with Max Weber) have learned to use it against Marxists. While we generally agree with Mannheim's historical interpretation of the equation of 'ideology' with 'a source of error,' we find his interpretation of the negative connotation of the term in twentieth-century non-Marxist thought (the claim that bourgeois scholars have raised the issue of 'ideology as error' only in reaction to, or as revenge for, the earlier Marxist use of the concept) difficult to accept. The idea of 'ideology as error,' and even as 'unredeemable error' (error that can never be removed by rational debate), fits neatly within the whole tradition of positivist, empiricist thought, and, as discussed below, it may not be purely by chance that this concept of ideology is quite widespread, at both the popular level and in the academic world, in the United States.
8. *PN*, 376.
9. In *Collected Works*, V (Moscow: Foreign Languages Publishing, 1961), 384.
10. *PN*, 423.
11. *PN*, 426–7.
12. *PN*, 461.
13. Antonio Gramsci, *Quaderni del Carcere* (*QC*) (Torino: Einaudi, 1975), II, 1277.
14. *PN*, 461.
15. *QC*, I, 430, and II, 1458–9. Gramsci's view resembles Habermas's later, more elaborate analysis of knowledge-making interests and science.
16. Gramsci's usage of the same term to refer to different concepts, especially when they are linked and complementary, has caused some authors to find incongruities and contradictions in his writings. We believe that Gramsci consistently takes the position we outline here throughout the *Notebooks*.
17. For a definition of folklore see *QC*, III, 2312. The relationship between philosophy, common sense, and folklore is clearly outlined in *QC*, III, 2271.

18. *PN*, 330.
19. *QC*, II, 1272.
20. *PN*, 419.
21. *PN*, 419, 421–2.
22. *PN*, 198.
23. 'Note the problem of religion taken not in the confessional sense but in the secular sense of a unity of faith between a conception of the world and a corresponding norm of conduct. But why call this unity of faith "religion" and not "ideology," or frankly "politics"?' (*PN*, 326).
24. *PN*, 323.
25. *QC*, III, 1727.
26. *PN*, 404.
27. *QC*, II, 1272.
28. *QC*, II, 1231.
29. Of course, 'merely didactic' distinctions are extremely important in clarifying concepts, the essential starting point of inquiry. Gramsci could not define his most important concept, 'historical bloc'—the unity of structure and superstructure in which 'material forces are the content and ideologies are the form'—without the distinction between structure and superstructure. In the same way, Gramsci's unified concept of ideology, as both worldview and political force, requires understanding the distinction between ideology as worldview and ideology as political force.
30. *PN*, 339.
31. *PN*, 338.
32. *PN*, 324.
33. *QC*, II, 1322.
34. *PN*, 327.
35. *QC*, III, 2267–8.
36. *QC*, III, 1875.
37. *PN*, 377. Gramsci's definition is one that he recalls from memory of Marx, '. . . men become aware (of the conflict between the material forces of production) on ideological grounds.'
38. Some scholars do argue for this simple 'dominant ideology' thesis, including many who find inspiration in Gramsci. The criticism of this approach contained in N. Abercrombie, S. Hill, and B. S. Turner, *The Dominant Ideology Thesis* (London: Allen & Unwin, 1980) appears to us to be fully justified, but cannot be leveled against Gramsci as much as it can be leveled against some of his interpreters.
39. *PN*, 420. We should point out here that while we have built our interpretations of Gramsci's theory on the original Italian texts, we have quoted from Hoare and Smith's English translation whenever possible. Their translation is excellent, but we were forced to change it in this instance. They say, '. . . an element of cohesive force *exercised by* the ruling classes . . .' rather than our '. . . *of the* ruling classes . . .' They refer to something that creates unity throughout society; we understand the passage as discussing something that provides unity within the ruling group. The two translations reflect different understandings of Gramsci's views. Hoare and Smith assume the dominant ideology thesis and the capacity of the ideology of the ruling class to

become common sense. Our (we believe, more accurate) translation helps illustrate that Gramsci sees the ideology of the ruling class mainly as a positive force for that class's solidarity and a negative factor impeding the thinking of the ruled, but not as the ideology of the ruled. The interpretation Hoare and Smith accept is widespread. We suspect that English-speaking readers have seen confirmation of this widespread, but incorrect, opinion in Hoare and Smith's translation.

40. See pp. 127–9, below.
41. *PN*, 333.
42. 'In this sense, Benedetto Croce has fulfilled an extremely important "national" function. He has detached the radical intellectuals of the South from the peasant masses, forcing them to take part in national and European culture; and through this culture, he has secured their absorption by the national bourgeoisie and hence by the agrarian bloc.' Antonio Gramsci, *Selections from Political Writings, 1921–1926*, ed. and trans. Quintin Hoare (London: Lawrence and Wishart, 1978), 460.
43. 'The first problem to resolve, for the Turin communists, was how to modify the political stance and general ideology of the proletariat itself, as a national element which exists within the ensemble of State life and is unconsciously subjected to the influence of bourgeois education, the bourgeois press, and bourgeois traditions. It is well known what kind of ideology has been disseminated in myriad ways among the masses in the North by the propagandists of the bourgeoisie: the South is the ball and chain which prevents the social development of Italy from progressing more rapidly; the Southerners are biologically inferior beings, semi-barbarians or total barbarians, by natural destiny; if the South is backward, the fault does not lie with the capitalist system or with any other historical cause, but with Nature, which has made the Southerners lazy, incapable, criminal and barbaric—only tempering this harsh fate with the purely individual explosion of a few great geniuses, like isolated palm-trees in an arid and barren desert.' Gramsci, *Political Writings, 1921–1926*, 444.
44. *PN*, 331.
45. *QC*, II, 1222–23.
46. *QC*, II, 1084.
47. *QC*, II, 1230.
48. Albert O. Hirschman's analysis of the origins of liberal thought in *The Passions and the Interests* (Princeton: Princeton University Press, 1977) parallels Gramsci's perhaps because of their similar historical starting point, the breakdown of feudal order in the early Renaissance, long before Hobbes.
49. '... individuals cannot be conceived outside of society and therefore ... it is impossible to conceive of any individual as not historically determined' (*QC*, III, 1686).
50. 'Question of the "Law": this concept will have to be extended to include those activities which are at present classified as "legally neutral," and which belong to the domain of civil society; the latter operates without "sanctions" or compulsory "obligations," but nevertheless exerts a collective pressure.' (*PN*, 242.)
51. *PN*, 323–24.
52. *PN*, 353.
53. *PN*, 328.
54. *PN*, 298.
55. *PN*, 138.

56. *PN*, 139.
57. *QC*, II, 1229–30.
58. *PN*, 181.
59. *PN*, 5.
60. Gramsci's analysis of the function of intellectuals suggests the mechanism through which, 'the ideas of the ruling class in every epoch . . . 'can actually become, 'the ruling ideas,' as Marx and Engels argued in *The German Ideology.*
61. *QC*, II, 690.
62. A thesis of this kind can be found in the theory of 'countervailing power' describe by John Kenneth Galbraith in *American Capitalism—the Concept of Countervailing Power,* revised ed. (Harmondsworth: Penguin Books, 1970).
63. Cf., T. J. Jackson Lears, 'The Concept of Cultural Hegemony: Problems and Possibilities,' *American Historical Review*, 90 (1985): 567–93.
64. Gramsci himself (*PN*, 331) realizes the difficulty of identifying the elements of common sense in actual societies without suitable primary research, but he considers it possible to reconstruct them by making reference to the general development of the country's culture, i.e. to its ethical-political history.

# 2 Elements of common sense in America

To apply Gramsci's ideas about ideology to American political history does not mean to search either for an idealist's explanation of American politics or to search for a unitary, dominant ideology which serves the interest of the ruling class. It is important for us to reiterate this point at the beginning of our historical discussion because many of the authors we rely upon to help us understand what has passed as common sense in America do, in fact, believe that a single dominant ideology has been shared by virtually all Americans since the seventeenth or eighteenth century. Moreover, even many of those authors who do not accept this 'consensus' view of American history, see American history as the unfolding of a limited number of conflicting ideas.

Most Americans learn their own history this way.[1] High schools often present the drama of the American past as a centuries-long conflict between the eighteenth-century philosophies of 'founding fathers,' Alexander Hamilton versus Thomas Jefferson, or Benjamin Franklin versus Jonathan Edwards. Pedagogy tends to reflect out-dated scholarship. For almost forty years active historians of the United States actually have denied that deep ideological battles have marked American history. In elite high schools and universities Americans learn the views of this 'consensus school' which affirms that a single philosophy has animated American politics from its beginning.[2]

Surveys of public opinion can be marshaled to support the position of the consensus school. In an exhaustive analysis of the results of surveys of American public opinion made over the last half-century since systematic polling began, Herbert McClosky and John Zaller demonstrate that Americans almost universally affirm certain principles that university professors would say are associated with political and economic liberalism. Moreover, support for these principles has changed little from generation to generation.[3]

Yet, the consensus historians' case remains far from completely convincing. McClosky and Zaller also demonstrate that ideological *conflict* has been important throughout recent American history. Even if the range of ideological conflicts that have emerged in the United States since its beginning may appear to be narrow when compared to ideological battles in some other nations, Americans have often disagreed about how the world works and what should be done about it.[4] Moreover, McClosky and Zaller's evidence makes it clear that long-standing differences in belief have a lot to do with differences in social position, just as Gramsci would expect.[5] What is common sense to privileged

Americans is not always common sense to the general public. Even though the differences may be subtle, they are real.

It is necessary to exaggerate our argument to make the point: The consensus historians tend to overemphasize the role that liberalism, which is, indeed, still at the center of the ideology of those who dominate the United States, actually plays in the lived philosophy of the average American. At the same time the consensus historians have undervalued the role that what might be called *actual* religious values (belief in God, etc.) as opposed to 'civil religion' plays in the lives of many Americans. The consensus historians may have done this, in part, because real religious values play such a minor role in the lives of the American elite of which they are a part. Nevertheless, despite these shortcomings, the works of these historians provide an excellent guide to part of what is common sense in America. They tell us a great deal about American cultural history and they elucidate the sources of much of the contradictory consciousness of many Americans. They just do not tell us all.

In this chapter we use the works of consensus historians of American politics along with critical analyses of American religion and culture and evidence from surveys of American public opinion to identify the range of what passes for common sense to most Americans. Whenever possible, we suggest the part of the American public most likely to possess one set of ideas rather than another. In a number of cases we repeat what we think are reasonable historical explanations for some particular pattern of American beliefs.

We begin with religion, in particular with the ideas at the heart of the Protestant denominationalism that began in America in the seventeenth century. We then turn to economic and political ideology, to liberalism, which has been at the center of American political history since the end of the eighteenth century. Finally we look at scientism, the faith that the systematic methods of the natural sciences can be applied with advantage to all fields, an idea that has been part of the common sense of American managers, both public and private, since the end of the nineteenth century. Each ideology began as an historical philosophy, as a coherent, well-developed system. Here we are less interested in the philosophical status of the ideas that animate American politics than we are in the residues that each of these three historical philosophies has left in the consciousness of Americans. We are interested in the ways that each of these historical philosophies has become and remained a vital factor in American social struggles.

Readers already familiar with Gramsci's work will remember that he, himself, had something to say about the ideological face of American society in his notes on 'Americanism and Fordism.'[6] Our account relies very little on his analysis, which he recognized was very partial and tentative. Gramsci did not intend to provide an account of the range of politically-relevant ideas that appear to be common sense to different Americans. Rather, his aim was to isolate one, potentially positive, element of one American ideology in order to explore its relevance to Italian society at his time. Gramsci was not equipped to carry-out a sustained analysis of the common sense of Americans at the time that he wrote 'Americanism and Fordism;' he simply did not know enough about the United States and he did not have access to materials that could inform such a study. This lack of information makes it particularly remarkable that his comments on the American social system are so astute in at least three ways. First, he recognizes the significance of the lack of an entrenched aristocracy and the existence of relatively easy access to land in the development of American society. Second, he recognizes the unusual interplay between religion and politics in the United States. And third, he has an unusually prescient understanding of the roles that science and technology, and the ideas that fostered them would play in the American political economy of the twentieth century. We return to this third issue, and to what Gramsci calls 'Fordism,' in the last part of this section when we look at scientism, the most recent historical philosophy that has left a politically important residue in the consciousness of many Americans.

### Denominational religion: American destiny, isolationism, evangelism, and crusaderism

Of course, long before many Americans turned to science to provide answers to ultimate questions most Americans had perfectly serviceable answers provided to them by their religion. The particular faiths of the early European colonists still influence many Americans today, even many in that minority of Americans who are not religious. Colonial religion can be understood as the source of three sets of ideas that are common sense to most Americans. One idea has to do with identity, with who Americans are, with the view that many American's have of their own exceptionalism and destiny, the idea of Americans as a chosen people. The second has to do with how to deal with dissent, how to deal with people whose views differ from your own. For many Americans the only ways to deal with people whose ideas differ from your own is to isolate yourself from them (or them from you), convert them, or destroy them. This impulse has its roots in the religious philosophies of the dissenting Protestants who first isolated themselves in North America and employed all three means to deal with dissent in their own society. Finally, we look at the limited American idea of charity which is bound up with assumptions about the exceptionalism of the American people.

Relatively few Americans reject the idea of American exceptionalism. The colonial faith's most pervasive legacy is the American sense of national destiny. In his recent investigation of the cultural sources of the American war in Vietnam, Loren Baritz states that a single sentence written by one of the country's most respected novelists summarizes all that it is to be American. In *Whitejacket*, Herman Melville said:

. . . we Americans are the peculiar chosen people; the Israel of our time; we bear the ark of the liberties of the world.[7]

Baritz, along with most of the historians of the consensus school, traces messianic American nationalism back to the experience of the first European Protestants who settled in New England in the seventeenth century. Yet, of course, the contemporary transcontinental industrial nation hardly resembles the underpopulated and rough agrarian societies of the early Plymouth and Massachusetts Bay Colonies, at least on the surface. Even the ideologies of government are quite different. While the Plymouth Colony of 1620 may have been a place that was unusually democratic and tolerant in comparison to Britain at the time, New England quickly became a land of religious oligarchies, suspicious of foreigners with different beliefs and completely intolerant of any internal dissent. The modern American republic gives a much higher proportion of the population some access to political power and it awards more significant legal protection to dissenters than the Puritan settlements in North American ever did. More than a century ago (and more than two centuries after the foundation of the first European colonies in New England) Karl Marx even used the United States, and even New England's New Hampshire in particular, as examples of the most advanced form of religious toleration in the world.[8] And in America today the nemesis of New England's Puritans, the Roman Catholic Church, has the largest following of any faith. Yet, the sedimentations of seventeenth-century dissenting, Calvinist Protestantism make up the deepest strata of the common sense of many Americans.

Central to the doctrine of the New England Puritans who left England because of their dissent from the established Protestant church is the Calvinist notion of the Elect; God has chosen some people to enter the Kingdom of Heaven while others, the vast majority suffer preterition. They have been passed over. In the Massachusetts Bay Colony (the most successful of the early dissenter communities in America) the idea of God's election of individuals was transformed into a belief in his election of a whole people; the New England Puritans became the new Israel.[9]

Even before the American colonies declared their independence from Britain in 1776, New England's Puritans had modified their own self-assured belief that God had only saved a few and that their leaders were surely among the elect. To perpetuate the oligarchy from generation to generation Puritans began to allow the presumption of election to pass from parents to children. From there it was only a short step to accepting the possibility that the Kingdom of Heaven might be open to all, or at least that all should be encouraged to act in this life as part of the Elect by being good members of the faith.[10]

The New England Puritans replaced their older view of personal salvation, individual membership in the Elect, with an understanding of their community as Elect, the idea of a collective covenant. The notion of Puritan New

Englanders, and later, of all Americans, as an Elect people lived on long after the original historical philosophy began to be forgotten. Many reasons can be offered for the persistence of the idea. American history has been marked by periodic religious revivals when new (usually Christian, Protestant, and Calvinist) denominations are created, assuring that at all times there are at least some Americans whose self-assurance about their own position as the Elect is as great as that of the seventeenth-century Puritans. Perhaps even more significantly, American politicians, novelists, poets, song-writers, playwrights, and scholars have consistently identified the United States as an exceptional society, a society of destiny, or the new Israel. What began as the core concept of a specific religion in the English colonies of North America, became the core of a civil religion that every American is exposed to throughout his or her life.[11] Baritz ends his book on Vietnam by quoting California Governor Ronald Reagan's set speech from his first triumphant campaign for president. Most of Reagan's themes, and many of his phrases, were the same as those used by the first governor of Massachusetts to his own people three and a half centuries before when the Bay Colony settlers were the first Americans to be told that they were God's chosen people and that their nation must be 'a city on the hill,' a new Jerusalem.

What common experiences do so many Americans have that would make it reasonable to continue to think of themselves as a chosen people, a new Israel, or an Elect? What real events do politicians and writers play upon, reaffirm, and help explain? Perhaps the most important experiences are those that make up the repeated drama of immigration, the experience that most American families share. The drama opens with membership in a despised or downtrodden community, a characterization as valid for today's Indo-Chinese immigrants as it was for the seventeenth century dissenters from England, and just as valid for all immigrant communities in-between: Irish laborers escaping famine in the early nineteenth century, German-speaking liberals in flight from the repression following 1848's unsuccessful revolutions, or farmers leaving the dearth in south-eastern Sweden at the turn of the century. Immigrant survivors have to explain their own success, what makes them different from those they have left behind. American exceptionalism helps provide that answer. Americans have actively worked for their own deliverance simply by immigration. In that way they are like the Israelites who followed Moses. And like the Biblical chosen people, Americans, too, can make their country a holy land.

As Moses himself learned, a community that is to be 'that shining city on the hill' must be one cleansed of all impurities. This was one of the overriding concerns of the early Calvinist communities in America. They had three, usually effective, means of dealing with internal dissent. These means continue to make up much of the repertoire of ways that contemporary Americans deal with internal dissent: exclusion, reconversion, and repression.

By far the most likely to be preferred one of these three means of dealing with organized dissent in early Calvinist America was the first, exclusion. Dissenters excluded from the chosen community could continue to think of themselves as Elect and wisely isolated from the impure community which had rejected them. The Puritan's North American environment was particularly conducive to this policy. When religious schisms took place dissenters could simply move west, obstructed only by the less-technologically sophisticated military forces of the native population. The geography of human settlement in the United States records a history of constant, often seemingly petty, religious disputes followed by the removal, isolation, and reaffirmation of the chosen status of the members of the new community, especially in New England, where most towns can trace their founding to a religious conflict in another town (often with the same name) further east. Many American colleges and universities, especially those founded before the civil war (1861–65) have similar histories that can be traced eastward through a chain of older colleges, and older religious schisms, to the first college in America, the Puritans' Harvard. Even after the 'closing of the frontier' at the end of the nineteenth century (the end of the long era in which large tracts of arable land were available at low cost), Americans continued to turn to exclusion of dissenters before considering other politics for keeping the elect community pure. Thus, throughout the Vietnam War, those who protested American policy would be greeted by signs that proclaimed, 'America: Love It or Leave It,' a very hard choice for those who believed in the unique destiny of their country to make.

The Puritans had other, less benign, ways to deal with dissent. They could demand the dissenter choose either to reconvert and then live a closely-watched life within the norms of community, or else be destroyed. In New England Puritan society, unlike (say) in some Catholic cultures, it was never enough for dissenters to confess and propitiate for their sins. Other members had to keep former sinners (and all others who were particularly susceptible to the blandishments of the devil: women and children) under close surveillance to make sure that deviations would be detected and properly punished.[12] For those who refused reconversion matters could be much worse, as the history of the Salem witch trials attests.

The same process of reconversion and surveillance still goes on in the contemporary American religious groups that identify themselves as the Elect, but other residues of this Puritan practice are more pervasive. McClosky and Zaller's figures indicate that many Americans, especially those who identify themselves as more religious, are not particularly tolerant of behavior that deviates from relatively narrow norms, even though the same people are likely to profess an adherence to an abstract principle of 'liberty for all.'[13] As a result, many Americans accept a relatively authoritarian concept of 'community,' one that entails indoctrination and little real dissent.[14] For many Americans it is the only concept of 'community' they understand.[15] Yet, many Americans remain frightened by those who limit a dissenter's alternatives to reconversion or repression, and they fight against every manifestation of this impulse in American political life.[16] For example, in *The Crucible*, the playwright, Arthur Miller, offered a powerful depiction of the seventeenth century Puritan witch trials as a condemnation and partial explanation American anti-communist hysteria in the 1950s, and Miller's play became a standard part of the high school curriculum in many American schools in the 1960s.

In Puritan New England the impulse to isolate, convert, or repress dissenters played as much of a role in the society's external relations as it did in its internal affairs. The early Puritans believed that the world outside New England was made up of societies less perfect than their own. Certainly there were Elect individuals outside Massachusetts, but there were even more preterite ones, some of who were positively evil. At the very beginning Massachusetts was happy to exclude the rest of the world from the colony and the colony from the rest of the world. How then could the colony be 'that shining city on the hill,' the light to all nations? It could do so only by supporting evangelical movements designed to convert those in the external world who could be converted. In the same way that the Puritans were capable of hysteria and violence when internal dissenters refused to be isolated or reconverted, so the Puritans were just as capable of hysterical crusading violence against those outside their community who refused isolation or conversion. In particular, the Puritans periodically savaged their Native American neighbors who had refused conversion.[17] Many Puritans eventually saw the recalcitrant Indians as a positive evil, as much of an incarnation of the Devil as the endless savage land of North America itself, land which also had to be conquered and civilized.[18] As the next chapter discusses, these Puritan images continue to play a role in the way some Americans deal with foreign relations.

For now we want to focus on the question: why has this Puritan repertoire of isolationism, evangelism, or crusaderism continued to have such a role to play in American political life? Before we can even suggest a hypothesis it is important to point out that this impulse does not characterize the way all Americans deal with all types of dissent. It is much more characteristic, as McClosky and Zaller make clear, of Americans with a strong religious orientation, and, to narrow the group even further, of Americans who are members of conservative Christian denominations.[19]

Two things are important to note about the most conservative of America's denominations: some Baptists and Methodists, Mormons, Pentecostalists, 'Pentecostalist' Roman Catholics, and various 'Fundamentalist' churches. First, all these religious movements can trace some of their roots back to the British dissenting, Calvinist, Protestant churches of the seventeenth century; today's conservative American Christians, even though most may be found in the American south or west are, in a very real sense, the true descendants of the New England Puritans. Second, almost all of the conservative American churches began during the periodic 'revival' movements that have swept through American society since the eighteenth century.

American revivalists have always found their greatest successes during periods of social upheaval,[20] most recently in the late 1960s and early 1970s,[21] and they have found most of their converts not among the wealthiest, best-educated, and most secure members of the American population, but rather among some of those likely to be victimized by rapid social change, the marginal land-owning rural poor and those without capital.[22] Revivalism, various 'returns' to 'fundamental' ideas of Protestant Christianity, e.g. ideas similar to those of the Puritans, offer converts a way to accept social change as well as a way to act together to respond to it.[23]

The role new Protestant denominations have in facilitating collective action may be the key to understanding the success of revivalism. In general, it is difficult for Americans to create new political groups through which collective, self-interested social action can be carried-out. For example, in the two centuries of American government under the present constitution only four major national political parties have been created, the Democrats, Federalists, Whigs, and Republicans. Gramsci sees the widespread American tendency toward (private) repressive political violence as part of the reason for this development:

> The history of political parties and factions cannot be separated from the history of religious groups and trends. Precisely the U.S.A. and Japan offer us exceptional terrain to examine and understand the interdependence between religious and political groups, that is, to understand that any legal hindrance or obstacle of private violence to the spontaneous development of political trends and to their formation as a political party gives rise to a multiplication of religious sects. From this standpoint the political-religious history of the U.S.A. may be compared with that of Tsarist Russia (with the important difference that in Tsarist Russia, while there was no legal political freedom, religious freedom was also lacking and hence religious sectarianism took on morbid and exceptional forms.) In the U.S.A., both legally and in actual fact there is no lack of religious freedom (within certain limits, as the action against Darwinism brings out), and while legally (within certain limits) political freedom is not lacking, it *is* lacking in actual fact due to economic pressure and also due to open private violence. From this point of view, a critical examination of the judicial and police organization becomes important, showing that they give impunity to and even support private violence intended to prevent the formation of other than the Republican and the Democratic parties. The birth of new religious sects, too, is almost always urged and backed by economic groupings, to channel the effects of cultural-political compression. The huge sums earmarked in America for religious activity serve a very precise political-cultural purpose.[24]

Even creating trade unions and cooperatives appears to be more difficult in the United States than it is in many other countries.[25] Yet it is relatively easy to create new religious denominations. Some scholars even argue that America's liberal legal guarantees of religious toleration explain why Americans are so much more involved with organized religion than people in other industrialized nations tend to be. Religious toleration has assured that every American can find a church where she is comfortable.[26]

But the comfort that religious Americans feel with their church probably has little to do with a conscious belief that their church's theology is the best; religious Americans rarely are people who have time to study comparative theology. Instead, it may have quite a bit to do with the way that the 'lived philosophy' of many Protestant denominations has helped marginalized Americans cope with their social position. Perhaps this relationship can be seen most starkly among black Americans. Even before the civil rights movement of the 1950s and 1960s, which was led by black Protestant ministers, the major black denominations had played a central role in the black social struggle after the civil war. Churches of the National Baptist Convention and the African Methodist Episcopal denomination, as well as many others, provided a way for black Americans to live principles of mutual support and self-help, ultimately providing most of the services (higher education, disaster relief, and support in old age) that would be provided by the welfare state.[27] Contemporary black leaders may disparage the churches before the civil rights movement for supporting a conservative version of black separatism,[28] but those leaders recognize that the older church role was as much a social one as the one taken on by churches today.[29]

Christianity's highest norm, charity, enjoins all of America's Protestant denominational churches to be, at minimum, sources of mutual support for their own members. Many American churches apply the norm well beyond their own inner community by helping the poor in their locality, country, and the world at large. Even outside the churches, public 'charitable' activities are much more central to life in the United States than in most other industrialized countries. Elite social clubs of college students within the so-called 'Greek System' of fraternities and sororities vie with each other for doing local good works. Every American city houses half-a-dozen or more businessmen's philanthropic clubs building hospitals, repairing homes of the elderly, and raising money for needed traffic lights. Almost every American employer provides a way for employees to give part of every paycheck to local charities. And the average American is much more likely than his or her European or Japanese counterpart to have personally contributed time or funds to an international welfare agency like UNICEF or Oxfam.

Yet, the idea of charity plays an unusual role in American common sense because many Americans tie charity to another residue of Puritanism that glorifies those who give 'charity.' One source of this residue is the New Testament parable of the Good Samaritan, Jesus of Nazareth's story of a member of a despised and outcast minority who was the only one who would help a stranger in need. One interpretation of the story says that the Elect, those who have followed the commandment to be charitable, will long be a despised minority, like the Samaritan, or like the Puritans escaping religious persecution in the old world, and like so many American immigrants. Thus, the act of giving charity can become an act of affirming the belief that one is of the Elect. The burden placed on the recipient of charity is not only one of gratitude, it is also one of recognizing the 'despised' donor as, in reality, something quite different, as one of the Chosen. Moreover, those who accept this line of thought can have little sympathy for the apparent 'charity' of others who are well-off but who appear to revile or despise the latter-day Samaritans.

As a result of this assumption of their own Election, many Americans are uninterested in the view of their charity that other donors or recipients might have. This can often lead to a kind of misunderstanding between donor and recipient that the Good Samaritan view of charity easily explains away: many Americans do not expect to be thanked for their charity; the Elect must accept that they are a despised people.

Some authors have gone to great lengths to show how this assumption of being a despised but charitable people has played itself out throughout American history.[30] For our purposes it is more important to try to identify a bit more precisely what groups in the contemporary United States would be the most likely to share this view. The most significant group are fundamentalists. As George M. Marsden writes, 'Certainly the most immediate heritage of the fundamentalists comes from their twentieth-century experiences of being a beleaguered and ridiculed minority.'[31] American fundamentalism grew as a reaction to a new phase of industrialization and scientism, the new ideology of the elite. It was beleaguered in a world of Protestants who had 'strayed from the fundamentals,' joining the false religions of non-Christians, Catholics, and Communists. The fundamentalists, a primarily white, lower middle class religion growing outside the geographic centers of power in the United States, perhaps have the most fully-developed Good Samaritan view of charity of any group in the United States, and they share the suspicion and potential for misunderstanding of others that this view entails.

Even though this understanding of charity may tend to characterize non-elites, it can support an elite view that philanthropy should reinforce power, as Barry D. Karl and Stanley N. Katz argue in their Gramscian analysis of American elite philanthropy. The system of charity in the United States has served to justify a minimal state, emphasize the benefits of 'self-help' for the disadvantaged, and excuse the lack of deeper expressions of love by rich 'philanthropists' to poor recipients, and *vice versa*.[32]

## Liberalism: competitive individualism, property, and the market

Protestant denominationalism may have had the most wide-ranging impact of any historical philosophy on what most Americans take to be common sense, but it is probably not the most significant part of the common sense of the ruling classes in the United States. That distinction belongs to liberalism.

Liberalism is the source of that lived philosophy of many of the more privileged Americans; it emphasizes social atomism and competition and suggests that people have few responsibilities for each other. Liberalism is also the source of the even more pervasive American insistence upon the importance of private property and the need for private accumulation. Finally, liberalism is the source of the preference that many Americans have for dealing with all social relations through the market.

If one of the United States's founding fathers could be transported from the end of the eighteenth-century to the present day they would probably not be surprised at the degree to which liberal doctrine is taken to be common sense by Americans. If anything they might be surprised at how much some liberal dogmas have lost ground to what to many of the founding fathers would have appeared to be archaic religious sentiments. In 1776 the United States may have been a more liberal nation than it is today. It was certainly a less-religious one. While one scholar estimates that only one in ten Americans would have identified themselves with any established religion at the time of the American war of independence,[33] today the United States is the most religious of the industrialized nations.[34]

Religion, particularly the denominations of the disadvantaged that grew with social upheaval and immigration, probably has encroached upon the mass appeal of some liberal ideas in the United States, especially the appeal of individualism. But, as if to compensate, Protestant denominationalism has served to strengthen other liberal dogmas: private property and the market. At the same time that newer 'scientific' ideologies, especially Social Darwinism, have reinvigorated almost all the elements of liberalism that are common sense to Americans.

Whether one wishes to start with Thomas Hobbes or John Locke or wait until the beginnings of modern political economy with Adam Smith, the core problem faced by liberal theorists has always been what to do in a world in which individuals are social atoms, driven by passions, without responsibility for one another and in relentless competition with everyone else. Albert O. Hirschman's brilliant analysis of the origins of liberalism reminds us that the original problem was one of philosophers worrying about a world in which the passions that drove the war-like princes had come to motivate a significant proportion of the population.[35]

At the time of the American war of independence the British colonies of North America may well have been the sort of place where such anti-social individualism looked like it could run amok. The country included a significant population of men who had little reason to develop any sense of community responsibility. Using relatively comprehensive statistics of one year's emigration from Britain to America in the late-eighteenth century, Bernard Bailyn figures that the new American population was made up of two distinct groups. One, family groups, often Scots–Irish, hardworking, and already Protestants or ripe for conversion in the new Methodist and Baptist revivals, were hardly people suffering from a fearful competitive individualism. The other group, primarily younger men, fortune seekers, men willing to sell their immediate liberty to get to America where their liberty might be total, were another matter.[36] The American frontiers soon filled with super-individualistic, often socially irresponsible adventurers, the men of American frontier novels and Westerns. They accepted, lived, convinced others of the importance of the liberal assumptions of competitive individualism.[37]

A number of American films of the last generation (e.g., *Butch Cassidy and the Sundance Kid*), mourn the passing of American competitive individualism along with the loss of the frontier to settled agriculture, families, churches, and responsible communities, but the idea has not been completely removed from the American common sense. Attitude surveys demonstrate that it shows up periodically. In the 1970s in particular there was a clear move toward a more aggressive individualism, especially among American men.[38]

The liberal assumption of competitive individualism has also retained its place in the consciousness of Americans by its attachment, since the late nineteenth century, to the philosophy of Social Darwinism. While most Americans might no longer believe that life is and should be a struggle of each man or woman against all others, most Americans do believe that life involves the struggle of groups against one another. Liberalism even contributed to white racism in the United States: because life is a struggle and people only have duties to themselves Native Americans could be eradicated and black people enslaved. When Social Darwinism gave white Americans a 'scientific' basis for their racism, the competitive struggle could be identified as the war between whites and the rest of the world.[39]

Yet, liberalism's concern with competitiveness, even as buttressed by Social Darwinism, has not left America with a monolithic, uniform racism.[40] On the other hand, respect for the basic means that the classical liberals saw for dealing with a world of competitive individualism pervades American thinking. American support and respect for private property is almost universal.[41]

In classical liberalism property, especially landed property, became the *sine qua non* of human character, the bridge between anti-social drives of the individual and the various market-like means through which the public interest could be served by those pursuing private vices. In Locke's system America itself acts as a sort of safety-valve of less-developed land that can be used to give property to those who will live under the British social contract. American history actually proved something similar to Locke's point. The availability of relatively inexpensive land until well into this century helped make 'The American Dream' of self-sufficient property ownership within the grasp of many Americans. In the United States, more than in many other societies, the popular defense of property is a defense of self-interest, or defense of the system in which one's own goals can be achieved, as much as it is a defense of the interests of the dominant class.

Yet, if liberalism were the *only* ideological underpinning of private property in the United States the institution would probably be much less legitimate that it is. Within the contradictory consciousness of most Americans there is a great fear of great accumulations of power, prestige, and wealth. It would be difficult for most Americans to fully justify the massive and continuous growth of the private fortunes that capitalism generates if it were not for the way that American religious doctrine works to support private property. At a very superficial level (important, perhaps, to early capitalism but less to the United States today) the Calvinist legacy leaves many Americans with the feeling that accumulations of wealth are a sign of virtue.[42] Today, or at any time in the last century, that argument is more likely to be put in Social Darwinist terms even if it is linked to religion, and it is an argument more likely to be given by ideologists of the American upper classes than as the religious argument of those who speak for and to the less-privileged.[43]

More significantly for most Americans today, neither liberalism nor Protestant denominationalism provides them with any positive command for taking huge fortunes from those who have them even when those fortunes appear to be ill-gotten; yet, religious ideology, especially the typical American idea of community, presents clear negative injunctions against breaking up such fortunes. It would be 'unfair:' it would be 'stealing.' Not surprisingly given the high inverse correlation between religiosity and social status, the largest group of Americans most committed to defending private fortunes are those whose social condition assures that it will be others' fortunes that they defend.[44]

Of course, liberalism only sanctions the accumulation of property as a private vice turned into a public virtue under certain conditions. The struggle to accumulate must go on under conditions that are the same for everyone. No special favors and no use of private (non-economic) power can be granted. Ideally, the market, unregulated by state or private power produces such conditions.

Critiques of the liberal analysis of markets are legion, and part of the normal political discourse in most countries, but they are neither particularly well known nor accepted in the United States outside of some quarters of the academic community. In a recent attempt to conceive of how Americans could move beyond their faith in markets one of the country's leading political behaviorists, Robert E. Lane, catalogs the vast amount of survey data on American perceptions of the fairness of markets and the unfairness of governmental regulation and concludes that, like it or not, this preference is a 'deep structure' of American politics, even though this 'structure' is largely a matter of perception. Lane argues that such perceptions could change if Americans developed a stronger community point of view (one that extended to the entire nation, not simply to a particular locality or denomination).[45]

While Lane advocates such a change, he recognizes how difficult it would be simply because the market preference most Americans have is based on real political experience, the partial proof provided by the American political history in which the market has always been valued even by the most successful reformers. As Vernon Parrington argues, since at least Lincoln's time successful American political entrepreneurs have argued that the egalitarianism preached by the revolutionaries of their time can be achieved through equality of opportunity in the marketplace.[46] In the US, political institutions that restrict the market to reinforce a broader view of community and demonstrate that government can be just have always functioned in opposition to ideas that are common sense to most Americans. Roosevelt's New Deal is, of course, the most important example, and Roosevelt was able to justify his New Deal on the basis of a new idea of community which attacked the presumptive superiority of the market-place, he justified on the basis of a sort of scientism, the need to experiment within the bounds of the liberal dogmas.

One consequence of the deep support given to the market in America is that even non-elite American movements for social change tend to work for the perfection of the market economy rather than for its restriction. Thus, in the 1970s, in the years before Reagan's election to the presidency, the most significant social movement in the United States was one which defined all Americans as 'consumers,' as people equally interested in perfecting the economic market and, therefore, in doing away with unfair business practices that raise consumer prices, flood the market with shoddy products, or force people to buy things that they do not wish to buy, for example, the electric power produced by nuclear power plants.[47]

Writing in the early 1970s Garry Wills, a perceptive American social critic, argued that the liberal notion of the market was not confined to the popular understanding of the economy but had permeated many Americans' understandings of their own morality.[48] Wills argued that many Americans metaphorically link their Calvinist concerns about Election and their Social Darwinist beliefs about the survival of the fittest in an idea of 'the moral market,' a struggle to prove the superiority of ones' own morality and ones' own being. Wills, who styles himself a conservative, finds this idea of competing in a moral market for individual virtue frightening and incoherent. But other academic commentators on American society see it as a virtue. People who compete in the moral marketplace are 'achievement oriented,' the essential citizens of a 'modern' society.

## Faith in science

Wills's study was written, in part, as a commentary on what he believed to be the passing of liberalism as the dominant ideology in the United States. He predicted that Richard Nixon would be the United States's last 'liberal' president. Wills argued that Nixon, who always considered himself an outsider in the higher circles of American power, was animated by what Gramsci would call an 'historical' philosophy that was going more and more out of favor with the American elite, even if it remained at the core of the beliefs of the American middle class.

Wills overstates the case. McClosky and Zaller's analysis clearly demonstrates that the American elite remain, for the most part, 'nineteenth century liberals,' dedicated to the free market and competitive individualism.[49] Still, arguably, a new historical philosophy has begun to supplant liberalism as the central ideology of American corporate managers and has become part of the common sense of most Americans, but it still owes a great deal to liberal roots. Scientism could never have developed its hold on the American consciousness if the ground had not already been prepared by the acceptance of Social Darwinism as means of explaining the rightness of the inequality created in a market society and the acceptance of an extension of the market metaphor to the creation and evaluation of ideas. To many Americans ideas compete and survive in an intellectual marketplace; they are proven by their practical application to existing problems.[50]

American faith in science also finds support in the Enlightenment faith in progress.[51] It was reinforced by the economic success of the first wave of American inventions[52] and the relatively benign history of the first experiments in industrialism in the United States,[53] as much as by the Social Darwinism that many Americans turned to explain those who failed in the new industrial economy. But a version of scientism did not become an historical philosophy and an ideology associated with an historically important social group until late in the nineteenth century.

The importance of professions in the applied sciences grew in America in the middle of the nineteenth century. The professions, in turn, had a major impact on the growth and development of American industry at the turn of the century, the so-called 'second industrial revolution.' The philosophy of 'systematic management' developed as a guide to controlling the engineering-dominated industries of mid-century, especially the railroads. From there the ideology was adopted as the managerial philosophy of the new industries that developed in the larger, continent-wide markets created by the railroads, industries which, themselves relied upon new scientific applications: the electrical and chemical industries and the industries producing packaged foods and other mass consumption goods. The engineering philosophy came to dominate management in the first gigantic firms that managed the second industrial revolution and it remained central to the management of all of America's major manufacturing industries of the twentieth century: the aerospace and telecommunications industries and, beginning even earlier, the most important, the automotive industry. This was what Gramsci called 'Fordism.' 'Science' was extended to labor-management relations, marketing, and even to institutions for constantly generating inventions that could be turned into new products.[54] Scientism became the ideology of the new part of the American governing elite, the managers of the growing private firms and (later) the managers of the growing bureaucracies of American government. Political analyst, Mona Harrington, calls the scientism that the American managerial class applies to problem after problem a 'functionalist' version of the old American 'dream of deliverance;'[55] the shining city on the hill will be created by experiment, efficient planning, and the application of technology.

It is important that it was engineering, applied science, rather than theoretical science that was the source of American faith in science and technology. The particular American faith in science supports an essentially anti-theoretical attitude. Most Americans expect science to give results, to show that things can be done and they have an extreme distrust of theories, abstractions that often suggest that certain things just cannot be done. This distrust of theory explains why many Americans, especially American managers or those who aspire to be like them, insist that they have accepted no ideology, no system, but are only guided by practical considerations.[56] The theoretical unities so essential to scientific investigation and to the accumulation of scientific knowledge leave many Americans unimpressed. Thus, we should not be surprised that in a country where the vast majority of people express some faith in scientific progress, about half of the adults find the Biblical account of creation preferable to Darwin's.[57]

This faith in science yet distrust of theory created an interesting paradox when the tools of the systematic management movement were first applied to government. American social sciences grew at the turn of the century with an explicit goal of applying scientific knowledge to the problem of government. This led to a call for government regulation that one historian notes was, quite self-consciously, 'an impulse without a philosophy, an instinct rather than a conviction.'[58] In part because America's early reforming social scientists distrusted moves to set the principles behind their proposals in a broader theoretical context, later 'scientific' economists operating on the basis of the liberal principles that have such a 'matter of fact' and 'non-ideological' status in the US, found it easy to dominate the new professions. Similarly, when systematic management actually was extended to government, first in the regulatory movements at the turn of the century and later in the Franklin Roosevelt administration, the move was justified as experimental and anti-theoretical leaving the reforms presumptively suspect and only waiting for any evidence that they were 'not working' as well as might be expected.[59]

Experimental method, then, not theory, gives Americans their trust in science. Scientific experimentation produces solutions to problems and makes things possible, or, at least that is the presumption. Some historians would put down the American faith in experimentation, tinkering to get things to work better, to the laziness and carelessness of a people whose ancestors went searching for pots of gold at the end of the rainbow, a free lunch, in the new world. A better explanation might be the one Gramsci seems to favor in his work on 'Americanism and Fordism,' the experimental tinkering and systematic application of technology that many Americans like has some positive results. It assured that American industry would grow to dominate world markets and it gave workers in the privileged sectors where science was first applied a relatively good deal.

Of course, not everyone in America was happy with the rise of scientism in the late nineteenth century. Traditional American intellectuals, disgusted by the factory and the engineer, searched for alternatives.[60] And the churches of the newly disadvantaged, the rural poor and the lower middle classes excluded from the new privileged sectors, rebelled. Today's fundamentalism began as an anti-modernist, anti-scientific, and anti-industrialist movement directly before the first world war.[61] Not surprisingly, the managers and owners of industries of the second industrial revolution responded in kind. The Rockefeller family, for example, supported the movement for social modernism by endowing the University of Chicago and the Federal Council of Churches (which was designed along engineering-management lines to 'administratively consolidate the denominations along the lines of big business') and by creating the *anti*-fundamentalist Riverside Church in Manhattan, a massive modern-gothic cathedral complete with Darwin and Einstein carved under a statue of Christ on a side portal.[62]

The Rockefellers were no more successful in uniting the denominations into one Calvinist conglomerate than they were at stopping the rise of fundamentalism. Yet the view of science held by the fundamentalists of the late twentieth century differs a bit from the views of their founders. As George Marsden argues, the fundamentalists' 'empiricist' search for the truth of God in basic texts has easily been assimilated with the technological side of American society, technological thinking that does not wrestle with theoretical principles.[63]

## Elements of contradictory consciousness in America

Political scientists who follow America's consensus historians tend to emphasize the compromises and accommodations that go on when a new ideological strain, like scientism, confronts older assumptions. That is in keeping with their conclusions, exemplified by Samuel P. Huntington's that there is a single liberal 'American Creed' that pervades American society.[64] It is hard for those who accept this 'dominant ideology thesis' to explain why those American commentators who most identify with classical liberalism act like it is so embattled.[65] Our starting point in Gramsci's understanding of ideology makes us emphasize something different, the contradictory historical sources of contemporary American visions and the uneven distribution of faith in different elements of the American Creed across different parts of American society.

Our starting point also makes us cast our net a bit wider than the scholars of the consensus school do. We must be concerned with the contradictory consciousness of the mass public as much as the lived philosophies the American elite. In contrast, a Harvard Business School professor, George C. Lodge, whose *New American Ideology* remains one of the most thought-provoking studies of American contemporary American consciousness, ends up writing only about the changes in consciousness that have occurred because of the rise of technologically-sophisticated production processes and the large firm. He assumes that these ideas have been set on top of a bedrock of liberal principles shared equally by all Americans. But, in the end, because he ignores the religious convictions that are at the base of the contradictory consciousness of most Americans, Lodge focuses on a conflict (liberalism versus the philosophy of systematic management) that may only be relevant in that simplified form to a small part of American society, the corporate and intellectual elite.

A historian of American Protestantism, Martin E. Marty, provides a better general analysis. Marty argues that the battle between technological philosophies and nineteenth-century liberalism represents rapid changes and ideological ferment in the upper strata of American society which belie the real stability of what we would call the contradictory consciousness of the general public, the affirmation of the principles of denominational Protestantism along with the liberal faith in property and markets.[66] That constellation of (often contradictory) beliefs has as much claim to be called the single 'American Creed' as does liberalism *per se*.

Yet, Lodge does make an important point by emphasizing the unresolved ideological contradictions created by the extension of the faith in science through larger firms and big government. Bureaucratization of work and politics undermines both the popular legitimation of American society provided by the liberal belief in the overarching good of individual action in markets and the denominational belief in the maintenance of community by isolation, conversion, or repression; neither the welfare state nor the big corporation nor even the big union maintain themselves primarily through repression and all of these institutions make implicit claims about the importance of communities larger than the ones many Americans accept. It may well be correct to argue, 'a serious legitimation problem has existed for American institutions since the Great Depression.'[67]

## Notes

1. Frances FitzGerald, *America Revised* (Boston: Little Brown, 1979).
2. Important and representative works in this school include, Daniel Boorstin, *The Genius of American Politics* (Chicago: University of Chicago Press, 1953), Richard

Hofstadter, *The American Political Tradition*, 2nd ed. (New York: Vintage Books, 1973), and especially Louis A. Hartz, *The Liberal Tradition in American Politics* (New York: Harcourt, Brace, and World, 1955). Analyses of contemporary political events based on the conclusions of the consensus school include Mona Harrington, *The Dream of Deliverance in American Politics* (New York: Knopf, 1986) and George C. Lodge, *The New American Ideology*, 2nd ed. (New York: New York University Press, 1986).

3. Herbert McClosky and John Zaller, *The American Ethos* (Cambridge, MA: Harvard University Press, 1984).
4. McClosky and Zaller, 228–33.
5. McClosky and Zaller demonstrate clear differences in the ideological makeup of elite groups as compared to the mass public. Their own distinctions tend to emphasize the political activism among the elite rather than job category, income, wealth, or other factors more clearly indicative of social class. Nevertheless, they use the relatively well-documented correlations among political involvement, education, and wealth in the United States in their own analysis.
6. Antonio Gramsci, *Selections from Prison Notebooks*, Quentin Hoare and Geoffrey Nowell Smith, ed. and trans. (London: Lawrence and Wishart, 1971), 279–80, 306–18.
7. Quoted in Loren Baritz, *Backfire* (New York: William Morrow and Co., 1984), 26.
8. Karl Marx, 'On the Jewish Question,' in T. B. Bottomore ed. and trans., *Early Writings* (New York: McGraw-Hill, 1963), 9, 23.
9. Perhaps the most elegant scholarly discussion of the genesis of the American idea of Americans as a chosen people is Sacvan Berkovitch's, *The Puritan Origins of the American Self* (New Haven: Yale University Press, 1975).
10. Berkovitch, 94.
11. A key source of this argument is Robert N. Bellah, *The Broken Covenant* (New York: Seabury, 1975). In Karl Lamb's in-depth study of the political attitudes of twelve American families during the Watergate era he found that in his small upper-middle class sample, religious affect had been almost completely transferred to the state and nation. His respondents believed in God, but they believed even more in America, and believed that part of being a good citizen was to be involved in some way with organized (usually Christian and Protestant) religion. The pattern he saw was consistent with survey data on American religious attitudes. *As Orange Goes: Twelve California Families and the Future of American Politics* (New York: W. W. Norton, 1974), 154.
12. Edmund S. Morgan, *The Puritan Family* (New York: Harper and Row, 1966).
13. McClosky and Zaller, 38.
14. David Little even argues that Calvinism's original force comes from this ability to impose a legitimate, authoritarian order on a confused world, *Religion, Order, and Law* (Chicago: University of Chicago Press, 1984).
15. In *The New American Ideology* George C. Lodge suggested that this was changing. The book was written in the early 1970s and, perhaps, represented a bit of wishful thinking on Lodge's part. Lodge, a professor at Harvard Business School, felt that Americans needed a stronger idea of community (a notion that membership in society had a long list of rights and duties associated with it) in order for the United

States to successfully reemerge in its position as the leader of the world economy at the end of the structural adjustments in the world economy that he saw appearing in the early 1970s. The last decade did not live up to his hopes. (On the contrary, Marsden, in fact, argues that fundamentalists have created some of the most successful 'new' communities in America in recent years, and these are on the old Puritan model, 'Preachers of Paradox,' 161.) Lodge's most recent project is both an attempt to develop a comparative explanation of America's lack of a deeper idea of community and a political tract aimed at convincing American industrialists and (to a much much lesser extent, labor leaders) that they should foster the development of such a concept. The result is a series of comparative case studies of something like the 'common sense' in nine industrial or semi-industrial countries. Despite the grounding of the work in an idealist research design, it provides an excellent basis for indicating what is unusual in American common sense and what is typical of the ideological basis of all industrial, capitalist societies, George C. Lodge and Ezra F. Vogel, eds, *Ideology and National Competitiveness: An Analysis of Nine Countries* (Boston: Harvard Business School Press, 1987).

16. One noted American historian sees American conformism and intolerance primarily as reflections of American class consciousness, a sort of immigrant's fear of slipping back down the status ladder to become just like those off the boat. This makes the impulse hard to fight against, but makes the fight even more worthwhile. Henry Steele Commager, *The American Mind* (New Haven: Yale University Press, 1950), 414.
17. In *Righteous Empire: The Protestant Experience in America* (New York: Harper and Row, 1970), Martin E. Marty argues that Protestantism was always a major support for those who wanted to remove Native Americans.
18. The earliest American novels even grew out of 'captivity narratives' that emphasized the conflict between the 'good' settler and the Indian 'savage' and his vast continent as a source of evil and terror, Richard Chase, *The American Novel and Its Tradition* (Garden City, NY: Doubleday Anchor Books, 1957), 11.
19. McClosky and Zaller, 43.
20. On the longer historical picture see Robert T. Handy, *A History of the Churches in the United States and Canada* (New York: Oxford University Press, 1976) and Linda K. Pritchard, 'Religious Change in Nineteenth-Century America,' in Charles Y. Glock and Robert N. Bellah, eds, *The New Religious Consciousness* (Berkeley: University of California Press, 1976.), 297–330.
21. George M. Marsden, 'Preachers of Paradox, in Mary Douglas and Stephen Tipton, eds, *Religion and America: Spirituality in a Secular Age* (Boston: Beacon Press, 1983), 160.
22. From 1955 to 1965, for example, during the childhood of the post-war 'baby boom' generation, almost all American denominations grew. But after 1965 the middle-class and upper-class churches diminished while lower-class Protestant churches continued to grow; see Wade Clark Roof, 'America's Voluntary Establishment: Mainline Religion in Transition,' in Douglas and Tipton, 135. The other side of the same phenomenon is that it is only in the religions of America's upper classes, for example, Episcopalianism and Unitarianism, that the 'crisis of religion' or the idea of 'God's death' has ever been much of a problem; see Peter L. Berger, 'From the Crisis of Religion to the Crisis of Secularity,' in Douglas and Tipton, 14–24.

23. Stephen Tipton demonstrates that the most successful of the new American religions of the 1970s, even those rooted in Asian philosophies or psychoanalysis rather than Calvinism, spread an achievement ideology similar to the Puritan's, 'The Moral Logic of Alternative Religions,' in Douglas and Tipton, 79–107.
24. Antonio Gramsci, *Quaderni del Carcere* (*QC*), (Torino: Einaudi, 1975), III, 1666–7.
25. Gramsci argues that because religion and politics are both conceptions of the world, where you have an apparent political unity you find a proliferation of churches and religious sects and where you have apparent religious unity you find a proliferation of parties. The difference between (say) Italy and the United States, has to do with the particular historical traditions of the countries not with any greater fundamental agreement in one country or the other (*QC*, II, 1021).
26. Marty (p. 74) argues that American denominations are like price fixers sharing a single market. The only way an American can 'buy' cooperation with others to deal with new social problems is to choose a denomination.
27. See Handy, 174, 271.
28. The criticism made, for example, by Jesse Jackson and earlier by Martin Luther King, Sr. and his son.
29. Robert N. Bellah reminds us that the American cultural revolution of the 1960s began in the civil rights movement, in the black churches, and ultimately in the integrationist Martin Luther King, Jr.'s call for a universal return to the Christian imperative of love. The counter-culture, as much as resurgent right-wing fundamentalism, were both responses to the same social pressures and both were cast in similar language. Interestingly, it was only the upper-class counter-culture movement that lost the religious language retained by the civil rights movement and by the fundamentalists; see, 'New Religious Consciousness and the Crisis of Modernity,' in Glock and Bellah, 337.
30. Walter Allen, *The Urgent West: An Interpretation of the Idea of the United States* (London: John Barker, 1969), 105–10.
31. 'Preachers of Paradox,' 160.
32. 'Foundations and Ruling Class Elites,' *Daedalus*, 116 (1987): 1–40.
33. Handy, 145.
34. David Martin, 'Received Dogma and New Cult,' in Douglas and Tipton, 112–13.
35. *The Passions and the Interests* (Princeton: Princeton University Press, 1977).
36. *Voyagers to the West: A Passage in the Peopling of America on the Eve of the Revolution* (New York: Knopf, 1986).
37. Allen, in *The Urgent West*, finds much deeper roots in Western society for this sort of individual and is surprised that the philosophical justifications for such individualism did not appear until much later, perhaps (say) with Max Stirner and his deep belief in the privacy of property and his moral justification for letting others fend for themselves. Cf., Pio Marconi, *La liberta selvaggia* (Venice: Marsilio editori, 1979).
38. J. C. Veroff et al., 'Comparison of American Motives: 1957 Versus 1976,' *Journal of Personality and Social Psychology* , 39 (1980), 1249–62, cited in Baard B. Knudsen, 'The Paramount Importance of Cultural Sources: American Foreign Policy and Comparative Foreign Policy Research Reconsidered,' Paper presented at the annual meeting of the International Studies Association, Anaheim, 22–9 March 1986.
39. Russell Blaine Nye notes that as early as 1854 influential works were published in

the United States ranking the various races and setting out the doctrine of the struggle between them. *Society and Culture in America, 1800–1860* (New York: Harper and Row, 1974).

40. McClosky and Zaller (p. 70) report that only about half of the American public believe in general racial hierarchies or abstract racist theories.
41. McClosky and Zaller report over 90 per cent approval of private property on a variety of different measures (p. 122).
42. Handy notes, 'John Locke, the "philosopher of the American Revolution," drew on the political capital of the Reformed tradition in his seminal essays. Therefore many Calvinists could accept his political philosophy even though his theological views were tinged with Enlightenment thought.' (p. 139.) Little emphasizes that for the early Protestants business was a special realm of human freedom because it helped assure that men would not be idle, following the liberal argument, it turned the vice of greed into the virtue of diligence (p. 123).
43. See Jim Moore, 'Herbert Spencer's Henchmen: The Evolution of Protestant Liberals in Late Nineteenth Century America,' in John Durant, ed., *Darwin and Divinity* (Oxford: Basil Blackwell, 1985).
44. McClosky and Zaller, 140.
45. 'Market Justice, Political Justice,' *American Political Science Review*, 80 (1986), 383–402.
46. Vernon L. Parrington, *The Romantic Revolution in America* (New York: Harcourt, Brace, and World, 1927).
47. See Robert D. Holsworth, *Public Interest Liberalism and the Crisis of Affluence* (Boston: G. K. Hall and Co., 1980). Holsworth demonstrates that consumer movements of the 1970s replicated the arguments and political tactics of earlier, largely unsuccessful movements for social change in the United States.
48. Garry Wills, *Nixon Agonistes: The Crisis of the Self-Made Man* updated version (New York: Bantam Books, 1979).
49. McClosky and Zaller, 248.
50. Wills's analysis of the consequences of this phenomenon, which builds upon Herbert Marcuse's, is especially cogent, 318–25.
51. Nye, 24.
52. Ibid., 29.
53. In the United States, unlike earlier in England, the availability of free land helped keep wages in the first factories relatively high and working conditions far superior to those in Europe. However, with the first cyclical downturns in the American industrial economy things changed somewhat. Capitalists encouraged immigration to lower the wage bill. Still, industrial workers in the United States began and remained the highest paid in the world, at least until the nineteen seventies.
54. The most important works on the rise of the large American firm and its relation to the engineering philosophy are Alfred D. Chandler, Jr's *Strategy and Structure* (Cambridge: MIT Press, 1962) and *The Visible Hand* (Cambridge: Harvard University Press, 1977). Also see David A. Hounshell, *From the American System to Mass Production, 1800–1932* (Baltimore: Johns Hopkins University Press, 1984) and JoAnne Yates, *Control Through Communication* (Baltimore: Johns Hopkins University Press, forthcoming).

55. See Harrington.
56. Commager, 3.
57. Eileen Barker, 'Let There Be Light: Scientific Creationism in the Twentieth Century,' in Durant, 186.
58. Commager, 217.
59. This is Hartz's basic analysis and critique of the Roosevelt reforms and is the basis for Lodge's argument as well.
60. Nye, 277.
61. John Durant, 'Darwinism and Divinity,' in Durant, 36.
62. Moore, 88.
63. Marsden, 161.
64. *American Politics: The Promise of Disharmony* (Cambridge, MA: Harvard University Press, 1981).
65. E.g., R. Q. Armington and William D. Ellis, *More: The Rediscovery of American Common Sense* (Chicago: Regnery Gateway, 1984).
66. 'Religion in America Since Mid-Century,' in Douglas and Tipton, 274.
67. Dick Anthony and Thomas Robbins, 'Spiritual Innovation and the Crisis of American Civil Religion,' in Douglas and Tipton, 232.

# 3 Ideology and American foreign policy

The authors who claim that the United States has suffered a legitimation crisis since the beginning of the Roosevelt era often go on to argue that the post-war American anti-communist crusade helped Americans manage this crisis. We believe this is a partial truth and an important one, but it may not be as central to understanding the role that the ideas that are common sense to many Americans have played in governing American foreign policy as it might appear at first glance. The American anti-communist crusade can be explained as the result of the way ideas much older than Leninism have played themselves out in the United States after the country became a world power.

Ideology plays two roles in the foreign policy process. On the one hand, mass ideologies must exist to legitimize the roles played by foreign-policy-makers; ideologies help constitute decision-makers as separate actors. On the other hand the ideologies of foreign-policy-makers themselves let them apprehend the world and ideologies act as guides to policy. The Gramscian perspective suggests two important things in regard to ideology in these roles. First, the ideologies that legitimize decision-makers,—the ideas that the mass public of a nation refers to explain why a special elite does and should make policy for them—are unlikely to be coherent within any group in society and they are unlikely to be exactly the same for all groups in society. Foreign-policy-makers will be legitimized by common sense, by the contradictory consciousness of the public. Second, we have no particular reason to believe that the operational ideologies followed by foreign-policy-makers will directly reflect the contradictory consciousness of the mass public more than minimally, that is, at the level needed to maintain the foreign-policy-makers' independent role.

In this chapter we will begin with the ideas that have given popular legitimation to foreign-policy-makers in the United States, in particular the notion of America's special destiny and mission. Then we will turn to the slowly changing mix of operational ideologies which have influenced the practice of American foreign policy from the foundation of the nation. Finally, we will look at foreign policy problems created by the conflicts within and between both sets of ideas, examining the form that any contemporary 'crisis of legitimation' in foreign policy is likely to take.

## American destiny and the legitimation of American foreign policy

It is a commonplace of the history Americans teach themselves that American foreign-policy-makers have been a distinguished lot. The United States has been blessed with diplomats like Benjamin Franklin, John Adams, and John Quincy Adams who could charm victory out of military defeat. They worked with authors of bold world visions, men like George Washington, James Monroe, and Woodrow Wilson.

We suspect that part of what makes American foreign-policy-makers look so good to the American public is that the public has put surprisingly few demands on them. In a country where foreign commerce only recently became important to most people, where international wars have not been fought on home territory for generations, the public has little reason to be interested in foreign affairs. Foreign-policy-makers, as compared to officials in other branches of American government, have unusual leeway to define what they want to do and how to do it.

Perhaps the most widespread popular belief about foreign affairs is that the United States has a peculiar destiny. American foreign-policy-makers need to, and have almost always wanted to, treat the US as a country with a special mission.

Yet, Americans have come to no particular agreement as to how that mission should be pursued, although the basic repertoire of political means provided by American religion offers something of a guide. Where and when the United States is powerless to change foreign affairs, foreign-policy-makers can isolate the United States from the rest of the world, or isolate parts of the world from the US. When American policy-makers confront people who it can be assumed because of their race, culture, or behavior could be convinced of the superiority of the American system, then policy-makers can work to convert them. When that is impossible and foreign powers threaten the United States value system or the nations that have been converted to its system, then repression must be tried.

Those who accept this Calvinist repertoire have difficulty approving of any attempts their government might make to make long-term deals with any foreign nations that do not accept the 'American system.' That is why it is difficult to find popular support in the United States for certain, non-idealistic visions of international law or for the maintenance of foreign spheres of influence, or, some would argue, for almost all of the traditional forms of diplomatic practice which are all about interacting in good faith with people with whom you disagree. In the real world, they say, American evangelism and attempts at domination have always been frustrated, thus forcing policy-makers into long periods of inactivity demanded by a brooding, isolationist public.[1]

No matter how real these cycles of 'introversion' and 'extroversion' are (and there is debate about that) they do not tell the whole story of the relationship between popular beliefs and foreign policy action. If Calvinist principles by themselves ruled American foreign-policy-making it would be difficult for American diplomats and statesmen to have been as successful as they have been. But really only one of these ideas, the idea of American destiny, has almost universal support in the United States. Samuel P. Huntington argues quite correctly that the American assumption of special destiny functions as the core of American nationalism,[2] and what an unusual focus of nationalist sentiment it is because the idea of American destiny has no concrete content. Arguably, foreign-policy-makers are constrained by this view to act to maintain and extend 'Americanism,' but 'Americanism' can mean many things to many different people. Policy-makers have a wide range of choice among different concrete meanings of American destiny.

Huntington, like many American scholars, believes that 'Americanism' means only one thing: the liberal principles of individual liberty, property, and preference for the market. But this has not been what all Americans have demanded from their government as expressions of American destiny at all times in the past. At the turn of the century people from the Bible-belt of the midwest and south demanded that the national government support 'Americanism' by supporting the Christian missionary movement that had made those the parts of the country where public knowledge and concern about international affairs was the greatest. For whites in the post-reconstruction south, pursuing American destiny might mean pursuing Anglo-Saxon superiority, taking the scepter of white domination of the world from England's weakened hand. For first or second generation Americans in the Roosevelt era, especially those in industrial working class families, it might mean extending the American system of equal opportunity and the newly won right to organize to all workers throughout the world.[3] For the urban poor at the end of the eighteenth century it might mean supporting the extensions of the Rights of Man, and the revolutionary program of the French Republic, just as today for the many Americans who supported Jimmy Carter, 'Americanism' entailed his campaign for human rights.

Popular attitudes about foreign policy place only a very loose constraint on the action of American foreign-policy-makers. Governments need only make a convincing case that they are pursing the United States's special destiny by designing a policy that satisfies the different visions of American destiny of a set of American social groups sufficiently powerful to give the government necessary support.

## The United States as a minor power

The American foreign-policy-makers who have been so slightly constrained by popular ideologies have been a surprisingly small group of men centered around the American president. When the 'founder' of American foreign policy, John Quincy Adams, became Secretary of State under the fifth president in 1817, no more than a dozen men could be considered 'decision-makers.' The State Department, the United States's foreign ministry, had only nine employees in Washington. Eight of them were clerks. And the US had foreign diplomatic establishments in less than a dozen countries.[4] Even when the United States became a great power, after the second world war, the group of foreign policy decision-makers remained small. In 1972 Richard J. Barnet estimated that less than 400 people, only one a woman, had filled the major decision-making positions in the American foreign policy establishment since the war.[5] These decision-makers stand over some twenty-five thousand civilian foreign policy officers in various branches of government, well over one hundred thousand employees in American intelligence services, and a professional military of over two million.[6] The vastness of today's foreign policy administrative system relative to the small number of administrators creates a host of problems of foreign policy implementation that John Quincy Adams never had to face. Yet, John Quincy Adams would still feel at home among today's American foreign policy elite. Many of the assumptions, goals, and interpretations of events that he accepted still motivate American foreign policy today.

It would be possible to paint a romanticized picture of the foreign-policy-makers of the early American republic that would have men like John Quincy Adams aghast at the power and pretensions of those who occupy their jobs today. Critics of the United States's globalism often recall George Washington's 'Farewell Address' which warned future American governments not to become involved in power politics and the entangling alliances of European statecraft and preached a modest, republican isolationism.

But Washington was also the man who called the United States a 'new empire' and dreamed of incorporating the entire new world into it and acting as a model for all governments raised after the destruction of Europe's atavistic monarchies. Washington's warnings against entangling alliances have more to do with his vision of American uniqueness and destiny than they have to do with any modesty. The United States was a new type of nation, a moral nation, that should not sully itself in Europe's deceitful bickering.

The founding fathers of American foreign policy shared the popular belief in American destiny. For them, American isolationism was the proper policy only because the United States was yet an embryonic empire, a new order not yet powerful enough to dominate the world.[7] They expected that the American system would expand, as the United States did from the very beginning.[8] As new English-speaking settlers moved west, north, and south across the continent they would set up their own republican governments and then ask for independence (in a commonwealth of republics) or inclusion under the American constitution. These new reflections of the American ideal need not be colonies formed on American territory. They might, like Texas, be parts of neighboring states or foreign empires.[9] Even long-settled places might sue for inclusion in the American system. At the beginning of the nineteenth century, for example, most American policy-makers believed that the English-speaking colonists of Canada would eventually join the United States.

It is worth noting as more than an aside that from the beginning American foreign-policy-makers had little trouble using the traditional diplomatic categories of 'nation' and 'people.' American policy-makers thought in terms of whole nations, English Canada, choosing to enter the American union, not of individuals, a flood of Canadians, asking for citizenship. This may seem surprising given what we have argued is the central role of liberalism in the consciousness of American elites from the beginning. Liberalism, after all, is a philosophy of the individual, not a philosophy of 'peoples.' But American exceptionalism, with its deeper roots in religion, already provided American elites with a notion of themselves as a people. In international affairs, liberalism's focus on the individual was simply displaced to nations. American foreign-policy-makers have always tended to treat international society as no more than the sum of nations. Moreover, nations, treated as individuals writ large, are assumed to have the same goals as liberalism's human individuals: the pursuit of self-interest, especially in terms of wealth and power. America's imperial goals were simply those of any nation. Finally, nations could be discovered to be successful or unsuccessful using the same measures that applied to individuals. A hierarchy of nations and people based on wealth and power appeared when the world was viewed through the lenses of early American foreign-policy-makers.

The early American foreign-policy-makers' vision of a growing and maturing empire even involved an explicit racism that, oddly, had its roots in liberalism as much as any other historical philosophy. Michael H. Hunt's recent comprehensive study, *Ideology and U.S. Foreign Policy*, even considers the white racism of the American elite one of only three principles that have motivated American foreign policy from the beginning.[10] Writing for a contemporary audience that would tend to see white racism as an unfortunate characteristic of lower middle class and working class men and women in declining industrial cities and the rural south, Hunt forcefully demonstrates that in the United States it began as an elite ideology and remained central to the views of foreign-policy-makers until well after the second world war. Racism was not just an elite ideology in the slave south, either; Hunt begins by quoting the racist writings of the most urbane and progressive of the founding fathers from the north, Benjamin Franklin.[11]

The ideological sources of American elite racism were twofold. On the one hand, religious doctrine allowed distinctions to be made between Christian and savage, distinctions that easily translated into categories which no longer reflected professed religion, but to 'unchanging' states of being. On the other hand and perhaps more significantly, the liberal Enlightenment idea of progress made it easy to distinguish between 'backward' and 'advanced' peoples and encouraged the search for explanations of those differences. Ultimately, those explanations would take the form of Social Darwinism, but much earlier, even at the time of the American revolution, the idea of a hierarchy of races was firmly implanted in elite consciousness.

Because American foreign-policy-makers believed in a hierarchy of races, in lesser and greater people, they could justify double standards in diplomacy. The occupation of the American continent by Native Americans imposed no impediment to the development of the continental empire and treaties with such 'lesser' people need not be thought to have the same force as treaties with Northern European whites. Similarly, from the very beginning of the American republic at least until the United States became a global power, American foreign policy makers have denied the validity of republican experiments carried on by 'lesser' peoples, which explains America's paradoxical lack of support for most revolutionary and nationalist independence movements. The white republics of Texas or California (or, later, the Boer republics of South Africa) could be expected to actually follow the American example, but not so the republics founded by blacks, like Haiti or Liberia, or Native Americans, like the Cherokee state, or 'debased,' 'mixed' people like Latin Americans.[12]

The hierarchy of race also assured a hierarchy of diplomatic treatment for these 'misshapen reflections' of the American system. The republics of the mixed races could be recognized and treated as slow-learning children, constantly under the protection of the United States. The Native American nations were given the dignity of diplomatic recognition but of an inferior sort, and the moral strictures against the use of force against them were always fewer. Finally, the black republics, governed by the people American foreign-policy-makers placed the lowest on the hierarchy of race, should not even be recognized as second or third class states. The United States recognized neither Haiti, the first republic in the Americas after the United States, nor Liberia, arguably the country that has tried to copy the American system the most faithfully, until generations after their independence.[13]

Some authors who recognize the continuity of the American imperial vision as an extension of the pre-independence idea of American destiny and who recognize the significance of elite racism in American foreign policy still argue that the nineteenth century witnessed a significant falling away from original, more benign ideals embodied in the 'Farewell Address' and the later policy of John Quincy Adams.[14] Washington and Adams, along with all the presidents and top decision-makers in between, tended to conceive of extending the American empire by private settlement and a sort of evangelism, the conversion of those who would be converted to the American way. Later, beginning with the war with Mexico in the 1840s and with Spain in 1898, the United States extended its territorial empire across the continent and the Pacific Ocean by force.

The use of force may be a less just means for extending American empire than evangelism, but it is part of the same Puritan complex of ways to deal with the world. When the United States was still an embryonic empire, a weak New Jerusalem in a wicked world, isolation was the sensible policy. As the country became stronger it could more boldly attempt to convert its neighbors and the world. When those attempts failed, American policy-makers felt it to be not only justified, but benevolent, to impose conversion to the American way by force.[15] As many authors have noted, whenever the United States has used force to gain territory it has done so with self-determination as the justification, forcing the American southwest, Hawaii, Cuba, and the Philippines to convert to the freedom they would have under the American system.

It would be easy to say that this kind of language represents a cynical and self-serving justification for territorial expansions that benefit the class of which American foreign-policy-makers are a part, but it is not quite that simple. Bits of the script of the unfolding of American destiny from isolationist republic to forceful empire have been played out even when only a fraction of the elite could expect immediate economic gain, as for example, during the war with Mexico when southern cotton growers stood to gain vast new territories suitable for their crop which had destroyed the fertility of the soil in the old south.

Scholars who claim economic interests are always more important than ideology suggest another way in which the ideas guiding American foreign policy appear to have changed during the nineteenth century.[16] At the beginning of the century the American empire grew by annexing neighboring territory where European and American settlements had sprung up in areas under Native American or Mexican sovereignty. By the end of the century the United States was annexing territory, but it was often far afield from American settlements. The new American empire in the Pacific served more as bases for an American navy dedicated to the 'open door' policy of giving the American merchants equal or better access than the European powers had to the vast markets in China and Japan. This 'open door imperialism' became the model for American expansion in the twentieth century when the United States has not been concerned with acquiring territory or settling Americans abroad to create new states, but has been concerned with establishing a military presence in a vast territory outside the United States and has been concerned with creating and monitoring international agreements that liberalize international trade and favor American business.[17]

This change, too, was anticipated at the founding of the Republic. The first American Secretary of the Treasury, Alexander Hamilton, the man who 'phrased' Washington's 'Farewell,'[18] called the new nation a growing 'commercial empire.'[19] The United States always had an interest in most-favored nation trade relations with other nations and the United States has always been willing to use military force against weaker nations, even those very far away, to protect American business interests. The hymn of the American Marines (the force maintained, in part, for this precise purpose) celebrates early twentieth century battles in Mexico, 'From the halls of Montezuma,' and then goes on to invoke earlier, *nineteenth* century, battles much further afield, in North Africa, 'to the shores of Tripoli.'

The long-standing 'open door' or liberal trade policy, which the United States has supported with its military might ever since the founding of the republic, reflects the content given to 'American destiny' by American foreign-policy-makers: America's destiny is to extend the liberal economic creed to the entire world. It should hardly be surprising that this view of American destiny rather than, say, the view that would see the United States as extending Protestant Christianity or democratic government to the entire world would be one that would predominate among American foreign-policy-makers. As Hunt argues, American foreign policy decision-makers have always been drawn from a narrow elite base, from (say) the most privileged one per cent of the American population,[20] the strata where the full liberal economic creed predominates. Barnet notes that even after the second world war, after the United States became a global power, foreign policy decision-makers were still predominantly men from big business or corporate legal backgrounds who attended the same schools and worked in the financial districts familiar to John Quincy Adams and the founders of American foreign policy.[21]

Thus, from 1776 to 1945 American foreign policy can be thought of as playing out a single script, 'The Rise of the Liberal Empire,' written by the colonial elite that founded the American foreign policy system. The script defined America as the white, Anglo-Saxon, republican commercial empire that the founders created, but it relied as much on older, Calvinist notions of how men should relate to each other as it did upon the liberal ideas of exchange and contract that could be found in Adam Smith. The script could be played out for so long because it was so successful. The American empire did expand in just the way that Hamilton, or Washington, or John Quincy Adams imagined it would. As the young republic grew stronger it extended itself across the continent and then the Pacific and even acted as the paternal guardian of republican experiments of 'lesser' people who tried to follow the American example, from the Latin Americans in the beginning of the nineteenth century to the Chinese at the beginning of the twentieth.

Still, its success may not have been the only reason that the American foreign policy script changed so little in the United States's first century and a half. It also had few challengers. The intellectuals consulted by American foreign-policy-makers developed no understanding of the American role in the world. In fact, the intellectual support that American foreign-policy-makers had before the second world war was surprisingly narrow and parochial. American foreign-policy-makers learned how to deal with the world from their business experience, from the prior history of American diplomacy, and from the lessons of the ancient world, not from the study of foreign nations and cultures. Most of the elite American universities, the breeding ground of American foreign-policy-makers, did little to inform their students about the modern world, the languages, cultures, and diplomatic practices of other nations.[22] What instruction they did give was most likely to be about Europe, and especially

England, and least likely to be about the places where the American empire was expanding, Latin America and East Asia.

As Hunt argues, racism and the Social Darwinism[23] that later supported it provided an easy way for foreign-policy-makers and the class that spawned them to reduce the mass of information about the rest of the world that they might otherwise have to consider.[24] There were, of course, American schools of higher learning where a great deal of information about these parts of the world were taught, the schools that generated the bulk of the American middle class missionary movement, but only one of these, Yale, was one of the elite schools that foreign-policy-makers might be expected to attend.[25] The continuity of the ideas underlying American foreign policy was reinforced by the fact that American diplomatic history remained the major relevant source of knowledge that American foreign-policy-makers had about how to deal with the world. Certainly the teaching of American diplomatic history changed from decade to decade. For example, after the defeat of the Confederacy in the civil war historians came to see the earlier war with Mexico as more of an unfortunate 'un-American' imperialist incident than earlier historians had reckoned it.[26] But the unfolding of American destiny remained the dominant theme of American diplomatic history until well into the twentieth century.

## The United States as a great power

The script of American foreign policy only began to be rewritten when the players prepared for the penultimate act in which the once downtrodden and despised nation becomes one of the two great powers struggling for dominance on the world stage. Sacred ideas of American destiny remained, as did the equation of the United States with the liberal economic principles long-favored by American business, but something new was added to the old Calvinist repertoire of ways to achieve change in the world. Science, technology, and systematic management began to influence American foreign policy.

The philosophy of systematic management, of the application of science and technology to human problems, 'Fordism,' entered American international policy directly from its source in American society, the gigantic firms responsible for the second industrial revolution at the end of the nineteenth and beginning of the twentieth centuries. Under the sway of Social Darwinism, the leaders of large American firms at the end of the last century developed the conviction that the American economy needed to expand outward, to extend American enterprise abroad not just by selling goods in all markets but by building factories, loaning capital, and struggling to dominate wider and wider economic spheres.[27] Initially this more aggressive private interest behind the open door had little implication for the foreign policy of government, but after as businessmen schooled in the new scientific philosophies of management entered government and as the idea of a scientifically-organized state promoting business took hold, American foreign policy took on a new role as a promoter of US business interests abroad.[28] Of course, this new role was justified with altruistic rhetoric, but not with the old religious view of America's manifest destiny; instead America was destined to rule the world because of the advanced position of its science, and science should guide America's further expansion.[29]

The success of the business-government partnership, the technologies created by it, and the seemingly limitless possibilities of extending that system were all central to Henry Luce's famous declaration of 'the American Century' at the war's end. The United States would become:

> ... the dynamic center of ever-widening spheres of enterprises, America as the training center of the skillful servants of mankind, America as the Good Samaritan ... and America as the powerhouse of the ideals of Freedom and Justice.[30]

As Stephen Ambrose argues, American technological leadership gave American policy-makers the confidence to seek a global role, to become the policeman of the world as well as the world's technological savior. In this context the American nuclear monopoly at the end of the war was 'a godsend,' promising to enable the United States to impose its will like it never had before.[31]

One consequence of the addition of faith in science and technology to the underpinnings of American foreign policy was the legitimation it gave to United States's growing national security establishment, a world-wide peacetime army, air force, and navy with immediate access to a larger world than that available to any previous imperial army. But perhaps a just as significant, and often overlooked, way in which faith in science entered American post-war foreign policy was in the *scientific* faith that American policy-makers developed in the dictates of classical diplomatic theory, *Realpolitik*, newly discovered in the United States after the war. For more than a generation, American policymakers and the intellectuals that support them have treated certain incidental historical lessons as scientific truths about international relations. Most significantly, the 'lesson of Munich' can be variously read as saying one can never cooperate with totalitarian states or that the use of force is the only effective way of dealing with great power conflicts.[32]

As Hunt argues, one of the major purposes of the policy-makers' attempt to create a 'science' of foreign affairs for the United States after the second world war was to preclude extensive public involvement in the professional matter of managing the new, extensive American empire. Intellectuals and policy-makers considered the public too moralistic and fickle to be involved in dangerous matters of state.[33] As Barnet points out, for the new American national security managers of the post-war era American public opinion became another variable in their equations, something else to be scientifically managed.[34] Significantly, this professional distrust of public involvement in the important business of foreign-policy-making was a view widely shared across the apparent ideological divides that split the American ruling classes after the second world war. George Kennan, who could be called the premier intellectual of American foreign policy directly after the war saw public involvement as one the greatest problems policy-makers had to face, but so did his sharpest and most respected contemporary critic, Walter Lippmann.[35]

Paradoxically, if rigid thinking and moralism were to be the criteria used for excluding people from involvement in managing the American empire, many of America's so-called 'realist' decision-makers would have had to have found other jobs. Scientific realism, like all of the other ideological strata that influence American foreign policy, was laid down in the policy-makers' minds on top of layer upon layer of other, often contradictory, historical philosophies. Therefore one the most celebrated of the realist thinkers, Reinhold Neibuhr, could write a messianic book on American destiny, saying that the United States was the new Athens and the new Rome, the holder of civilization against the barbarians, at the same time that he advocated what he considered a measured lack of idealism in foreign relations.[36] Some critics argue that America's national security managers have inappropriately applied a faith in science to a realm where most problems cannot be solved, leaving American policy-makers with an unwarranted sense of omnipotence.[37]

Perhaps the most prominent sign of the lack of realism of America's post-war 'realists' is the persistence of the American crusade against communism, and the communism of the Soviet Union in particular. The most widely-used text on American post-war foreign policy even organizes its argument around anti-communism and anti-Sovietism as two of the three constant goals pursued by the United States.[38] The other one, not surprisingly, is liberal internationalism, a relative constant in American foreign policy since Hamilton first thought about America's expanding commercial empire.

Where does American anti-communism come from and how did it become so strong? One logical answer might be that it has its source in interests of the same class that gave the United States its older, liberal foreign policy goals. Private businessmen have good reason to be rabid in their opposition to communism.

But that answer is not complete. Writing in 1950, in the first major empirical study of public opinion and American foreign policy, Gabriel Almond claimed:

> Every group of any size in the US sees Soviet communists as a threat, the believing Christian, trade unionist, democratic Socialist, liberal, conservative.[39]

Arguably, Almond could have been reflecting a peculiar time when anti-communist zealots like Joseph McCarthy and Richard Nixon were whipping up anti-Soviet hysteria. But other evidence from different times points in the same direction. Robert Dallek argues that in 1939, the majority of Americans, like the majority of Germans, preferred fascism to communism.[40] The preference for the allies in the European war which eventually led to American involvement at first came more from identity with the British than from opposition to systems imposed by the Axis.

Of course, popular opinion about communism need not matter very much as long as American foreign policy had other legitimations. Many realists argue that American foreign-policy-makers would have to be anti-Soviet because the Soviet Union was the only major challenger to the United States left after the war and that the fact that the Soviet Union was communist and the United States was not was reason enough to be anti-communist. President Truman's personal speeches and writings, for example, did not become strongly anti-Soviet and anti-communist until he developed the conviction that the United States would have to replace British power throughout much of the world.[41] Yet, anti-communism has always been more than just a tactical necessity of *Realpolitik* for many American decision-makers. For those with strong religious convictions it fit on top of and helped define the moral mission that the United States was expected to undertake. For instance J. Edgar Hoover, the leader of the Federal Bureau of Investigation for most of its existence and the one bureaucrat that no American president dared to fire, deeply believed that God had chosen the United States as his special instrument to overcome world communism.[42] With anti-communism already in place as a religious value of some American leaders, it has always been tempting for American national security managers to play upon popular religious and quasi-religious sentiments to 'sell' what otherwise might be unpopular imperial policies as part of an anti-communist crusade. Without the communists menace a whole host of innovative American post-war policies from the Marshall Plan to military assistance given to repressive regimes throughout the Third World might never have surmounted the hurdles of public opinion even though those hurdles are very low.[43]

Even with all of these innovations in American foreign policy, the new importance of the faith in science, 'realism,' and anti-communism, it is important to emphasize how much did not change when the United States finally became a great power. Most significantly, American foreign-policy-makers continued to define the core of the American national interest as an interest in 'open doors,' equal or better access for Americans to foreign markets and sources of supply, and to define the American dream that they were extending to the world in terms of the entire range of nineteenth-century liberal economic principles including the sanctity of private property and the special usefulness of markets.[44]

But it is equally important, and less often emphasized, that American foreign policy continued to be motivated by the invidious comparisons that American elites make about groups of people. Looked at from one perspective, elite white racism in the United States changed its form, not its substance, in the years since the US became a world power. For example, when the United Nations Education Scientific and Cultural Organization was created at the end of the war the Americans insisted that, because this was a cultural organization, its first director must be an Anglo-Saxon or, at worst, French.[45]

But looked at from a slightly different perspective—not the perspective of 'who are the best people' but rather 'what makes them best'—things have changed dramatically. The decades of civil rights protests in the United States have had their effect on American foreign-policy-makers. Yet, as Hunt points out, the invidious comparisons are still made, and the old hierarchy of foreign peoples still maintained not by Social Darwinism and 'scientific' racism but by the new science of development economics, which is, indeed, more color-blind, more able to imagine individuals as fundamentally equal, even while it maintains the older hierarchical distinctions among foreign people.[46]

## The troubled superpower

We concluded chapter 2 by mentioning how the growth of institutions of control, both firms and government, may have undermined both key liberal beliefs (the efficacy of individual action) and key religious beliefs (the sufficiency of the isolationist, evangelist, crusader repertoire) that have been important constants in American political life for generations. The ideological problems for American foreign-policy-making in the same period have taken quite a different form due to the historical dominance of foreign-policy-making by the American elite. On the one hand, there is a problem of elite ideology: at the moment that the United States achieved the historical, essential liberal goals that had formed the basic core of American foreign policy motivations since the founding of the Republic, those liberal beliefs were being challenged by members of the very class that had been served by US foreign policy from the beginning. On the other hand lies a problem of mass legitimation: the foreign policy of America as a great power has demanded more public sacrifice and, hence, greater attention to some of the most archaic themes of American common sense, than ever before.

The problem for the elite can be understood as one of whether some version of foreign policy 'scientism,' Mona Harrington's 'functionalist' version of the American dream, or the traditional script of America's expanding commercial empire will guide foreign policy. In the two major recent empirical studies of American elite attitudes toward foreign policy[47] this conflict appears as the difference between 'conservatives' who are anti-communist, who believe that America's great power status requires the US to crusade against alternative ideological systems, and who have great faith in unmanaged international economic liberalism, and 'liberals' who have become 'non-interventionist' due to the failure of the Vietnam war, who evaluate relations with communist regimes in functional terms, and who support the development of a 'managed' international liberal economy through growing international organizations. Jimmy Carter, with his emphases on restricting the use of US force, supporting international attempts to coordinate economic policy (at least among rich capitalist states), and looking for ways for the US to 'get past' its virulent anti-communism, epitomized the later group. Ronald Reagan exemplifies the former.

But knowledge of just these elite differences would hardly be enough to let anyone predict how American foreign policy will develop in the future. The foreign-policy-makers of America the great power have made unprecedented demands on the American public since 1941, taxing them to pay for a 'peacetime' military as well as massive wars, demanding further funds to re-construct allies and maintain friendly governments, and requiring young men to offer their lives in wars that, in historical terms, were the most massive and frequent in American history. After all, a key element in even the elite foreign policy debate in the US since 1970 was a response to the failure of the policy of conscription in Vietnam, a failure that led many American intellectuals to re-evaluate the efficiency of US foreign policy, if not its morality. As long as the United States has been a great power, the American public, not just the elite, has been able to make some effective demands on American foreign-policy-makers and American foreign policy has had to respond, more, to the interests and aspirations of what Gramsci would call the popular masses.

In the absence of a political process to illuminate 'good sense,' popular demands on the foreign policy of the United States as a great power emphasize all the contradictory aspects of American common sense, including the residues of religion that are less apparent in elite ideology. To many members of the American working class the lesson of the American failure in Vietnam is that the US should be less involved with the world; it should practice the isolation-ism of a chosen people unable to influence it preterite neighbors. To other non-elite Americans the lesson is that the obviously powerful United States should be willing to use its power and defeat its enemies not back away from conflict as it did in Vietnam.

Neither of these, albeit simplified, extremes of mass opinion in the United States provides much support, much legitimation for the type of foreign policy preferred by what many scholars consider the most progressive portion of the American elite the 'post-cold war internationalists'[48] or the businessmen who support a non-interventionist United States.[49] The kind of foreign policy that unreflective American common sense is unlikely to support is precisely the sort of policy that Jimmy Carter followed in his first years in office. Conversely, probably the type of American foreign policy upon which it would be easiest to get some level of agreement between an unreflective elite and unreflective mass public would be the conservative policy that Reagan followed, a continued enactment of the traditional American foreign-policy script, that gave the American mass public a desired role: part of a successful global crusade.

## Notes

1. This is the so-called 'mood-interest' theory of American foreign policy; see Frank L. Klingberg, 'The Historical Alteration of Moods in American Foreign Policy,' *World Politics* 4 (1952): 239–73, and *Cyclical Trends in American Foreign Policy Moods* (Lanham, MD: University Press of America, 1983).
2. *American Politics: The Promise of Disharmony* (Cambridge, MA: Harvard University Press, 1981), 27.
3. Mona Harrington, *The Dream of Deliverance in American Politics* (New York: Knopf, 1986) would call this the 'democratic' version of the American dream of deliverance.
4. Samuel Flagg Bemis, *John Quincy Adams and the Foundation of American Foreign Policy* (New York: W. W. Norton, 1949.), 255.
5. Barnet, *Roots of War* (Baltimore: Penguin, 1972), 48.
6. Charles W. Kegley, Jr. and Eugene R. Wittkopf, *American Foreign Policy: Pattern and Process*, 2nd ed. (New York: St. Martins Press, 1982), 322, 374.
7. Bemis, 182.
8. Fredrick Merk, *Manifest Destiny in American History* (New York: Knopf, 1963), 4–7.
9. Merk considers this innovation to represent a degradation of the original ideal.
10. The others Hunt discusses are the idea of American destiny and American aversion to revolution. (New Haven: Yale University Press, 1987). The same prominent theme appears in one of the few recent monographs on American diplomatic history writing by a third world scholar, M. L. Gujral, *U.S. Global Involvement: A Study of American Expansionism* (New Delhi: Arnold Heinemann, 1975).
11. Hunt, 46–7.
12. Hunt links the American concern about revolutions by 'lesser' peoples to the development of a virulent opposition to revolution in general. Ibid., 100–37. We think perhaps he overstates the case for a general American opposition to revolution a bit. The US government has welcomed revolutions and independence movements of Northern European whites when they do not threaten property, even, for example, the 1905 revolution in Russia and the 1917 Revolution at the beginning. As explicit racism started to fade in the US after the second world war, the US was even able to support some independence movements in the third world.
13. Robert Dallek, *The American Style of Foreign Policy: Cultural Politics and Foreign Affairs* (New York: Knopf, 1983), 6–8.
14. This is Merk's view.
15. Barnet notes that Calvinism forces people to face the question 'Who will be the Sheriff?' Who will create order in an unruly world? And it provides the answer: Those whose virtue has been certified by world success. Thus, American use of force against the recalcitrant world can be thought of as responsibility incumbent upon the US because of its power (p. 70).
16. The most prominent is William Appleman Williams whose *Tragedy of American Diplomacy* (Cleveland: World, 1959), which inspired an entire generation of diplomatic historians for whom the dating of a 'change' in American foreign policy became less important. Williams's more recent work sees a continuity in American policy toward the outside world since colonial times, *Empire as a Way of Life* (New York: Oxford University Press, 1980).

17. Raymond Aron argues that only the annexation of the Philippines contradicted the original American national purpose, *The Imperial Republic*, trans. by Frank Jellinek (Cambridge: Winthrop Publishers, 1974), xxxiii. Aron claims that 'freedom of access' has been the guiding principle of American foreign policy since the beginning, but that this economic interest has not been the sole governor of that policy. He believes that *Realpolitik* considerations of power may have involved the US in military conquests and territorial acquisitions that would not have been dictated by economic interest alone (p. 187).
18. Bemis, 62.
19. Bemis devotes a section to the importance of equality of commercial opportunity to American policy makers before 1830. Ibid., 448–68.
20. Hunt, 15.
21. Note that some scholars have simplified the ideological sources of American foreign policy to liberal ideals espoused by the elite. This is perfectly reasonable as long we recognize what liberalism cannot explain: the assumption of America's special destiny, the methods American foreign policy maker prefer, and the reasons for the broader public's lack of interest or involvement in foreign policy. See Edward Weisband. *The Ideology of American Foreign Policy: A Paradigm of Lockean Liberalism* (Beverley Hills: Sage, 1973).
22. Robert A. McCaughey, *International Studies and Academic Enterprise: A Chapter in the Enclosure of American Learning* (New York: Columbia University Press, 1984).
23. A 'science' which, unlike the study of modern societies other than the United States, *was* developed and taught at the elite universities before the world wars.
24. Hunt, 52.
25. McCaughey, 52.
26. Jerald A. Combs, *American Diplomatic History: Two Centuries of Changing Interpretation* (Berkeley: University of California Press, 1983), 35.
27. Emily S. Rosenberg, *Spreading the American Dream: American Economic and Cultural Expansion, 1890–1945* (New York: Hill and Wang, 1982), 22.
28. Ibid., 5–56.
29. One of the sources of this view was the late nineteenth-century writings of John W. Draper quoted at length in Mansour Farhang, *U.S. Imperialism from the Spanish-American War to the Iranian Revolution* (Boston: South End Press, 1981), 86–94.
30. Rosenberg, 229.
31. *Rise to Globalism*, 3rd revised ed. (Harmondsworth: Penguin, 1983).
32. Combs, 197.
33. Hunt, 7.
34. Barnet, 266.
35. Oscar Handlin, *The Distortion of America* (Boston: Atlantic Monthly Press, 1981), 141.
36. Norman A. Graebner, *America as a World Power* (Wilmington, DE: Scholarly Resources, 1973), 86.
37. Stanley Hoffmann, *Gulliver's Troubles or the Setting of American Foreign Policy* (New York: McGraw Hill, 1968).
38. Kegley and Wittkopf, 36.
39. Quoted in Francis E. Rourke, 'The Domestic Scene,' in Robert E. Osgood, et al.,

*America and the World from the Truman Doctrine to Vietnam* (Baltimore: Johns Hopkins University Press, 1970).
40. Dallek, 138.
41. Deborah Larson, *The Origins of Containment* (Princeton: Princeton University Press, 1985), 323.
42. Michael J. Parenti, *The Anti-Communist Impulse* (New York: Random House, 1969), 261.
43. Cf. Barnet, 270–6.
44. One of the best pieces of evidence for this assertion is Stephen D. Krasner's *Defending the National Interest: Raw Material Investments and U.S. Foreign Policy* (Princeton: Princeton University Press, 1978). Krasner looks to what policy makers do to give an 'inductive' definition of the American national interest and concludes that the creation of competition and the protection of property are the only concrete goals that stand out from the rest.
45. Frank A. Ninkovich, *The Diplomacy of Ideas: U. S. Foreign Policy and Cultural Relations, 1938–1950* (Cambridge: Cambridge University Press, 1981), 150.
46. Hunt, 161.
47. Bruce M. Russett and Elizabeth C. Hanson, *Interest and Ideology: The Foreign Policy Beliefs of American Businessmen* (San Francisco: W. H. Freeman, 1975) and Ole R. Holsti and James N. Rosenau, *American Leadership in World Affairs: Vietnam and the Breakdown of Consensus* (Boston: Allen and Unwin, 1984).
48. Holsti and Rosenau's term.
49. To use Russett and Hanson's language.

# 4 The case of foreign assistance

In this chapter we turn to a specific area of America's great power foreign policy and apply Gramsci's conceptual tools slightly differently. First we look at American foreign assistance from a philosophical perspective, contrasting what the main historical philosophies shaping American common sense would have to say about aid to the views of an advocate of the Third World's New International Economic Order, Mahbub ul Haq.[1] Then we go back to a more historical and sociological perspective to analyze the policies of successive American administrations in order to identify the changing mix of ideas informing US action and the nature of conflict over US-Third World relations at the end of the 1970s.

## Philosophical perspectives on American aid policy

Few people from the countries that receive foreign assistance ever hold powerful positions in the major agencies that provide it. Mahbub ul Haq, once Vice President of the World Bank, is an exception. At one point, late in Jimmy Carter's administration, after Carter had suggested the radical idea that the Bank's top job should go to a citizen of one of its major clients, Haq's name was even mentioned for that, the most-powerful of the jobs in the multilateral aid system. It is not surprising that Haq was never appointed; his philosophy on international assistance runs counter to most of the views heard in the United States, which is why his position can give us an interesting perspective on American philosophy.

Haq argues for applying the same criteria to domestic and international economics and laments the fact that while, at the national level, in most countries measures have been taken to offset the inequities produced by the market (public ownership of utilities, redistributive taxation, welfare schemes, and social insurance) nothing of this kind has yet developed in international society, even though a few individual governments and multilateral agencies may be guided by a notion of human solidarity in their foreign-assistance policies. Haq wants to see an evolution of welfare policy on the international level such as the one that has taken place at the national level. For a start, he would like to see a mechanism of international taxation to provide regular funding for development projects and he would like to see a global central bank to coordinate macroeconomic policy in the global, rather than the national, interest.

### *Liberalism: aid to open markets and enhance power*

From the point of view of classical liberalism, Haq's arguments look like part of a strategy for increasing the wealth and power of Third World states at the expense of the people in wealthy nations like the United States. Haq appeals to the democratic spirit, the liberal belief in equality, and to the idea of progress, but only in order to advance Third World economic interests. It is not surprising, therefore, that much of the American scholarly literature on New International Economic Order responds to arguments like Haq's by trying to expose the self-interest underlying the Third World position, thereby emptying Third World requests for redistribution of any moral content.[2]

Liberal political philosophy's assumptions about human motivation only suggest Haq's argument is self-interested; classical liberal economic theory provides a moral foundation for *opposition* to the redistribution of the world's wealth: its theorem that the market is not only efficient but fair. If we all get what we deserve from this simple and fair mechanism, poverty can only be the result of a lack of individual initiative or capacity for which the victim has only himself, or adverse nature, to blame. An independent state facing international society is no different from the free man facing the opportunities of the free market in this respect.

Bearing in mind the residues of both liberal political and economic theory consider the common-sense reaction that many Americans would have to Haq's argument: his arguments look at the same time arrogant and naive; they certainly have no moral foundation. Global redistributive taxation would penalize those who have worked for their wealth and give resources to those who have demonstrated the least capacity to use them properly. Therefore, it would be unlikely to help poor nations develop. The damage could be even greater because aid must be channeled through Third World governments that typically distort local markets.

If foreign assistance is neither morally due nor useful to the recipient, it can only be given, rationally, if the donor country thinks it serves its interests. Of course, liberals support aid as a temporary *quid pro quo* for the long-term liberalization of a recipient's markets. More significantly, liberal theory justifies foreign aid given in a self-interested attempt to acquire power: to obtain recognition of the donor's leadership in international affairs or to secure support on critical issues. In this context, a liberal may see no difference between military and economic aid. Neither is likely to really contribute to economic development but both represent a transfer of wealth, for which the donor should demand something in return.

### *Religion: evangelical developmentalism and aid in the crusade against communism*

Foreign assistance looks a bit different when approached from the point of view of denominational Protestantism and the civic religion of American exceptionalism that arose from it, the source of that part of American common sense that must influence foreign-policy-makers when they call on the support of the American mass public. Even though America's religious tradition at first helped constitute and later reinforced the liberal approach to the world, its lessons for foreign assistance are a bit different. For example, liberalism places less emphasis on charity, even though John Locke urges us to consider charity a moral obligation. In *Two Treatises on Government*, he says, '*Charity* gives every Man a Title to so much out of another's Plenty as will keep him from Extream want, where he has no means to subsist otherwise.'[3] Yet, to most liberal thinkers, charity is not a duty, as it is in Christian doctrine.

Even so, Haq's views would find little more support from the religious elements of American common sense than from the liberal ones. Third World countries could ask for charity, but, as we have seen in chapter 2, even that may entail the *quid pro quo* of actively reinforcing the superiority already felt by the donor.

Residues of American Protestantism can provide further justification for foreign assistance. As discussed in chapter 2, in the United States Protestant ideas were supplemented by the philosophy of the Puritans whose most significant innovation was their belief that they were chosen by God for a special mission, the founding of the new Israel, the 'city on the hill.' From the Puritans' collective covenant with God arose the idea of America as a 'chosen' country. A second theme connected to American Puritanism has to do with the three ways the 'chosen' community deals with dissent, as isolationists, evangelists, and crusaders.

The isolationist impulse was coherent with and organic to Puritan philosophy. It wanted to eliminate any contact between a pure community governed by God's law and an external world full of Evil. The evangelical and crusader impulses emerged when Puritans began to credit themselves with more power to influence this world. The mission of fighting Evil and spreading Good abroad became the chosen country's specific task.

As discussed in the last chapter, in foreign policy, the isolationist impulse was particularly appropriate to the American economy when it was still very localized. But from the beginning of the American republic foreign policy was guided by a vision of the United States becoming increasingly powerful with isolationist policy giving way to evangelical policy, that is, to the replication of the American system in other white republics (e.g. Texas and California) and territories that might ask to become part of the union, and then evangelical policy giving way, when the United States was powerful enough, to a positive crusade against Evil in the world. Not coincidentally, by the time that America's transnational economic links became so important that isolationism was unrealistic, many Americans were ready to imagine that the US's role was to convert the world and fight against its evils, although isolationism remains common sense to many Americans.

From the standpoint of an isolationist, Haq's recommendations, and any program of foreign assistance, make no sense. Trying to redistribute wealth to the world could even undermine harmony in the United States. This is one of the few views that many conservative members of Congress share with many of the older religious leaders of the civil rights movement. Both groups' views rest on the bedrock Puritan idea that the social harmony of the United States is something very special, perhaps even ordained by God. For some of the Americans most consciously influenced by religion, foreign assistance can suggest aiding countries that God has not favored as much as the United States, countries whose role in this world may even be that of Babylon.

This view is not shared by all Americans influenced by religion. It is contradicted by the evangelical impulse which starts from the same assumption of America as the chosen country. Unlike isolationism, national evangelism could only develop when the idea of predestination had been called into question. To desire to convert the world is to admit the possibility of salvation, of being 'born again.' The chosen people had a new obligation, to use their knowledge and resources to help sinners redeem themselves. For Americans with the evangelical impulse, foreign assistance is not only conceivable, it may be obligatory. The United States has to help Third World countries build proper institutions and choose the correct path to economic development. Secular theories of political development share this impulse, although, of course, political scientists tend to turn to liberal political philosophy as their guide for understanding what aid is needed, not to the residues of Puritanism that may give them their zeal for aid in the first place.

Still, the evangelists of development rarely believe that the transfer of resources should be made the way Haq proposes. In the same way that sinners must learn how to redeem themselves from the lives of the saints, so must Third World countries follow the example of the most developed countries and accept suggestions on how to organize themselves internally and externally. Therefore, foreign assistance must be conditional and a distinction might be made between military and economic assistance. The former may waste resources while the latter is much more likely to be useful.

Development crusaders rarely make the same distinction. The American crusader impulse has its own religious background in the Manichean idea of absolute Good and absolute Evil which will have their last battle in Armageddon. A powerful chosen people cannot accept Evil. Evil must be turned-back or at least contained. All of the resources of the chosen people should be devoted to this end. Systematic management's cost-benefit analyses have no place here. Haq's proposals are out of place to the crusader. After all, the great global conflict is not one between the rich and the poor, as Haq implies, but one between Good and Evil, and for many Americans that means between the American Way and communism. The real battle is between the United States and the Soviet Union and transfers of resources are just ammunition. From this perspective foreign assistance can be given quite generously to those who join the fight, to those who are in danger of being overcome by Evil, and to those tempted by Evil offers. In this conceptual scheme there is no difference between military and economic aid because both can be instrumental in stopping the evil of Soviet communism.

### *Scientism and the most efficient use of aid*

Liberalism was born from Protestantism and found support for its conceptual structure in Protestant beliefs. Similarly, scientism, the latest of the historical philosophies that has left a residue in the American consciousness, can be thought of as a child of liberalism and as an ideology which has always resonated with American liberal beliefs even though it was, at the beginning, at odds with many American religious precepts. Not surprisingly, in many ways what America's faith in science would say about aid is poles apart from the dictates of America's crusader self-image.

From the later half of the nineteenth century faith in science challenged faith in religion. Darwin's theory of evolution appeared to refute the Biblical thesis of God's creation of the world. Nevertheless, the scientific faith reinforced liberal optimism, infusing it with the confidence that the solution to every problem not only can be found but will prove easy. This optimistic philosophy has diffused the most among elements of the American upper classes, intellectuals as well the engineering and managerial elites for whom faith in science is organic. At the same time popular versions of the faith have developed. In its many versions, scientism has helped Americans think of the problem of social progress not as one of building human solidarity, as evangelism might suggest, but as one of waiting for inevitable scientific and technical improvements. To someone with faith in science, poverty must be seen as a consequence of our ignorance or, more likely, of the ignorant practices of the poor.

Those with a strong faith in science can be quite sympathetic to the idea of foreign aid. Still, they find Haq's proposals unreasonable because the problem of underdevelopment cannot be solved by simply increasing the availability of resources. Resources need to be used correctly. Scientism moves the makers of American foreign aid policy to experiment with new types of projects and to support massive technical assistance. The technical orientation of the American faith in science assures that it has its greatest impact on American aid policy only after the decision to aid has been made for other reasons—in pursuit of American self-interest, as part a movement to convert other states to the American Way, or as part of a global crusade. The American faith in science helps in deciding on means not ends. American scientism could easily support Haq's views, as long as his egalitarian end was accepted and as long as the means he proposed proved to be the most efficient.

*Conclusion*

We now turn to answer the question implicit in comparing Haq's perspective to the philosophies underlying American attitudes toward aid: why does America give aid primarily for geopolitical purposes and not simply to promote international solidarity? Because giving for the pleasure of giving, sharing what you have with others as a means of communication, redistributing wealth only to raise the standard of living of others who are not part of the 'chosen' people are all concepts that are alien to every aspect of American common sense except the notion of charity. Individual Americans may be unusually generous, but in the majority of cases the contradictions of their consciousness are likely to make them limit their actions to private compassion, the provision of personal charity.

Does that mean that American aid really is given mainly for political purposes? Yes, but not just because, as Gramsci would say, 'everything becomes political through ideology,' but because of the explicitly geopolitical content of most of the motivations for aid that US ideology allows. Aid may be given either to promote the American national interest, usually to enhance American power—according to the liberal conception of the world–or as part of an evangelical or crusading movement, political movements designed to spread the 'American Way.'

Similar conclusions have been reached by analysts whose research approaches the problem differently. For instance, Seyom Brown, analyzing the attitude of Congress toward foreign assistance says:

> The legislature, acting as the broker for constituent domestic interests jealous of any diversion of resources to foreign objectives, needs either a grand moral crusade or a clear and present danger to the nation to forge a consensus in back of altruistic acts.[4]

Congress, the part of the national government kept the most in touch with the public by frequent elections, often expects aid to be given only in response to clear signs of Evil in the world, as we would expect from an institution influenced by the religious residues in the American common sense. At other times we would expect policy to respond to the liberal criteria: aid would be used to enhance American wealth and power.

## The changing mix of motivations for American aid

Congress does not make most American aid policy. The dominance of the executive branch in foreign policy means that we must look at different presidential administrations to see how different ideological elements have combined to influence American foreign assistance policy. Robert A. Packenham's *Liberal America and the Third World*[5] remains the best study of that issue to date. But Packenham has blind spots that we hope a Gramscian analysis can remove. For example, he ascribes the persistence of simplistic liberal assumptions about political development to America's 'happy history.'[6] Yet, American history has been 'unhappy'—brutal and violent—for many,[7] even though elites may remember it differently.

Packenham's belief in America's 'happy history' convinces him that the frustration felt by American development policy-makers results from a lack of experience with such failures. But most policy-makers expect success primarily because they have faith in economic science, a motivation with very different consequences.

Packenham tends to overlook the religious as well as the scientistic elements of American common sense. By failing to recognize the evangelical impulse he distorts American efforts to build democracy in the Third World. He is correct to argue that the US has actually done that at times. But he fails to adequately explain why administration after administration has embraced right-wing dictatorships when confronted with the slightest risk of communism. The remnants of the American religious conception of the world and the twentieth-century identification of Evil with communism provide a clearer explanation.

Last but not least, Packenham himself puts some faith in the power of a conception of 'world community' that, at present, simply is not part of what common sense is to most Americans, unless we want to consider as 'community' a relationship between the United States as a teacher and the rest of the world as students or unless we think of world community as equivalent to the perfection of the world market.

The limits of Packenham's analysis derive from his assumption that liberalism has been the pervasive ideology in America. He shares the 'consensus' view of American history. Liberalism, still the main philosophy of American ruling elites, provides the ideological explanation most-readily available to American intellectuals. And in Louis Hartz's interpretation of American history, the source of Packenham's insights,[8] liberalism becomes a defining characteristic of a nation born free of the original sin of feudalism and the economic and political bondage it entailed. The United States is better than the old and corrupt European nations from whom it took world leadership in Hartz's own day, in the early 1950s, when American aid policy began.

We do not make assumptions about ideology as bold as Hartz's or Packenham's. We have tried to observe the whole range of historical philosophies that have affected American policy toward the Third World in order to assess their relative influence on contemporary thinking. We turn to the historical record of successive American presidents to assess the significance of the distinctions we have made and to see if we can uncover any constants, cycles, or trends in the relative impact of the different ideologies.

*Truman: aid and the origins of the cold war*

Directly after the second world war liberalism dictated most American attitudes toward the less-industrialized nations. During its first few months the Truman administration answered requests for foreign economic assistance or reform of the international economic system by saying that the only road to economic development was to keep the government away from the market. A prudent monetary and fiscal policy, international trade liberalization, and a favorable climate for foreign investment would accomplish the task of economic growth in 'backward' countries.[9] This policy, of course, served American economic interests as well.

Yet, Truman would provide economic and military aid to Greece and Turkey in 1947, to European countries through the Marshall Plan starting in 1948, and to east and southeast Asia between 1948 and 1950. President Truman remained a liberal. He opposed MacArthur's crusading 'no substitute for victory' against China and North Korea,[10] emphasizing, instead, the importance of western Europe. Truman used aid as one way to help prevent Soviet inroads in western Europe and thus assure access to important markets. Nevertheless, in presenting requests for foreign assistance, Truman had to appeal to the crusader impulse of a Congress more connected to the religious strata of the American common sense:

> I believe that it must be the policy of the United States to support free peoples who are resisting attempted subjugation by armed minorities or by outside pressures. . . . The free peoples of the world look to us for support in maintaining their freedoms. If we falter in our leadership, we may endanger the peace of the world, and we shall surely endanger the welfare of our own nation.[11]

George Kennan's 'scientific' concept of 'containment' reinforced this 'Truman Doctrine,' because it appealed to the religious foundations of American consciousness. Appeals to self-interest would never have been as powerful. Keeping European markets open may have appealed to many powerful people in the US, but other elements of American common sense were needed to justify aid to the public. For liberal leaders concerned with developing the most rational possible policy, the result was less than optimal. In his memoirs George Kennan remarks:

> Throughout the ensuing two decades the conduct of our foreign policy would continue to be bedeviled by people in our own government as well as in other governments who could not free themselves from the belief that all another country had to do, in order to qualify for American aid, was to demonstrate the existence of a Communist threat.[12]

Yet, Kennan's scientism was a more integral part of Truman's aid policy than any religious anti-communism. 'Point Four' of his inaugural address of 1949 announced, 'a bold new program for making the benefits of our

[American] scientific advances and industrial progress available for the improvement and growth of underdeveloped areas.'[13] Truman's faith in science made him believe that American technical assistance, channeled through advisory missions, could raise the world's standard of living by 2 per cent each year. This would assure America's prosperity by opening vast new markets in the rapidly developing nations. And, Truman argued, it would assure peace would be guaranteed, because, he believed, wars were caused by countries that wanted 'something that didn't belong to them.'[14] In aid policy, Truman's faith in science worked well with American religious ideas and with his fundamental liberal beliefs. Technical advisory missions took a new gospel, a combination of liberal economics and the managerial science that developed along with American industry, to the world.

The concepts that motivated and justified Truman-era aid policy remained important for decades. This is especially true of the policy's anti-communism, a point worth analyzing in more detail.

Two conceptions of communism have alternated in America. The first holds that communist governments stem from external pressures or the violent action of an armed minority which imposes dictatorship on a subject population. This concept relies on the image of the Soviet army shaping eastern Europe after the second world war. Extended to the whole world, this image suggests that no communist regime could arise with public consent. This image was widely disseminated by the popular press throughout the Truman years. In December of 1950, for example, the *New York Herald Tribune* promoted a 'Declaration of State of War Against Mao's Faction,' intending it, 'not ... [as] war against China or the Chinese people but against one fraction in China, namely the Communists.'[15]

The second American image of communism originates in social scientific analysis, but remains quite simplistic. According to this theory, detailed in Price's 1955 analysis of American foreign assistance programs in Asia, 'hunger and want [were] so severe and widespread that people were ready to grasp at any new hope, any utopian promise. What was there to lose?'[16] Poverty causes communism.

Both concepts of communism allow America a special position in the world. The first sees this special quality in more overtly religious terms; it justifies American crusades against communism. The second incorporates religious impulses into liberal theory: America is a model that all would like to emulate, but, not being able to, some are driven to communism in desperation or envy. If the first image of communism leads to crusades and military assistance so people can resist violent communist minorities, the second image leads to liberal evangelism and using economic assistance to avoid the desperate turn to communism.

Truman's liberalism and the scientific bent of his advisors attracted them more to the second image of communism rather than the first. After all, in the geopolitical terms of the new science of international relations promoted by men like Kennan, the cold war was simply the result of growing Soviet influence. If the resulting threat to American clients could be met by economic development which also helped American industry, all the better.

Yet, to many Americans the cold war was much more. Joseph McCarthy's accusations and MacArthur's aims in Korea found wide public support.[17] As a result, the public demanded changes in Truman's original goals for aid and Congress passed the Mutual Security Act of 1951, which stated that every kind of American foreign assistance—economic aid, technical cooperation, and military aid—should be oriented to, 'strengthen the free world in its resistance to Communism.'[18] The act, in force until 1961, required that no country was to be considered eligible to receive aid if it were not aligned with the West. At the same time the ratio of economic to military aid, which was about four to one in the second half of the 1940s, was reversed to favor the military by about two to one during the 1950s.

### *Eisenhower: aid and the anti-communist alliance*

When Eisenhower became president in 1953 observers predicted that the United States would step-up its crusade against communism. The general had campaigned as the man who could confront the Soviet Union. But, he actually did little more than allow members of his administration to give greater rein to crusader rhetoric. He overruled those who pushed for direct American involvement in Indo-China and he insisted on reducing public expenditure and keeping government out of the market, even if that meant the government did not have the resources to wage a crusade against communism. Eisenhower, like Truman, was basically a liberal.

Still, Eisenhower's administration did not sound like Truman's. The president did not take as active a role in foreign policy. Its active Secretary of State, John Foster Dulles, unlike most members of the American governing elite, was as swayed by the crusading elements of American common sense as he was by liberalism or faith in science. The son of a Presbyterian minister and himself a devout Christian, Dulles saw the cold war as a decisive struggle between Good and Evil. He once said that Bolshevism was a product of the Devil, but God would wear out the Bolsheviks in the long run.[19] Dulles considered containment immoral because it meant leaving people under communist rule. He preached the need to roll back communism and liberate people living under communist systems.

Despite this rhetoric, Eisenhower just reinforced containment by encircling the Soviet Union with military alliances. American foreign assistance, regulated by the Mutual Security Act, was central to that policy. The Eisenhower administration conceived of aid as a way to strengthen the military capability of allies under communist pressure. The administration's preference for military over economic assistance was, at the same time, supported by the liberal assumption that economic aid was basically useless.

Based on these premises, the Eisenhower administration refused to give foreign assistance to non-aligned countries. This exclusion was not just an elaboration of the containment policy, for men like Dulles, it was grounded in religious ethics; non-alignment was the refusal to fight the Evil. During his controversy with Nasser over the financing of the Aswan Dam in 1956, President Eisenhower himself, reading a speech prepared by Dulles, said: 'Neutral doesn't mean neutral as between right and wrong, or decency and indecency.'[20]

The American policy of sending aid only to loyal allies changed in the late 1950s as a result of Soviet initiatives. After the death of Stalin in 1953 the Soviet Union began to take an interest in the Third World. In 1955 and 1956 the Soviets concluded arms and economic assistance agreements with a number of countries including Egypt, India, Syria, Indonesia, and Afghanistan. Khrushchev told the Central Committee:

> These countries, although they do not belong to the Socialist world system, can draw on its achievements in building an independent national economy and in raising their people's living standards. Today they need not go begging to their former oppressors for modern equipment. They can get it in the Socialist countries, free from any political or military obligations.[21]

A complete and rapid reversal of US aid policy in response to Soviet moves would have been too difficult for many in the administration. Nevertheless, changes began to appear as early as 1957, after the Suez crisis, especially in US policy towards the Middle East. American geopolitical strategists most feared Soviet advances in that region where two-thirds of world oil deposits were at stake. In a joint resolution, since called the 'Eisenhower Doctrine,' Congress authorized the president:

> ... to cooperate with and assist any nation or group of nations in the general area of the Middle East desiring such assistance in the development of economic strength dedicated to the maintenance of national independence ... to undertake ... military assistance programs with any nation or group of nations of that area desiring such assistance ... to employ the armed forces of the United States as he deems necessary to secure and protect the territorial integrity and political independence of any such nation or group of nations requesting such aid against overt armed aggression from any nation controlled by international communism.[22]

The Eisenhower Doctrine meant that some aid could be given to some non-aligned states; the direct threat of communism was no longer paramount. The Doctrine reintroduced the basic liberal principle of the pursuit of national interest into a strategy that had been dominated by the crusader impulse for a number of years. The administration took further steps in the same direction in 1958, creating the 'Development Loan Fund' with an appropriation of

$300 million, and ending its opposition to the establishment of the Inter-American Development Bank, for which the US provided $350 million of its initial one billion dollar capitalization.

In the end, the foreign assistance experience of the Eisenhower administration was just as ironic as that of his predecessor. American foreign assistance to the Third World began in the Truman administration as a policy aimed at achieving limited liberal and economic ends. The policy was dictated by the new, more objective and scientific, study of foreign affairs exemplified by George Kennan's work. Yet, by the end of the Truman years, the policy became the center of a new American global crusade. In the Eisenhower years the US followed the same path in the opposite direction. What began as part of an all-out crusade against international communism ended up as a modest policy concerned with fostering American economic and political interests around the world, one that saw the Soviet Union as the United States's primary geopolitical rival, but not as the source of all that is Evil.

*Kennedy and the quintessence of American common sense*

John F. Kennedy returned some of the waning religious zeal to American aid policy. He revitalized American foreign policy without really changing its post-war direction; he simply intensified all of the somewhat contradictory elements of the foreign policy of the US as a great power. Kennedy's policy direction, as well as his immense popularity, were functions of his ability to fuse all the disparate elements of American common sense. Political and economic liberalism, American exceptionalism with its related crusader and evangelic impulses, and faith in experimental science merged together in 'The New Frontier.' Kennedy was schooled in the lessons of liberal political theory. He could act the rational egotist and understood the threat of an atomistic universe, as he demonstrated in the Cuban missile crisis. Private enterprise and the free market remained sacred to him, even though he presided over a partial renewal of the American economy on the basis of Keynesian theory and he paid less attention to the federal deficit than many traditional liberals would have hoped. Nonetheless, the Keynesian recommendations he chose were the ones most consistent with traditional liberal economics, i.e. tax reduction rather than income redistribution. In foreign policy, the evangelic impulse dominated: Kennedy's 'New Frontier' was the world. He thought the US had a duty to promote economic development and democracy in the Third World on the basis of the American historical experience and on the model of present American economic and political institutions. Kennedy occasionally even became a crusader, as he did in the Bay of Pigs and started to do in Vietnam. Kennedy's faith in science was just as important. He believed that most problems could be solved, it was just a question of finding the right technique. Therefore, he surrounded himself with 'the best and the brightest' political scientists and economists to apply their systematic methods to foreign policy.

Events at the end of the Eisenhower administration led Kennedy to reassess American foreign policy toward the Third World. Not only was the Soviet Union more active, the friendship of even traditional American allies could not be assured. In the spring of 1958 Vice-President Nixon made a goodwill tour of Latin America and confronted rioting university students in Lima and a mob who tried to overturn his car in Caracas. In January 1959 Fidel Castro took power in Cuba, later nationalized foreign assets, and ultimately established friendly relations with the Soviet Union.[23] Many in the Eisenhower administration saw the violent reaction to Nixon only as proof of a communist conspiracy, but Kennedy's intellectuals accepted it as a sign of widespread anti-American feeling. Eisenhower did not dismiss the Cuban revolution. He recognized that Castro was 'a hero to the masses.'[24] The Kennedy administration was forced to see that as well, after the failed Bay of Pigs invasion.

That failure convinced Kennedy that the mixture of Soviet activism, anti-American feeling, and Castro's charisma was potentially devastating to American interests in Latin America. In response, he turned to analyses elaborated in the 1950s by economists and political scientists at Harvard and MIT, the men he had put in charge of US–Third World relations.[25]

Kennedy's intellectuals saw poverty and want at the root of the illusion that communism could solve the Third World's problems. Therefore, strengthening the military capability of friendly governments (the goal of the Mutual Security Act) would not be sufficient to prevent communism from spreading. The US had to help eliminate the poverty that made communism attractive. Fighting poverty became an important instrument in the policy of containment and gave American foreign policy a humanitarian drive that could be legitimated by the evangelical themes Kennedy invoked in his inaugural address. Still, for his policy intellectuals the justification of this humanitarian drive was quite different: It was a rational, scientific instrument for advancing American geopolitical and economic interests.

How could poverty in the Third World be eliminated? The first answer American intellectuals offered was not redistribution of the world's wealth, but straightforward economic growth. Few scholars would betray the principles of economic liberalism, but they could endorse the thesis that poverty was the result of the relative lack of capital in the Third World. An influx of capital through foreign assistance, preferably in loans that required discipline to pay back, could fill the gap. Loans could be used to build up the infrastructure that private banks considered too risky to finance. And the discipline demonstrated in building the projects and paying off the loans would create a favorable economic environment for the expansion of both national and foreign private investment. This would lead to economic development. The most widely-publicized theory of this kind was Walt Whitman Rostow's conception of stages of economic development, leading to a 'take off' into self-sustaining economic growth like that in the United States.[26] The prevailing intellectual consensus in the US during the late 1950s and 1960s was that economic development would eliminate poverty, as the new wealth created trickled down to the lower social strata so that everybody would enjoy a better way of life.

However, some American scholars felt that economic growth alone would not eliminate poverty. Their challenge was more difficult because most Americans understood redistribution as limiting people's rights to enjoy the fruits of their labors. At the end of the 1950s, progressive American intellectuals identified anti-market forces in Latin America that made the distribution of wealth suspect even to liberalism. Opposing this 'feudalism' became a Kennedy mission as part of the global battle with communism. Land and tax reforms to stimulate savings and investments became the new gospel. As Kennedy declared:

> For too long my country, the wealthiest nation on a poor continent, failed to carry out its full responsibilities to its sister Republics. We have now accepted that responsibility. In the same way those who possess wealth and power in poor nations must accept their own responsibilities. They must lead the fight for basic reforms which alone can preserve the fabric of their own societies. Those who make peaceful revolution impossible will make violent revolution inevitable.[27]

Kennedy's mission went even further. Economic development and social reform were not enough: He wanted to establish democracy. Ultimately, he aimed at the wholesale transfer of the American historical model to the Third World. As he said:

> [The] fundamental task of our foreign aid program in the 1960s is not negatively to fight Communism: Its fundamental task is to help make a historical demonstration that in the twentieth century, as in the nineteenth—in the southern half of the globe as in the north—economic growth and political democracy can develop hand in hand.[28]

Kennedy replaced the Mutual Security Act with the 'Foreign Assistance Act' and created the Agency for International Development (AID), Peace Corps, and a special program for Latin America, the Alliance for Progress. By 1963 American foreign assistance grew to $4 billion per year and the ratio of economic to military aid reversed in favor of the former by two to one.[29]

The evangelical vision underlying Kennedy's policy was a slippery one. Missions have a way of becoming crusades by their own logic, as this statement of American preferences in the Dominican Republic after Trujillo's demonstrates:

> There are three possibilities in descending order of preference: a decent democratic regime, a continuation of the Trujillo regime, or a Castro regime. We ought to aim at the first but we really cannot renounce the second until we are sure that we can avoid the third.[30]

Kennedy's advisors, both during his life and after his death, when many continued on Lyndon Johnson's staff, easily justified supporting dictatorships in societies where leftist governments might be the alternative and they demanded the use of overt and covert force to prevent communism in developing countries: counterinsurgency programs and economic assistance went hand in hand.

### *Johnson: a return to liberalism*

The American war in Vietnam can be considered the tragic result of the application of a number of self-reinforcing lessons from American common sense, all of which the Kennedy administration accepted: the reality of America's mission, the need for force when evangelism fails, the faith in science. Yet, even though Lyndon Johnson carried out the war that reflected the quintessence of American common sense, Johnson's aid policies, in sum, did not stem from quite the same tragic combination of ideological elements inherited from Kennedy.

Johnson was less of an evangelist. In Latin America he was primarily concerned with American geopolitical interests and the liberal world economy which supported them. Undersecretary of State Thomas C. Mann articulated the shift in policy by citing four main objectives in Latin America:

> (1) to foster economic growth and be neutral on internal social reform; (2) to protect US private investments in the hemisphere; (3) to show no preference, through aid or otherwise, for representative democratic institutions; and (4) to oppose communism.[31]

To be sure, evangelism did not completely disappear in the Johnson years. It was a powerful source of legitimation for the potentially quite unpopular war in Vietnam and a 1966 Congressional amendment to the Foreign Assistance Act of 1961 stressed political democracy as an aim of American aid policy.[32]

Still, Johnson's liberalism and faith in science guided what he thought was really possible much more than any legislative mandate. For instance, Johnson believed that North Vietnam would apply cost-benefit analysis in deciding whether to continue the war.[33] Johnson's faith in technology made him feel that sophisticated American weapons would eventually assure American victory[34] and his faith in the ubiquity of liberal motivations assured him that the North Vietnamese would eventually recognize their defeat. Equally, it was ultimately his own cost-benefit analysis of the effect of a continued war on American national interests that led Johnson to withdraw from the presidential race in order to devote his time to finding a way to end the war without the US having to suffer a humiliating defeat.

With the escalation of the Vietnam war Johnson increased development assistance to Asia. He contributed to the establishment of the Asian Development Bank and proposed a regional program of assistance which was as ambitious as Kennedy's for Latin America. The Johnson administration continued to see economic development, coupled with military assistance, as the best way to prevent communism from spreading, but Johnson was not interested in a global crusade, 'Johnson was not against foreign aid; he was merely against handing it out without a clear cut return, either in terms of demonstrable economic improvement, or in political favors, or both.'[35]

Throughout most of Johnson's administration the budget for aid remained high, although slightly lower than during the Kennedy years. In the last year of the administration Congress reduced the aid budget as a sign of their displeasure with the administration's conduct of the war in Vietnam.[36]

### *Aid in the 1970s: national interest and a more 'scientific' attack on poverty*

Throughout the Nixon and Ford administrations Henry Kissinger dominated American foreign policy. His primary concern was America's geopolitical role in a hostile world of egoistic states. He was not very concerned with the nation's historical 'mission' or even, many observers argued, with the immediate economic interests of its people; his orientation came under attack from both crusaders and evangelists and, toward the end of his tenure, from economic liberals as well.

Jimmy Carter's general approach to foreign policy revived American evangelism and redefined the country's mission to be the promotion of human rights globally. Tragically for Carter, this revival of America's missionary impulse contributed to his later humiliation, which may not have been as great had he continued to present the US as an ordinary power, which is what both the defeat in Vietnam and Kissinger's traditional realist policies suggested. Carter failed the public by failing to demonstrate the US's special power in the Iranian embassy hostage affair, something the public had not demanded of the less-evangelical Lyndon Johnson in the very-similar Pueblo incident.

Still, for those concerned with expanding America's foreign assistance role, Carter's evangelism was a boon. Liberal *Realpolitik* has never convinced Congress to make large aid allocations. The aid budget was a much smaller percentage of national expenditures at the beginning of the 1970s than throughout the 1960s. Not only was Congress reluctant to support many Third World countries after the Vietnam debacle, Kissinger's orientation toward the Third World made aid a less significant foreign policy instrument; the Third World was never as central to the Nixon and Ford administrations as it had been to Kennedy or even to Eisenhower and Truman. Aid was no longer needed to fight Third World forces of Evil, nor was it seen as a tool for the implementation of political and economic reforms following the American model. In real terms, the annual American aid budget dropped by over 40 per cent from 1967 to 1973. After 1974 foreign assistance started to grow again. It even grew sharply in the first two years of the Carter administration under the influence of the administration's revival of a US global mission. But even with that growth spurt, throughout the 1970s (a decade of recession) increases in the US aid budget fell behind the growth rates of the US and global economies. In the last two years of the Carter administration, American aid as a percentage of GNP reached its lowest level ever.[37] Moreover, due to the Egyptian-Israeli conflict the proportion of the aid budget going to that region alone (which had always been high) nearly doubled. Real US foreign assistance to most of the Third World shrunk dramatically.

Not surprisingly, when the Kissinger years began (entailing the prospect of reduced aid funding for years) American aid officials began to experiment with ways to get the most 'development' out of each, increasingly scarce, aid dollar. In the first few years of the Nixon administration the major US aid agency, AID, focuses on controlling Third World population as the most efficient means to assure development. The logic of that policy can be summarized in all-too simple terms, without significant distortion: If development = GNP/population, and prior efforts had focused on the numerator (with mixed success), it might prove more efficient to focus on the denominator.

This policy immediately resonated with the World Bank's new president, Robert S. McNamara, a quintessential 'Fordist.'[38] As Kennedy and Johnson's Secretary of Defense McNamara introduced the cost-accounting methods of modern business. As president of the leading aid agency he promised to apply the same management science to development.

Critics of this new direction in aid policy were apt to see zealous US support of Third World population control as evidence of none-too-veiled white racist fears of a world in which people of 'good European stock' were becoming a smaller and smaller minority.[39] But AID and the World Bank's rapid search for alternative means to encourage cost-effective development after population control proved not to be a panacea indicates that faith in the experimental method rather than semi-conscious racism may have been the more important motive.

The next experiment both AID and the World Bank tried was a 'direct assault on poverty.' McNamara's experience was an important source of support for this experiment. The war in Vietnam taught him that popular communist movements cannot be stopped by force. And his short experience at the Bank taught him that even remarkable economic growth might do nothing for the poor; the 'trickle down' mechanism regularly failed. Growing poverty would provide a breeding ground for violence and communism in the years to come.[40] A new combination of American science and evangelism, different from that which had supported the failed experiments of growth without redistribution or the fight against Latin American 'feudalism' had to be elaborated to understand this persistent poverty.

McNamara put forward his new conception in a speech to the Board of Governors of the World Bank in 1973, saying:

> The fact is that very little has been done over the past two decades specifically designed to increase the productivity of subsistence agriculture. . . . I suggest that the goal be to

increase production on small farms so that by 1985 their output will be growing at the rate of 5 percent per year. If the goal is met, and smallholders maintain that momentum, they can double their annual output between 1985 and the end of the century.[41]

The proposal concerned 40 per cent of the population of the third world, 550 or 700 million people according to different assessments, living in rural areas with an annual income of $50 or less in 1970 prices.[42] AID, McNamara's World Bank, and the many agencies they influenced tried to achieve the desired results with 'integrated rural development programs' which would turn the 'inactive' peasantry into productive workers.

The new rural development policy did not contradict liberal economics. Its aim was growth achieved through market mechanisms. More significantly, it was concerned neither with relative poverty nor with active redistribution, but with absolute poverty; thus, it managed to avoid references to international disparities of income.[43] The new policy's guidebook became a study jointly conducted by the World Bank and the Institute of Development Studies at the University of Sussex, *Redistribution with Growth*[44] which recommended targeting investments to the poor in order to increase their income through economic growth. Despite its title, the study does not advocate active income redistribution. Just changing the targets of investment would, over time, result in a radically different distribution.

Inside the World Bank and other UN development agencies the focus on poverty elimination led to an elaboration of another, related, approach: meeting 'basic human needs.' Because it assumes that material well-being is everyone's basic right, this is a much more radical approach, implying a return to Locke's doctrine on charity which most liberals have subsequently ignored. To accept that would require, as one observer of aid policy in the 1970s argues, 'larger changes, and perhaps profound ones, in the structure of production and in the role of government in the economy'.[45]

US government aid policy never became quite as radical as the most far-reaching proposals made by the World Bank staff, but amendments made to the U.S. Foreign Assistance Act in 1973 did emphasize poverty elimination and they remained the guidelines for official American aid policy through Carter's administration. They state:

United States bilateral development assistance should give the highest priority to undertakings submitted by host governments which directly improve the lives of the poorest of their people and their capacity to participate in the development of their countries.[46]

## Conflicting ideologies as constraints on American aid policy

Gramsci argues that ideology sets some of the limits on human action as it helps establish patterns of conduct. Overcoming those limits requires a critical, intellectual effort to understand the world better and, in doing so, to develop new aspirations and more inclusive values. Arguably, the history of American aid policy until 1980 shows something like that kind of creative learning. If one just took the first statements the Truman administration made on aid at the United Nations, before his 'Point Four' speech, and compared them to the doctrine of the 1970s summarized above one could say that a self-interested policy established without consulting the real interests and aspirations of its ultimate clients had been transformed into altruistic policy consciously directed toward serving the world's least-advantaged people. But, of course, the reality is not quite that simple and neither the straightforward liberal goals that the Truman administration wanted American foreign assistance policy to serve, nor the global welfarism of the supporters of 'basic needs' development strategies nor Haq's vision of a worldwide Keynesian state ever dominated US foreign assistance policy. But it may help us see the nature of the ideological constraints on American aid policy to think about why neither of these ideals came to pass.

First, consider the liberal ideal of using foreign assistance only as an instrument of a self-interested foreign policy: as a spur to liberalization of the world economy and as a political tool. Most elite Americans would want aid policy to approach this ideal. Unfortunately for them, the closer an administration approached this ideal, the fewer aid resources it found available: not enough for Truman to reconstruct Europe and not even enough for Kissinger to conduct effective policy in the Third World. To have foreign assistance available as an effective instrument American presidents have had to rely on some of the religious residues in American common sense—especially the idea of the US's special mission in the world. This can legitimate a costly policy to a public equally influenced by liberalism and, therefore, willing to ask, 'What's in it for us?,' when government proposes they fund policies so clearly aimed at others. Truman's invocation of anti-communism was essential to the reconstruction of Europe. Kennedy's conquest of the global 'New Frontier' assured that all his new ideas about US–Third World relations would become a reality. And Johnson was probably right: He never would have been able to carry-out his own, much more modest agenda if he had not continued to fight Kennedy's crusade in Vietnam.

Alternatively, consider Haq's ideal of a foreign assistance system funded by global redistributive taxation and targeted toward the least-advantaged in the Third World. Perhaps the best that Haq could hope for from America under today's ideological constraints would be an administration that considered the elimination of world poverty to be an end in itself and, at the same time, believed that economic science showed that the most efficient way to assure such development was by global redistributive taxation (something Haq believes). But, of course, to get an administration that wanted to eliminate poverty, Haq would have to accept one with some sort of evangelical mission, one that could tap into traditional American aspirations. This, of course, has its dangers; it may reinforce American feelings of superiority and evangelism easily slips into crusaderism. About the best that Haq could hope for would be an administration like Carter's, guided by evangelism and scientism. But, we know from Gramsci, that Haq could hope for something slightly more: for an American government that does not simply accept current ideological constraints but, rather, marshals American intellectuals to emphasize American 'good sense' about foreign assistance and convince the public to drop contradictory notions. Carter's government was notoriously ineffective at this.

That ineffectiveness stemmed, in part, from how tenuous the support for Carter's overall foreign policy position was compared to the massive support that could easily be mustered for an alternative position. Carter began as a 'post-cold war internationalist.' He even conceived of his evangelism in the Third World, his human rights program, as a way to provide America with some target for its international zeal other than Soviet communism. But he tried to legitimate his policy by telling the public about the limits of US power, something, that if many ever came to believe would only convince them of the need for a new American isolationism, not a new, less compelling, mission. At the same time Carter's scientism and his internationalist version of liberalism only appealed to one part of the American elite, those for whom America's anti-communist crusade had really only been a means to assure the realization of the old vision of America's global 'commercial empire.' To other members of the elite, often those more attached to domestic industry than to international trade and investment, anti-communism was a much more organic ideology; it had been a tool in their own struggles against more radical elements of organized labor and domestic poor people's movements. In contrast to Carter's views, while 'cold war internationalism,' invoking the old communist threat, may have been called into question by the defeat in Vietnam, its base of support was still easier to form by combining both elements of the American elite and emphasizing the strength of America to mass public, thus justifying a continuing crusade.

## Notes

1. *The Poverty Curtain: Choices for the Third World* (New York: Columbia University Press, 1976).
2. See Craig N. Murphy, 'What Does the Third World Want? The Development and Meaning of the New International Economic Order Ideology,' *International Studies Quarterly* 27 (1983): 55–76.
3. Quoted in John Dunn, *Locke* (Oxford: Oxford University Press, 1984), 43.
4. Seyom Brown, *The Faces of Power* (New York: Columbia University Press, 1983), 25.
5. Packenham, *Liberal America and the Third World* (Princeton, NJ: Princeton University Press, 1973).
6. Ibid., 20.

7. See Hugh Davis Graham and Ted Robert Gurr, eds., *Violence in America: Historical and Comparative Perspectives* (New York: Bantam, 1969).
8. *The Liberal Tradition in American Politics* (New York: Harcourt, Brace, and World, 1955).
9. Craig N. Murphy, *The Emergence of the NIEO Ideology* (Boulder, CO: Westview Press, 1984), 19–31.
10. See John G. Stoessinger, *Crusaders and Pragmatists* (New York: W. W. Norton, 1979), 82–96.
11. Quoted in Brown, 41.
12. Quoted in Packenham, 29.
13. Ibid., 43.
14. Ibid., 45.
15. Quoted in Stoessinger, 91.
16. Quoted in Packenham, 40.
17. Even before McCarthy had scrutinized more than one million Americans, 'three out of every four Americans disapproved of the way Truman was conducting the war,' and agreed with MacArthur's approach. See Stephen E. Ambrose, *Rise to Globalism: American Foreign Policy Since 1938* , 3rd revised ed. (Harmondsworth: Penguin Books, 1983), 183.
18. Packenham, 49–50.
19. Stoessinger, 98.
20. Ibid., 112.
21. Quoted in Joan Edelman Spero, *The Politics of International Economic Relations*, 2nd ed. (New York: St Martin's, 1981), 153–4.
22. Quoted in Brown, 124.
23. On the importance of Nixon's trip and Castro's actions for the reassessment of American foreign policy see Jerome Levinson and Juan De Onis, *The Alliance That Lost Its Way* (Chicago: Quadrangle Books, 1972), 44–6.
24. Brown, 131.
25. The 'action intellectuals' or the 'Charles River Group,' see Packenham, 61-3.
26. *The Stages of Economic Growth, a Non-Communist Manifesto* (Cambridge: Cambridge University Press, 1960), serialized prior to publication in the London *Economist*.
27. Quoted in Brown, 155.
28. Quoted in Packenham, 59.
29. Ibid., 59.
30. Levinson and De Onis, 95.
31. Ibid., 88.
32. Packenham, 98–109.
33. Brown says, 'The U.S. strategy in Vietnam, therefore, despite its turns and twists, had an underlying consistent objective: to increase the enemy's costs and diminish their prospects of success' (p. 292).
34. Loren Baritz, *Backfire* (New York: William Morrow and Co., 1984).
35. Packenham, 89.
36. Ibid., 87.
37. Spero, 162, 171.

38. Ironically, he led the Ford Motor Company before joining government.
39. On the debate in international forums see Murphy, *The Emergence of the NIEO Ideology*, 117–18.
40. Packenham, 52.
41. Quoted in Donald R. Mickelwait, Charles F. Sweet, and Elliott R. Morss, *New Directions in Development: A Study of U.S. Aid* (Boulder, CO: Westview Press, 1979), 2.
42. Robert L. Ayres, *Banking on the Poor* (Cambridge, MA: MIT Press, 1984), 92.
43. Ibid., 76–83.
44. *Redistribution with Growth* (New York: Oxford University Press, 1974).
45. Ayres, 85.
46. Quoted in Mickelwait et al., 2.

# 5 Reagan and American common sense

In 1980 Ronald Reagan's campaign did emphasize America's continuing strength and he did call upon the American people to join a new crusade. Of course, few of those who voted for Reagan knew or cared about the implications of his philosophy for American foreign assistance programs to the Third World. Probably most, if they were asked, would have predicted that aid would decline under a Reagan administration, that the United States would 'give less away' to ungrateful foreigners. Although that prediction would have been wrong, it would have mattered very little to most of the public that supported the Republican presidential candidate in 1980; the cost of foreign assistance was not even what bothered most Americans about their country's relationship with the Third World.

Reagan inspired Americans because he combined all the elements of American common sense to find answers to current dilemmas. To a soul-searching American people shaken by the Vietnam war and by internal social unrest, he reaffirmed America's special destiny. To those who had complained about Carter's inefficacy and confusion in foreign policy, he promised to guarantee national interests over and, if necessary, against the needs of the international community. To businesspeople he professed his belief in the 'magic of the market' to solve the country's and the world's economic and social problems. And to a nation disturbed about a growing inability to turn new inventions into competitive products, he expressed his certainty that 'progress' and 'human destiny' find their expression in scientific advancement.

Like Kennedy, whose popularity only he among America's post-war presidents has equaled, Reagan represents the quintessence of American common sense. This is not to imply that Kennedy, had he lived, would have supported Reagan's policies, nor that Reagan did what Kennedy would have done. They combined the basic elements of American common sense in different ways. Kennedy's evangelism, for example, involved preaching to the world about the desirability of the American political system, liberal democracy. Reagan is more concerned with teaching other nations how the free market can solve their economic and social problems. Reagan constantly reiterated the theme that too much government causes economic backwardness, a theme the Kennedy administration only harped upon when Third World governments impeded foreign investment or trade with the industrialized west.

## Understanding Reagan's ascendancy

In 1980 a whole host of issues worried the American public. The most troublesome were economic. The decade was ending the same way it began, with continuing stagnation and high inflation. After the second major oil shock of 1979 (occasioned by the Iranian revolution) matters appeared even worse than they had after the first. Interest rates were the highest they had ever been in America's history as an industrial economy. Unemployment seemed ready to rise, so soon after the modest gains that had been made during the Carter years. Many who would not normally worry that their own future might be destroyed by a recession worried this time because the late 1970s had seen the first major applications of 'affirmative action' principles in the American workplace. Groups that had traditionally been the most-discriminated against in the American job market—the last hired first fired—including women and blacks, now were protected by the federal government. White men in potentially marginal jobs feared layoffs that their fathers, in a less-enlightened era, would not have feared.

On top of economic changes, other more purely social changes (often reinforced by the economic hardships of the decade) bothered many Americans. The 1970s witnessed a significant increase in the proportion of women working outside the home. Even though most of the change can be accounted for by 'push' factors—by the need to make ends meet in families hard-pressed between rising prices and the stagnant wages of a male wage earner and not by the free choice of the new working women, many men and women feared the effect this trend would have on 'family values,' especially since so many of the women new to the workforce were single mothers supporting families that their husbands had abandoned. Many Americans understood this problem not as a one of irresponsible husbands but as one of irresponsible mothers not devoting themselves to their children as homemakers. The problem appeared to be of a type with other threats to the American family supported by 'radical feminists,' especially the legalization of abortion and the new assertiveness of lesbians and gay men.

An analysis of Reagan's appeal needs to take all these issues into account. It is easy to do so in terms of Reagan's ideology since in almost every instance what he offered the American public was a plausible reaffirmation of American common sense and not a critical rethinking of traditional ideas made outmoded by social change. As we outline the ideological sources of his triumph, we need to put them in the context of the political strategy that brought Reagan to power. In that way we will anticipate, and provide an introduction to, the theme of the second half of the book, Gramsci's insights on the consolidation of power, the creation of 'supremacy.'

Many scholars have written about the sources of Reagan's triumph–the reasons for his two landslide presidential victories as well his ability to achieve most of his political agenda, at least during the first seven of his eight years in office. The analysis that we find most compelling places Reagan's ascendancy in a larger social context, as part of a politically-orchestrated *Right Turn*[1] in American politics which had little to do with real changes in American ideology, but involved changes in the political economy of the United States and the creation of new social coalitions and transformation of old ones. The only problem with this view is its tendency to overemphasize the conspiratorial role of self-interested elites and underemphasize the significance of Reagan's recombination of traditional ideological elements. Emphasizing that aspect too makes this view compatible with Gramsci's understanding of political dynamics.

Thomas Byrne Edsall, whose *The New Politics of Inequality*[2] was one of the earliest insightful analyses of the Reagan phenomenon, does not even begin with crises in the American economy in the 1970s, but with the earlier breakdown of the dominant role of the Democratic party in American society. Edsall blames the party's weakness in the 1970s on its increasing identification with the interests of the poor, as a result of both its own democratizing reforms and of the power of the civil rights movement.[3] Even if it sounds a bit like blaming the victim to imply that the past political victories of the least-advantaged are to blame for their defeat in the 1970s, the weakness of the Democrats under Carter did provide the real background for Reagan's success.

The other major political development of the 1970s that Edsall notices is the increasing, and increasingly direct, involvement of American business in politics through the Republican party. He summarizes his entire argument by saying that in the 1970s an alliance between the ideological right and business began to form.[4] Reagan was both that alliance's major beneficiary as well as one of the key figures who helped forge it.

## Reagan as an intellectual

For Ronald Reagan's critics, who are accustomed to thinking of him as passive, befuddled, and more than a little stupid, it may be difficult to imagine him playing a central role in forming the most important domestic political coalition in the United States in half a century. If so, it will be even more difficult to credit that Reagan's role was that of an intellectual, a role he rarely even played in movies.[5] Yet, quite seriously, the role that Reagan played in America's 'right turn' was, more than anything else, one of those that Gramsci attributes to intellectuals: he articulated the point of view of a particular social group and helped convince those articulating the points of view of other groups to accept his position. Moreover, this sort of rhetorical activity was much more central to Reagan's entire political career than it has been to the careers of any other recent candidate for president, with the possible exception of the two ministers, Jesse Jackson and Pat Robertson, in 1988.

Reagan's strength as political intellectual, his trick as a politician, has always been his ability to reflect the common sense of his audiences back to them. Throughout his career, Reagan has been able to articulate dreams and fears and make them more plausible, all the more real, all the more like simple common sense, by the way he articulates them.

Garry Wills's central insight in his biography of Reagan[6] and his role in American life is that Reagan has not, as most observers say, had two careers (actor and politician) or even three (actor, union leader, and politician), but one. Reagan has always been a spokesman. He began as a radio announcer, reflecting the newly-returned confidence of the middle class of New Deal-era small mid-western cities back to itself. Given the opportunity to move up to Hollywood, he soon found himself in wartime propaganda films, boosting American confidence and belief in victory both when he worked on government-sponsored films and when he played archetypical 'American' roles in privately-financed movies. Soon after the war he became a key figure, and later president, of the Screen Actors Guild, acting less like a union leader defending the narrow self-interest of his members and more the spokesman for an ongoing compromise between actors, agents, producers, and a rabidly anti-communist government. (This was the Joe McCarthy era, the days when Hollywood blacklisted 'un-American' writers, actors, and directors.) In the late 1950s, after his acting career had reached its nadir, he continued as a full-time spokesman for General Electric.

Wills argues that it was at GE that the future president developed the vision, and even much of the wording of the vision, that would be central to his political career.[7] In a period of eight years, visiting every GE factory and speaking to businessmen's civic groups in every town where they were located, Reagan perfected a set speech attacking communism abroad and big government at home and calling for a return to 'American values.' It was significant that Reagan developed the core of 'The Speech' when he was a conformist middle-manager working in one of the most rigidly conventional American companies of the fifties. That is one reason why the core of Reagan's message has always sounded a bit like a caricature of big business ideology from Eisenhower's day. Nevertheless, as Reagan became more comfortable and confident, his GE speech came more and more to reflect the small-town business values of his audiences, views he had know well as far back as his days in radio. And even after he was dropped by GE (some suggest because he deviated too far from the company line) he continued to be wildly successful at business functions throughout the country in the early 1960s when the conservative wing of the Republican Party succeeded in having one of their own, Barry Goldwater, nominated for president. Wills argues, 'Thus The Speech was part of that body of right-wing rhetoric igniting the grass-roots Goldwater movement of the early 1960s.'[8] When Reagan gave the same speech in a nationally-televised address to boost Goldwater's campaign in 1964, Reagan's own political career was launched as well.

Reagan's shift to electoral politics entailed a slight shift in his well-developed professional role. As California's governor from 1967 to 1974 he acted not only as spokesman for a point of view, he also acted, as Wills argues, like the marketing chief of a large firm. Reagan helped identify and decided how to promote all the most positive points of the program that he and his financial backers and political advisors had brought to the statehouse.[9] More significantly, just like a marketing manager, when Reagan's well-developed knowledge of what the California public wanted told him that a particular program would never sell, he sent those that developed the product back to the drawing board.

After his second term as governor ended Reagan continued to articulate his philosophy, increasingly as the grounds for a grand coalition between broad business interests and groups with traditional, non-economic, right-wing concerns like rolling-back communism or protecting the American family. By 1980, after a decade of rapid social change and a decade of economic stagnation, these were traditional themes that many Americans wanted to hear.

Reagan is quite the opposite of a revolutionary intellectual—one who criticizes common sense, shows its inconsistencies, prejudices, and superstitions, and works with people to help find the good sense at the core of their contradictory consciousness. Reagan (very much like John F. Kennedy, in this way) reinforces contradictory consciousness. Reagan tells people what they believe is right. He will only tell an audience to think differently than it does if he assumes it to be hostile; this is the way he has approached Congress, the United Nations, and the national press, but not civic associations or a national television audience.

Reagan's ability to reflect back to audiences things that they want to hear, by itself, would hardly make him an intellectual in Gramsci's sense. But Reagan uses that ability to convince people. It would be better to say that Reagan is a master of one of the first rules of rhetoric: the listener's prejudices will always be the most convincing evidence for a proposition. Reagan uses his mastery of that rule not to be an undistorted mirror of preconceptions, but as a coalition builder. He addresses his audiences selectively. Some of his themes touch some of his supporters more. Others themes are addressed to others. In the process Reagan has helped meld together a new political bloc in the United States. True, Reagan's method can leave him delivering a message that is repetitive, trite, and that may, upon examination, appear to be a bit incoherent. He has never struggled to resolve his many views into a single philosophy. But therein lies his strength as a politician.

It is also his weakness as an 'intellectual' in Gramsci's terms. Gramsci still expects us to remember the traditional meaning of the word even after he has used it to name a new concept. Intellectuals, in the fullest sense of the term, are people who can and do take time to reflect on what they know; they are people who strive for a coherent synthesis. That kind of activity was never central to Reagan's role as a master of marketing.

## Reagan and old-fashioned liberalism

In Gramsci terms, Reagan is tied organically to the American bourgeoisie, but not to any one part of that dominant class. Reagan's strong attachment to individualism and the 'need to get ahead' (ideas that were organic to his upbringing in a petite bourgeois mid-western family, the son of an unsuccessful salesman) made it perfectly sensible for him to sell his talents to the highest bidders, from the radio station owners in larger and larger cities, to Hollywood, and finally to big business. Yet, to some extent, Reagan remained true to the interests of the class in which he grew up. Even at GE he was pulled toward the concerns of the local business leaders to whom he spoke, concerns that were less-cosmopolitan and less liberal than those expected in the corporate culture of even one of America's most conservative firms.

Reagan's liberalism is of the old school, the lived-philosophy of bourgeois Americans before the rise of the large corporation, the big union, and the welfare state. Reagan is a pre-Keynesian liberal. The one belief that Reagan most often repeats is his conviction that the twentieth-century welfare state has sapped individual initiative and led to widespread injustice by distorting the operation of the free market. Reagan articulates this view with the conviction of a convert. His first political identification was with Franklin Roosevelt's New Deal, in fact, in Gramsci's terms, both in some of his first jobs in the midwest and as an employee of the government in Hollywood, Reagan had been part of the ideological apparatus that set up that welfare state.

Reagan's campaign in 1980 promised to do away with every part of the welfare state except a minimal 'safety net' to catch the destitute. He promised further to end deficit spending. The two promises were intimately linked, but the first was always more important to Reagan than the second. Reagan did not want to balance the budget only to become, 'tax collector for the welfare state.'[10] Consequently, Reagan's major domestic initiative of two terms was a series of massive tax cuts, especially for the rich, which, in fact, accumulated a federal deficit in his 8 years about the size to that left over from the previous 205 years of the republic. Nevertheless, he was able to keep his more important promise, by cutting the size of federal welfare state programs by about 10 per cent, although his first budget director, David Stockman, considers this small cut evidence of the failure of the 'Reagan Revolution' from the point of view of traditional liberal economic values.[11]

Stockman fails to take into account that this 'Revolution' began long before Reagan entered the White House. In the late 1970s the massive direct political mobilization of American businesses behind an ideological attack on the welfare state through elite 'high-intellectual' think tanks as well as by sponsoring the appearances of more popular advocates of the same position (most significantly, Ronald Reagan)[12] had put enough pressure on the Carter administration that it began the 'Reagan' Revolution, by dramatically reducing most of the welfare state programs which affected the urban poor, the major focus of the essential bourgeois attack. Reagan had only to cut out most of the rest of those programs, leaving 'welfare' programs that actually provide more entitlements to the middle-class and the rich than they do to the poor—farm subsidies, veterans' benefits, and various forms of social insurance, as well as the minimal safety-net programs.

Reagan went further than Carter, and further than many of the business think tanks of the 1970s dared hope, in his direct attack on 'big labor' as well as 'big government.' The administration dismissed worker-safety regulations as anti-market and appointed labor regulators who consistently ruled against unions on the same grounds.[13]

## Reagan and the religious

Much of the support Reagan received for his more radical economic program came from a revitalized religious right wing, epitomized by the self-designated 'Moral Majority.' The success of the American fundamentalist revival of the 1970s, like that of Ruholla Khomeini's oddly similar movement in Iran, depended upon modern telecommunications technology. In the US it was television not the cassette recorder which brought the faithful authoritative opinions on every subject from family codes to world politics.

In many ways it is ironic that Ronald Reagan would be the political beneficiary of this fundamentalist drive and a trusted colleague of its leaders. Superficially, Reagan is the least-religious of recent presidents. The American public watched Kennedy go to mass, suffered with Johnson as the Episcopal parish priest in the church across from the White House lambasted the war in Vietnam from the pulpit, giggled at Nixon's awkwardness at his umpteenth inter-denominational service in the White House, and felt a bit guilty for their own lack of zeal when they heard about Jimmy and Rosalynn Carter learning Spanish by reading the Bible to each other each night before they went to sleep. Reagan's public displays of religiosity have been much less frequent. Moreover, his actual 'religion' is a bit of a mystery; everyone knows from his speeches that he is some sort of Christian and some sort of Protestant, but the fact that he is never seen in church leaves him denominationally ambiguous. Not only does Reagan appear to violate the commandment to keep the sabbath, he has violated a host of other norms that religious Americans hold dear. Most significantly, he is divorced, something that even a dozen years ago the common political wisdom in the US held to be an insurmountable obstacle to presidential ambitions.

Reagan has actually turned his lack of traditional outward signs of religiosity into a strength; it is impossible for religious critics to place an invidious denominational label on him. And he has more than compensated by constantly articulating religious themes in his political rhetoric, themes that other, perhaps more careful or more historically knowledgeable, politicians would never touch. For example, Reagan unlike almost every previous president, sees nothing wrong with publicly identifying the United States as a 'Christian nation.' Although this may send the eighteenth-century liberals who fought for religious tolerance spinning in their graves, many Americans love it and have never understood the reluctance of other politicians to state so obvious, and so praiseworthy, a fact.

Beyond Reagan's identification with religious Americans in the abstract, he has been a spokesman for fundamentalism's social agenda since the beginning of his political career. In very simple terms, American fundamentalists wish to preserve a traditional sphere of family relations untouched by modern extensions of liberal rights—the rights of women to work out of the home or to have abortions and rights of both women and children to protection from family violence—which are seen by fundamentalists as unnecessary extensions of the role of government.[14] The fundamentalist model is akin to the old Puritan family in its emphasis on repression: 'Spare the rod and spoil the child.'

Similarly, the new American religious right emphasizes the duty of powerful and righteous nations to use force against weaker societies that would stray from the path. 'Jesus,' as the Moral Majority's Jerry Falwell says, 'was no sissy.'[15] Neither should the powerful US act like one by following the Carterite dictum that a great power avoids the use of force whenever possible. The religious right of the 1970s shared the conviction that Reagan had been proclaiming since his first days with GE: that the United States must mount a crusade against world communism.

Two of the perceptive analysts of Reagan's rise to power, Thomas Ferguson and Joel Rogers, make a great deal of the fact that most Americans have never embraced the specific policy proposals that Reagan has enunciated. In the area of force projection, for example, extremely large majorities believe that the US should have a policy of 'no first use' of nuclear weapons and that new weapon systems should not be built as 'bargaining chips.' In fact they argue, the only concrete policy area where there was a clear 'right turn' in the distribution of popular attitudes in the late 1970s was in the area of the military budget. Half a decade after the end of war in Vietnam many Americans felt it should start to grow. But, Ferguson and Rogers point out, even that attitude had changed after *Carter* began the military build-up that Reagan continued.

Ferguson and Rogers use this as evidence for an elite theory of Reagan's rise; the American people were duped, given no real choices by a business elite that controlled the political process.[16] We do not find this completely convincing. After all, the American public very clearly did prefer Reagan and Reagan's message to Carter (despite the fact that Carter actually initiated many of the 'Reaganite' *policy* changes, which, in fact, the public may not have liked). And Reagan's first years in office did lead to a significant change in public attitudes about the position of the US in the world. Reagan's appeal clearly has been an abstract one. Ignoring what the public may feel about his (or any alternative) concrete policies Reagan offered an analysis of America's position in the world that reaffirmed things many in the American public wanted to believe: the reality of US power and the crusading responsibility that went with it.

The highly affirmative public response to Reagan's power projections, especially in Grenada, should confirm that fact. Observing the outpouring of support, one usually sanguine analyst suggested that it represented the recreation of the foreign policy consensus that had broken down during the war in Vietnam, the reunification of 'cold war internationalists,' 'post-cold war internationalists' and 'post-cold war isolationists' under a 'new cold war internationalist' banner;[17] it represented the triumph of a religious element of American common sense and a restoration of meaning and identity to many Americans.

## Reagan's faith in science

Reagan's close association with the religious right sometimes obscures his equally-strong faith in modern technology. Throughout the early stages of his 1980 presidential campaign the man who would become his vice president, George Bush, gained his greatest political mileage by pointing out Reagan's dismissive attitude toward standard economic science. Reagan's economics, Bush said, was 'voodoo economics.' Yet, Reagan would really be the last person one could imagine embracing the mystical. Even when he attacks the theory of evolution (which, of course, fundamentalists consider bunk) he does so in the scientific idiom, saying of evolution to a fundamentalist rally during his first campaign, 'It's a scientific theory, and in recent years has been challenged in the world of science.'[18]

Reagan's faith in science is not a faith in theory. Neither is it a faith in the wisdom of those who other scientists currently think are wise. This gives Reagan great flexibility. He will entertain the creative ideas of outcasts from the regular scientific community, people like Arthur Laffer whose theory that a tax cut could result in higher revenues for the government became part of Reagan's faith.[19] Yet, Reagan is hardly more likely to justify his views by turning to the *theories* of outcast scientists than he his to listen to mainstream scientific opinion. He justifies his ideas on the basis of experience, successful experiments. For example, the results of John F. Kennedy's tax cut, which led to greater economic growth and (arguably) increased government revenues even at lower rates, are more likely to be cited by Reagan than any of Laffer's curves.

The most remarkable example of Reagan's faith in science is, of course, his promotion of the concept of strategic nuclear defense, his promise to the American people that an invulnerable 'peace shield' could be built over the United States that would render Soviet missiles powerless. Although there are elements of the American scientific community who have long supported developing an anti-missile system to defend American nuclear weapons, as part of a modernization of deterrence, expert belief in the practicality of Reagan's vision of an invulnerable shield that would make deterrence obsolete is virtually non-existent.[20] Nonetheless, Reagan has convinced much of the American public that he is right. Congress, which cannot be convinced by *theoretical* arguments about its infeasibility either, has allocated significant funding to the project simply because its members are willing to experiment, willing to try any new industrial technology that might make nuclear weapons obsolete. And despite continued reservations about the ultimate vision, American scientists and American defense contractors have been happy to share in the bounty.[21] This reinforces the public's faith in the ultimate project; after all why else would 'real scientists' be conducting all those experiments; only impractical 'theorists' seem to oppose it. Moreover the public has 'seen' Reagan's 'Star Wars' technology work in the 'realistic' video animations prepared by defense contractors and the Defense Department and constantly aired on American news programs due to their high 'entertainment' and 'news' values.[22]

The same combination of Reagan's faith in technology with the eagerness of American scientists and corporations to absorb funds and experiment, and then those experiments themselves reinforcing the public's faith in the scientific merits of a particular public policy goes a long way to explain the almost uncontrolled growth in the American defense budget throughout the Reagan years. Reagan convinced Congress to approve 'high technology' weapon systems, many of which had been on the drawing boards for a decade: a massive new nuclear missile, two new intercontinental bombers—one using so-called 'stealth' technology to avoid radar, a 'stealth' fighter plane, and many new ships for the navy. And while public support for giving a blank check to the military has waned, approval of the high-tech war-fighting machines that Reagan purchased is widespread. American faith in science has not been shaken.

## Was there an alternative?

Nor has America's faith in its special destiny, or in Puritan ways of dealing with dissent, or in the market. Garry Wills sees in this fact a tragedy of world historical proportions. It seems unconscionable to him that wisdom relevant to a seventeenth-century religious commonwealth, an isolated eighteenth-century republic, or a nineteenth-century industrial nation on a still vast and hard-to-pollute continent would be treated as relevant to the problems of a society with global responsibilities. Equally tragic is the fact even most of what Americans remember from Protestant, liberal, and systematic management traditions are distorted, half truths. But that is the way common sense works.

Contrary to Wills, one could argue that what is significant about the contemporary American experience is that apparent solutions to so many of the problems its citizens faced could be found in that agglomeration of ideas. Reagan's triumph, after all, did not represent the injection of any new analysis, any new understanding into the organization of American social life. Rather, the 'right turn' of the 1980s was all about new political organization around old ideological themes—business pressure groups organizing to support their own interests behind a rather superficial version of pre-Keynesian liberalism, the fundamentalist churches that had grown during the social upheaval and economic troubles of the 1970s interjecting traditional Puritan themes in the American political process, and cold war internationalists pushing for technological solutions to the historical battle with the Soviet Union. Surprisingly, despite the fundamentally new problems it faced, Reagan's government, combining all these elements, succeeded in making most of the American public feel a lot better about themselves and their society, for a time.

Other analysts (Edsall, Ferguson and Rogers) make the right's triumph look much less significant; as if it only reflected the fact that the Democratic party failed to offer a convincing alternative. But offering as convincing an alternative would be hard, given the prejudice of common sense. The people Edsall and Ferguson and Rogers consider the 'good guys,' labor rather than business interest groups, the churches and social movements representing the poorest and most disadvantaged rather than the petite bourgeois fundamentalists, the peace movement rather than the war movement, cannot simply do the same things that the right did. And the left has no particular advantage just because the general public's attitudes on *concrete* policy issues, as opposed to abstract principles, is far from that of the right. Gramsci's analysis of ideology would suggest that to develop as successful an alternative to Reaganism would require a much greater ideological and intellectual effort. Rather than simply select among prejudices, the anti-Reagans need to help Americans confront their contradictory consciousness and search for the reasons why the abstract principles they accept contradict the 'good sense' of their attitudes on specific policies.

The simple one-way propagandizing that business round tables, TV preachers, and Ronald Reagan all specialize in would not be enough to convince people to change their minds in the ways Reagan's most sophisticated detractors would hope; something that America's largest labor federation learned in the 1984 presidential campaign when they tried the direct-mail and TV tactics pioneered by the new right.[23] To convince people to change their views, rather than just to reinforce them and suggest political actions that will further them, requires interaction, critical discussion, debate, and time, as well as a coherent intellectual effort to develop alternatives that can, in time, make sense and that do, in fact, advance people's interests as well as shape and transform their aspirations.

The crises that triggered Reagan's rise to power, the signs that America's long-planned global destiny would not be fulfilled, really only appeared in the

1970s. Perhaps it is only a matter of time before the more difficult intellectual and ideological work of responding to those crises will be done. In the meantime, because the ideological forces of the right had begun to organize before the crisis (through the Goldwater campaign and as part of the most recent religious revival) the lead established by those who had less need to present a new vision and encourage critical reflection and debate, was enough to assure Reaganism its day.

Jimmy Carter's partisans might claim that he attempted to develop a new vision of America's role in the world, but he was singularly unsuccessful in convincing the American public to adopt this vision. In particular, the concessions he made to the Third World made him appear weak and indecisive not only to the American public, but even to many of America's allies who not only shared his more forthcoming approach, but went well beyond it.

Carter's problems as the result of his policy toward the Third World began early. Because, in sharp contrast to Nixon, he believed that, in the long-run, the Third World was crucial to the United States he devoted his first months in office, and much of the political capital that any new president accumulates, to winning a fight with Congress over abandoning US control of the Panama Canal, a major sticking point in US-Latin American relations. This made his subsequent relations with Congress particularly difficult.

Ironically, Carter's fatal error in the Third World actually involved not having a more cynical idea of national interest at the forefront of his consciousness when he was petitioned by Kissinger and other luminaries of past administrations to bring the ailing Shah of Iran into the United States. When the American embassy hostages were taken in retaliation Carter was not willing to escalate the conflict into another US war in the Third World. He was not willing to match the revolutionary regime's own crusaderism, despite the popular support that such a policy would have found.[24] Instead, he turned to traditional diplomacy, which (in fact) eventually won the hostages' release, and to a brief bit of misplaced faith in American technology, hardly surprising for an engineer and former officer of America's sophisticated nuclear submarine fleet. But the American special commando which was supposed to fly into Teheran and rescue the trapped prisoners in a display of high-tech bravado floundered because not enough of the baroquely-complicated helicopters used in the operation were working at the time to provide the necessary backup, and some of those that went on the mission were grounded by the unplanned-for hostility of the desert sand. Carter's high tech military defeat in the Third World was all the more galling to many Americans because Canadians had succeeded in a similar operation; common sense suggested that the problem was not one of faith in high tech military solutions, *per se*, but of the incompetence of the particular leader who authorized this one adventure.[25]

The images Americans retain of the day Carter turned over the presidency to Reagan are blurred. Somehow at the same time the embassy hostages arrived back from Iran. Carter's supporters—those who saw hope in his ability to forget the anti-communist crusade without, at the same time, exalting narrow self-interest the way his immediate predecessors did—remember the hostages' return as a triumph of quiet diplomacy and reasonableness, the swan song of an administration more concerned with peace that with its own survival. Reagan's partisans remember the hostages' release as the first victory of the kind of tough-minded foreign policy the country had not seen for over a decade. America *was* back. Reagan did not even have to communicate directly with the hostages' captors. Fear of his stated willingness to use all of the power of the world's strongest government was enough for Iran to cut a deal with his more forthcoming predecessor.

No matter what point of view they take, Americans are hard pressed not to see in the day of Reagan's inauguration a strange reflection of the day twenty years earlier when Eisenhower turned over the office. In 1961 the old man who was leaving warned against the concentration of power inherent in the new empire's rising military-industrial complex, while the young man entering found it gave the American alliance a new mission, the promise of new crusades. In 1981 the old man entering renewed the crusader's call while the younger man leaving spoke of limits, restraint, and the realism of lower expectations. Had nothing been learned from Kennedy's day to Reagan's?

A case could be made that the intervening period had proved the futility of basing American foreign policy, especially in the Third World, on the tropes of American common sense. Isolation of the 'chosen nation' was no longer possible. Johnson had pursued America's crusade in Indochina to its logical conclusion, defeat at the hands of a 'seventh rate' power because no US government would ever be able to find a legitimate basis for using all the force at its disposal. Carter's human rights evangelism, his preaching of liberal political principles, appeared to many Americans as as unjustified and (ultimately) unsuccessful as Kissinger's self-interested *Realpolitik* with its glorification of the liberal understanding of human motivation. And, finally, when American faith in science was put to the test in foreign affairs either in high-tech military adventures, such as the Vietnam war or the hostage rescue attempt, or in those foreign assistance policies honestly concerned with development, the results were not especially heartening.

In electing Reagan, Americans rejected that case, not because they doubted that Johnson, Nixon, Ford, and Carter had failed—especially in the Third World—but, perhaps, because none of these administration actually provided a fair test of American common sense as whole. None subscribed to all the elements of American common sense—Protestant denominational, liberal, and scientistic—equally and at once. In fact, the closest thing to a complete test of American common sense as a guide for American foreign policy in the Third World, or anywhere, that had taken place since the United States had secured its post-war hegemony had been aborted by Kennedy's death. In electing Reagan, Americans opted to complete that test.

What the public felt Reagan was likely to do about changing the US–Third World relationship through common sense made a difference in the election. Reagan, unlike Carter, could be expected never to give up American strategic resources or advantages in the Third World. Throughout Carter's entire administration Reagan had thrilled audiences with attacks on Carter's Panama Canal policy. The issue had been the core of Reagan's platform in his unsuccessful bid for the Republican nomination in 1976, 'We bought it, we paid for it, it's ours, and we are not going to give it away to some tin horn dictator!'[26] By 1980 the issue was past. Carter had 'given' the Canal away. But Reagan promised the American people that no further humiliation of the sort, with its implied repudiation both of the sanctity of property and of America's special role in the world, would be tolerated.

More generally, Reagan promised that the United States would no longer be made to look foolish by the Third World and no longer taken advantage of by Third World governments. The US had the power to avoid the humiliations of the 1970s from the unprecedented defeat in Vietnam, to the gas lines of 1973 and 1979, to the more recent, and thus, more salient, embarrassment of the embassy hostages in Teheran. Common sense said that the US would not have had to suffer any of that shame if presidents had been willing to use the military force the US had at its command, if the US had bombed North Vietnam 'back to the stone age' as one of the architects of American air power, General Curtis LeMay, had counselled at the time. Oil prices would have remained stable had the US taken over some oil fields in the early 1970s (perhaps from Libya's upstart colonel who overthrew an American ally and started the upward price creep) or bombed the Ayatollah, as respected conservative international relations scholars had proposed.

Finally, and perhaps somewhat less significantly for an American public that become fast friends of the Chinese government despite its ideology and had enjoyed the decade of detente before the Soviet invasion of Afghanistan, Reagan promised that the Soviet Union would not get away with anything in the Third World. The United States would not 'lose' more states to communism. In 1980 most Americans would have been hard-pressed to name all the nations that made up the conservative litany of those recently 'lost to communism.' Angola, Cape Verde, Grenada, Guinea-Bissau, Mozambique, and Yemen were not exactly household words. Ethiopia was better known, but most Americans who thought about the revolution there remembered something about a sort of fair swap, the US getting a former Soviet ally when the Soviets found friends in Addis. In 1980, and, to a surprising extent, even at the end of the Reagan administration, Americans were as likely to treat the nearby Nicaraguan revolutionaries as friends as they were to consider them Soviet puppets. And to many Americans, even Cambodia, Laos, and Vietnam were much too old news. Nevertheless, it was easy recast each of these events as American 'defeats,' creating a blur of half-remembered cases to substantiate a 'trend' that the American public knew best through the more recent humiliation in Iran and the impotence in confrontation with the oil producers whose consequences every American felt. The litany also reinforced an older, if now half-forgotten, assumption that the world's problems stemmed from Soviet communism, a view reinforced by the easily-remembered Soviet invasion of Afghanistan with its easily-remembered negative consequences, not the least of which was the cancellation of American involvement in the 1980 Olympics. Reagan's election promised that there would be no more Afghanistans and that we would no longer have a president who could be fooled by the Soviet Union—the only 'real' challenger to American supremacy, or so many Americans believed.

## Ideology: summary and conclusion

Many people concerned with the Third World hope Reaganism will not last long because of the hardships caused by the new relationship between the United States and the Third World apparent since Ronald Reagan's first few months in office. We began looking at American ideology because we wanted to know whether this change simply reflected the whims of ideological zealots whose government will soon be forgotten, or whether it responded to deeper forces in American and world society. We turned to Antonio Gramsci's theories because in both most Marxist and non-Marxist social science tradition ideology has been treated as a derivative and unimportant concept. In the Marxist tradition it has been associated with false consciousness and in liberal social science it is simply contrasted with a pragmatic attitude in the search for truth. Yet, ideologies are alive in the minds of people even if they do not realize the extent to which their desires, choices, and actions are influenced by them. And the active ideologies of a powerful people can do much harm, or good, in the world.

Gramsci's views on ideology stand out from those of other thinkers both bourgeois and Marxist; he was an innovator in the theoretical school of which he considered himself a part. Unlike most of his Marxist contemporaries, Gramsci believed that ideologies make a difference in the world. He was not willing to assume that ideologies were mere distortions of the world, but, rather, he contended that every concrete ideology served both as the worldview of a particular group and as its political program; because every 'historical' ideology is linked to the self-defining action of concrete historical groups, ideology, for Gramsci, is a force in the constitution and transformation of society.

This does not mean that the ideology of the dominant group becomes the worldview and political program of every group in society. Rather, domination is achieved through the contradictory consciousness of the masses. For most of us, most of the time, our common sense understanding of the world is hardly a mass of unrealistic delusions, but a mass of contradictory understandings and prescriptions, bits of fact, rules of thumb, and undissolved residues of various philosophies, including, but hardly limited to, the ideologies that guide the actions of the people who dominate our society.

One part of Gramsci's revolutionary prescription is for the intellectuals who are tied to the dominated by bonds of family, work, and sympathy to persuade them to change the contradictory consciousness of common sense to a revolutionary ideology of 'good sense,' a coherent worldview and guide to action. Much of the initial work Gramsci demands of his revolutionary intellectuals differs little from the traditional role Western intellectuals have assigned to themselves for centuries. Armed with a few concepts as guides, they are to go out and critically study the world, to analyze, to experiment, and to synthesize what they have learned. Gramsci, of course, would require that progressive intellectuals go further, to teach, to listen to, to criticize, and to help transform the common sense of the dominated. We would be satisfied if, as we said in the introduction, armed with Gramsci's concepts about the role of ideas in society, we can inform some of 'those who are not in the know.'

We contend that an important part of what is common sense to most Americans involves residues of three historical philosophies: Protestant denominationalism, liberalism, the scientism that typified the engineering-based systematic management movement that has been so important in modern corporate America. These elements combine in complex, and often contradictory, ways. For example, we contend that it is religion, more than liberal political economy or engineering, that remains the source of widespread American idea of 'exceptionalism,' the belief that most Americans have in the special destiny of their nation, the core of what many observers call America's 'civil religion.' Religion, we contend, also remains the most important element in the worldview and personal guide to action of most of the American public while the newer historical philosophies, liberalism and scientism, are more significant to those who dominate.

The particular ideologies of the people who dominate American politics have guided the policy of American governments toward the rest of the world. From the foundation of the United States in 1776 until the emergence of the United States as the pre-eminent global power in this century the complex of ideologies buttressing American foreign policy has been remarkably consistent. For the most part, America's active governmental policy has been dictated by liberalism, the ideology of America's commercial elite. Yet, at the same time, American exceptionalism, and other historical residues of the Protestant foundation of many of the first European societies in North America, have influenced those American foreign policies which required legitimation by the mass public: policy during times of war and the policies of western and overseas expansion. After the second world war, when maintaining political order within a global empire first became a problem for American foreign policy, scientism joined liberalism as a major guide for American foreign policy while a cold war version of America's civil religion helped legitimate the massive social changes demanded by the country's new role in the world.

While American foreign assistance can be considered a tool for the systematic management of the American empire, American aid policy is not merely the reflection of the scientism of some of the groups that dominate American society. American aid prescriptions have always emphasized the liberal political economy that has been the main source of actual American foreign policy since its inception. Buttressed both by its identification as 'scientific truth' and, through civil religion, as 'the American way,' the market approach to Third World development occupies the center of American aid policy and, thus, the center of the American relationship with the Third World in general. When other states, whether aid recipients or even other donors, challenge that approach, they challenge much more than a bit of social scientific theory believed by a few technocrats trying to hold together the peripheral parts of the American empire; they challenge ideas that are at the core of many Americans' definition of themselves.

The definition Americans have of themselves also has a great deal to do with the success of Ronald Reagan and resulting change in US-Third World relations. Reagan is a reflection of American common sense. We dealt with the Reagan phenomenon in this first part of the book because we believe his capacity to mobilize the American will with his jokes and slips of logic has been a crucial factor in the reconstruction of American supremacy with all its consequences for the Third World. As Gramsci says of the constitution of a great power, one important element is the, '"internal tranquillity" that is the degree and intensity of the hegemonic function of the leading social group.'[27] Reagan, the spokesman for American common sense and 'intellectual' for the broad bourgeois coalition he led, helped provide that tranquillity in the 1980s, as US reconstructed its supremacy.

## Notes

1. The title of Thomas Ferguson and Joel Rogers' analysis (New York: Hill and Wang, 1987). Joel Krieger, *Reagan, Thatcher, and the Politics of Decline* (New York: Oxford University Press, 1986), provides a helpful comparative perspective.
2. Edsall, *The New Politics of Inequality* (New York: W. W. Norton, 1984).
3. Ibid., 62.
4. Ibid., 74–5.
5. 'Bedtime for Bonzo,' in which he played a college professor, being the notable exception.
6. Wills, *Innocents at Home* (Garden City, NY: Doubleday, 1987).
7. Ibid., 279–88.
8. Ibid., 287.
9. Ibid., 323–4.

10. His advisors believed that to do so would be to fall in a 'Hooverite' trap. David A. Stockman, *The Triumph of Politics*, 2nd ed. (New York: Avon Books, 1987), 57–8.
11. Ibid., 436.
12. Ferguson and Rogers, 104–5, details this activity.
13. Ibid., 133–7.
14. Krieger, 145–6.
15. Quoted in Alan Crawford, *Thunder on the Right: the New Right and the Politics of Resentment* (New York: Pantheon), 1980, 159–60.
16. Ferguson and Rogers, 19–24.
17. Richard A. Melanson, 'The Grenada Intervention: Prelude to a New Consensus?,' in Richard A. Melanson and Kenneth W. Thompson, eds. *Foreign Policy and Domestic Consensus* (Lanham, MD: University Press of America, 1985), 155–201.
18. Quoted in Ronald W. Clark, *The Survival of Charles Darwin* (New York: Random House, 1984), 339–40.
19. Stockman reports, second-hand, on Reagan's first meeting with Laffer and Reagan's immediate intuitive grasp of Laffer's point, 55.
20. A point explained in great detail and made repeatedly in the many publications of the Union of Concerned Scientists on the topic.
21. Wills, 359–60.
22. On sources of public attitudes toward SDI see Marion Just, 'Do the Missiles Really Go "Plink, Plink" on the Peace Shield,' paper presented at the annual meeting of the American Political Science Association, Chicago, September 1987.
23. The materials the AFL-CIO developed provide a wealth of information, perhaps one of the reasons they were ignored. See, e.g., AFL-CIO Department of Legislation, 'The People's Lobby' (Washington: AFL-CIO, 1983).
24. Popular posters of the day included one with messages like, 'Nuke the Ayatollah,' 'Ayatollah Assaholla,' and one of Mickey Mouse making an obscene gesture and saying, 'Up Yours, Iran.' There were also number of very popular songs with similar themes, including the catchy, 'Bomb, bomb, bomb! Bomb, bomb, Iran!'
25. Jimmy Carter's own analysis of his failures in the long concluding section to his autobiography, *Keeping Faith* (New York: Bantam Books, 1982), 431–596, is remarkably self-critical and more perceptive than a great deal of the more scholarly commentary.
26. Quoted in Wills, 330.
27. Antonio Gramsci, *Quaderni del Carcere* (Torino: Einaudi, 1975), III, 1577.

# PART II
# SUPREMACY

# 6 Gramsci's understanding of supremacy

## Gramsci on hegemony

This chapter clarifies the key concepts Gramsci uses to understand the consolidation of power: 'hegemony' and the broader concept, 'supremacy.' The attention scholars have paid to his views on hegemony has tended to obscure Gramsci's broader view. We do not want to contribute to this tendency; yet, the best way to illustrate what is distinctive about Gramsci's understanding of supremacy is to begin with his more familiar ideas.

Three important interpretations of Gramsci's views on hegemony exist. One sees him as a faithful follower of Lenin and equates 'hegemony' with the 'dictatorship of the proletariat.'[1] Another either tends to emphasize Gramsci's debt to Croce's idealism, by focusing on the paramount role Gramsci attributes to consensus in the exercise of power, or by pointing to evidence that he considers 'civil society' more important than the 'economic structure.' This view sees hegemony as consensus to be acquired in civil society; the idealist version of this view emphasizes the role of intellectual leadership.[2] The third interpretation, inspired by structuralism, sees Gramsci as the theorist of the 'dominant ideology,' as the person who first shed light on the function of ideology in the acculturation of the masses aimed at bringing about their acceptance of class exploitation and social inequality; it concentrates on the notion of 'ideological hegemony' as an instrument for the preservation of bourgeois domination.[3]

We believe that each of these views develops only one aspect of Gramsci's thought and loses the sense of his analysis as a whole. Gramsci's work appears to us to contain the principles of a sociological theory of power that goes beyond traditional Marxist analysis or Max Weber's theses on legitimation and leadership, a theory applicable to any ruling or subordinate group in society. We can illustrate the scope of Gramsci's theory by showing how he began with Lenin's concept of hegemony, which is primarily relevant to the political strategy of the Marxist working class, and built a broader theory upon it by adding elements from the theories of Croce, Machiavelli, and Hegel.[4]

### *Lenin's concept as Gramsci's starting point*

In the *Prison Notebooks* Gramsci repeatedly attributes the concept of hegemony to Lenin. For instance, in one of his most significant passages, he writes, '... the greatest modern theoretician of the philosophy of praxis [Lenin] ... constructed the doctrine of hegemony as a complement to the theory of the

State-as-force.'[5] Gramsci may be too modest about his own contribution. In comparison, Lenin's concept is much less well developed, and much less important to his revolutionary scheme.

'Hegemony' appears several times in Lenin's 'Two Tactics of Social Democracy,'[6] a pamphlet written in 1905 in Geneva for circulation in Russia. In it, Lenin attacks the Mensheviks for failing to respond to the then current historical phase in Russia. According to Lenin, the Mensheviks either mistakenly focused on problems which would only occur at a stage when democracy had already been attained or else they looked back to a revolutionary phase that was already over. Their slogan, 'the party of extreme revolutionary opposition,' forced their constituents, the working class, to be in a marginal political position (always 'in opposition') and thus allowed the monarchic bourgeoisie to maintain 'hegemony' over the revolutionary process. The Mensheviks' economism blinded them to the political aims and the historical role of the Russian proletariat.

In contrast, Lenin claims that the Bolsheviks responded to the actual revolutionary situation (of 1905) by demanding political power for the working class through the immediate establishment of a provisional revolutionary government and the subsequent convening of a Constituent Assembly. The Bolsheviks, unlike the Mensheviks, supported armed struggle and believed an autonomous proletarian political program to be essential. Lenin says that it was no longer sufficient to limit activities to propagandizing and organizing the workers, the tactics he himself had stressed in *What is to be done?* He argues that it was necessary to move on to armed struggle because, 'in the final analysis force alone settles the great problems of political liberty and the class struggle.'[7] Nonetheless, given the strategic goal of establishing the dictatorship of the proletariat, it was tactically essential to form temporary alliances with the peasantry and the petite bourgeoisie (through the revolutionary government and Constituent Assembly) in order to free the political arena of Tsarist oppression. This would help assure the 'hegemony' of the proletariat in the revolutionary process.

To Lenin, 'hegemony' simply meant dominance in a revolutionary alliance. Unlike Gramsci, Lenin continued to assume that the consolidation of power was ultimately a matter of armed force. He did not re-evaluate the significance of the cultural battleground as much as Gramsci suggests he did. Even in *What is to be done?*, another work that Gramsci no doubt knew, Lenin's conception of the 'cultural' side of revolutionary strategy does not seem to go beyond that of disseminating political propaganda. Moreover, Lenin's concept of hegemony applies to a very restricted historical phase, during a revolution. It does not elucidate the ways in which post-revolutionary proletarian power is to be maintained and consolidated, nor does it say anything about the ways bourgeois 'hegemony' was maintained in more normal times in more developed societies than Russia.

Lenin's narrow concept of hegemony was, nevertheless, crucially important to Gramsci simply because it had been proven in revolutionary practice. Gramsci firmly believe Marx's dictum: 'The philosophers have only interpreted the world; the point, however, is to change it.'[8] Ultimately, Gramsci recognizes, 'Illich [Lenin]'s greatest theoretical contribution to the philosophy of praxis,' is that he

> ... advanced philosophy as philosophy in so far as he advanced political doctrine and practice. The realization of a hegemonic apparatus, in so far as it creates a new ideological terrain, determines a reform of consciousness and of methods of knowledge: it is a fact of knowledge, a philosophical fact.[9]

Note, of course, that even in praising Lenin, Gramsci developed the concept of hegemony more thoroughly than Lenin had. What may be the most important point about the Leninist starting point of Gramsci's reflections on hegemony is that Gramsci found support in Lenin's revolutionary practice and writings for critical reflections on some of the tenets of orthodox Marxism which Gramsci's humanistic background had already led him to question. It is to those influences that we now turn.

### *Croce and the intellectual hegemony of the ruling class*

As we have already seen in Part I, Croce's idealism, which Gramsci had admired and adhered to in his youth, gave Gramsci the tools to go beyond Marxist economism, a debt he continued to recognize throughout his life.[10] Croce's views on culture and intellectual life became the point of departure for Gramsci's reflection on ideology and his conclusion that the ethical and cultural aspects of a people's way of life often have decisive effects on social dynamics. Nevertheless, Gramsci always maintained that Croce's method, by itself, was incomplete:

> Ethical-political history, insofar as it sets aside the concept of historical bloc in which economic content and ethical-political forms are concretely identified in the reconstruction of the various historical periods, is no more than a polemical presentation of more or less interesting philosophemes—but it is not history.[11]

Rather, ethics and politics must be reintegrated into materialist analysis, 'if it is desired to arrive at an integral history and not one that is partial and extrinsic (history of economic forces as such, etc.).'[12] Gramsci's philosophy of praxis, '"absorbs" the subjective perception of reality (idealism) in the theory of superstructures, ... [and] reduces [it] to one of its "moments."'[13] With Croce's contribution, Gramsci's Marxism goes beyond a material dialectic of pure economic forces and becomes a combined dialectic of interests (expressed through ideologies by economically-based social groups) and of ideal aspirations which social contradictions sometimes give people the opportunity to make real (as long as they become aware of their own role in society), both operating under material constraints.

The concept of hegemony plays the central role in Gramsci's incorporation of Croce's insights into Marxist analysis. [14] Indeed, according to Gramsci, the history of ethics and politics is not, as Croce believed, the history of the progressive realization of the most fundamental human aspirations (mankind's 'march toward freedom'). Instead, it is the history of ideologies which ruling classes, succeeding one another in the course of history, have adopted to maintain their role in society. It is the history of power. Croce

> ... thinks he is writing history in which the class element is exorcised, and instead he is describing very accurately and laudably the political masterpiece whereby a given class manages to present—and cause them to be accepted—the conditions of its existence and its class development as a universal principle, as a worldview, as religion, i.e. he is describing the ongoing development of the practical means of government and dominion.[15]

This became one aspect of Gramsci's concept of hegemony. A class with 'hegemony' has convinced subordinate classes that the conditions needed to maintain the dominant class in power are ethical and wise.

But, according to Gramsci, just focusing on the ideas originating in the ruling class would be insufficient. Subaltern classes, though subject to the influence of the ideology of the ruling class, preserve a culturally autonomous sphere of their own and attempt to express their interest and aspirations in opposing ideologies. When interpreted in this broader sense, Croce's 'ethico-political' history becomes, according to Gramsci, the history of class struggle waged at the philosophical level. It is the history of different groups trying to establish 'hegemony.' It must take into account, and explain, the ideas which have left traces in the culture of the masses. It is in this context that Gramsci developed his analysis of the role of the intellectuals as elaborators and disseminators of ideologies, as discussed in Part I.

Thus, Gramsci expands Lenin's concept to give 'hegemony' a larger and more long-term role in class struggle. It is not enough to develop some political propaganda temporarily instrumental in the struggle for power or to find the basis for temporary alliances of convenience. Revolutionaries must understand the culture created by a history of ideological stratification and they must elaborate a philosophical system (that can be applied to all spheres of knowledge) in keeping with the interests and aspirations of the masses. Ultimately, revolutionaries must learn how to spread this philosophical system throughout society, and learn where, why, and how it must be spread. In searching for answers to these questions of practical politics Gramsci turned from Croce's idealism to Machiavelli's practical political science.

### *Machiavelli and the need to transcend the pursuit of simple corporate interests*

Machiavelli provided Gramsci with an important source of inspiration and reflection. As Leonardo Paggi observes, Gramsci not only developed a Marxist analysis of Machiavelli's thought, he used aspects of Machiavelli's work to reinvigorate Marxism,[16] which is what interests us here.

In 'Two Tactics' Lenin urged the working class to go beyond merely defending its own economic interests and, instead, pursue political power. As a mere economic interest group, according to Lenin, the working class indirectly supported the bourgeoisie's political objectives. If it sought political power, it would be autonomously pursuing its own historical goals.

Gramsci related Lenin's problem of the range of goals the working class should pursue (a problem Gramsci's party had confronted in Italy, and every working-class party has had to confront) to Machiavelli's analysis of the strategies pursued by the nascent Italian bourgeoisie. Gramsci considered two specific historical experiences comparable: that of the medieval communes in Italy—in which the budding bourgeoisie tried to assert itself, dissolve the feudal structure, and create a new state to defend its aspirations—and that of the Workers' Councils in the period immediately following the first world war—in which the Italian working class manifested its aspirations for self-government and its ambition to establish a democratic proletarian state. In Machiavelli's analysis Gramsci finds confirmation that

> ... the Italian medieval bourgeoisie could not pass from the corporate to the political phase, because it was unable to free itself completely from the medieval cosmopolitan conception represented by the Pope, the clergy and also by the lay intellectuals (humanists)—in other words, it was unable to create an autonomous state...[17]

Similarly, the workers in the Councils never went beyond the corporate phase because they were unable to extend their influence to the rest of society. Both attempts failed to create a state based on the principles that they advocated, Gramsci argues, because they could neither universalize their experience and programs in a theory, nor, therefore, could they convince other social groups and protect what they already achieved through a system of alliances.

Scholars generally recognize that it was this analysis that led Gramsci to his conviction that the working class needed a party as a collective intellectual to guide spontaneous movements. However, just as Machiavelli, 'is unable to do away with the republic though he understands that only an absolute monarch can solve the problems of the epoch'[18] (that is, only an absolute monarch could allow the incipient bourgeoisie to assert itself), Gramsci also remains emotionally tied to the self-management experience of the Workers' Councils even though he considers it necessary to create a centralized party which will act as a 'Modern Prince.' Ultimately, Gramsci embraces, with all of Machiavelli's tragic irony, the formula that, '... those who want the end want the means to achieve it,'[19] unless they are prepared merely to pursue utopian ideals which are by definition unattainable.[20]

What is less widely recognized is that it is this very analysis that led Gramsci to the conviction that 'hegemony' (not merely as leadership of a revolutionary alliance, but as intellectual and moral leadership throughout society) must be at the center of any analysis of political and social change. Discovering the conditions under which hegemony could be exercised, thus, became a central focus of his own analysis.

*Achieving hegemony*

According to Gramsci, hegemony is the ability of a class or social group to exercise a function of 'political and moral direction' in society. Other social groups acknowledge the hegemonic group as having a leading role in society and a relatively wide political consensus supports the hegemon's policy goals. A hegemon expresses this leadership ability by responding to the 'interests' which derive from a group's position in the mode of production (one of the two basic motivations of human action recognized by Gramsci), and by both responding to and helping to shape the ideal 'aspirations' that emerge in each unique historical, economic, and cultural context (the other basic motivation).

Gramsci believes that in industrial societies only social groups that perform an essential role in the mode of production can become truly hegemonic, unlike, for example, in feudal societies where religious groups have exercised political and moral direction. He says:

> ... though hegemony is ethico-political, it must also be economic, must necessarily be based on the decisive function exercised by the leading group in the decisive nucleus of economic activity.[21]

It is precisely this essential role in the world of production that first confers prestige on a leading social group and makes its dominant social and political role acceptable to others. In Italy, at his time, Gramsci saw this potential in the bourgeoisie, which had, in fact, exercised an inadequate hegemony before the rise of fascism, and in the working class. New groups which possess this potential may have emerged in the industrial world since then. The profound evolution of capitalism has diminished the importance of private entrepreneurs and privileged the role of holders of financial capital and non-owner managers as new basic social groups. The managerial class in the west has its counterpart in the 'new class' of organizational leaders in eastern Europe.

Because hegemony involves understanding and responding to interests and aspirations, none of these groups can develop it without first understanding their own interests and developing their hegemonic aspiration. Members of the potentially-hegemonic class must attain self-awareness of the economic role they perform and of the political role that they could fulfill. In discussing Gramsci's understanding of ideology, in Part I, we looked at the way in which he elaborated the dynamics of aggregation of individual economic interests through successive stages—the movement from solidarity with people in the same job, to local solidarity with people in similar jobs, and ultimately to solidarity within the whole class. For Gramsci, as we said, this process corresponds to the development of self-consciousness. The would-be hegemon must go further and develop a 'critical' self-consciousness which sees beyond its own 'economic-corporate' interests, an understanding that can only develop in active political struggles. Gramsci says:

> Critical understanding of self takes place . . . through a struggle of political 'hegemonies' and of opposing directions, first in the ethical field and then in that of politics proper, in order to arrive at the working out at a higher level of one's own conception of reality. Consciousness of being part of a particular hegemonic force (that is to say, political consciousness) is the first stage toward a further progressive self-consciousness in which theory and practice will finally be one.[22]

With this critical self-understanding the potential hegemon must make alliances, taking a step beyond defending its economic-corporate interests (i.e., 'immediate and narrowly selfish interests of a particular category'[23]) in order to link itself to other groups involved in society's key political struggles. This is the process which Gramsci, using Sorel's language, defines as the establishment of a 'historical economic-political bloc.'[24] To create such a bloc the hegemon must be able place its ideal aspirations above its own economic-corporate interests:

> Undoubtedly the fact of hegemony presupposes that account be taken of the interests and the tendencies of the groups over which hegemony is to be exercised, and that a certain compromise equilibrium should be formed—in other words that the leading group should make sacrifices of an economic-corporate kind.[25]

Thus, the social group that wishes to exercise hegemony must take into account the interests and aspirations of allied social groups, renouncing part of the narrow economic-corporate benefits which its position might enable it to acquire.

Such action at the level of interests must be backed up by parallel actions on the ideological level. Here the work of the intellectuals becomes essential. 'The role of intellectuals is to represent the ideas that constitute the terrain where hegemony is exercised.'[26] They must supply intellectual and moral support for the hegemon's dominant political role to the point that, 'What is "politics" to the productive [and hegemonic] class becomes "rationality" to the intellectual class'[27] as a whole. The intellectuals organically tied to the hegemonic class must demonstrate in every field of knowledge that the interests of the group they serve coincide with the interests of society as a whole. The intellectuals of the hegemonic class must produce a philosophy, political theory, and economics which together constitute a coherent worldview, the principles of which can be translated from one discipline to another.[28] As actors in the ideological struggle, the intellectuals of the dominant class must prevail over the intellectuals of other classes by developing more convincing and sophisticated theories, inculcating other intellectuals with the dominant worldview, and assimilating them to the hegemon's cause. Potential hegemons fail when they fail to consolidate the support of intellectuals, the way the Italian bourgeoisie of the Communes (analyzed by Machiavelli) failed because intellectuals of this new class (like himself) failed to enlist traditional intellectuals who remained wedded to the ideas and interests of the feudal world.

Gramsci argues that, to further reinforce the solidarity of the historical bloc and go beyond it to extend the hegemony of the leading social group to the popular masses, it must ensure economic development. This is another reason why hegemons in modern industrial societies can only come from classes that play an essential role in the economy. The central role the hegemonic group plays in the world of production gives it great influence over the economy as a whole, but this potential to mold the economic development of society must be made a reality by conscious political action. Analyzing the history of the French bourgeoisie, which had to respond to a series of such crises, Gramsci argues, 'Political consensus is regained (hegemony is retained) by broadening and deepening the economic base with individual and commercial development.'[29] In this process of economic development, which Gramsci sees as one of the progressive functions of the hegemonic social class, the extension of new productive activities and the social ascent of those who are, 'more endowed with energy and spirit of enterprise,'[30] take place. Indeed, it was the breakdown of this dynamic process which, according to Gramsci, led to the crisis of bourgeois hegemony in Europe after the first world war.

Thus, in Gramsci's view, a class that wants to achieve hegemony today must take into account all these requirements—developing a critical self-understanding, making alliances, and capturing the ideological realm, and, if it intends to extend its hegemony to the mass public, assuring economic development. A society in which any one of these requirements is absent experiences a 'crisis of authority.' And a hegemonic group that fails to maintain at least those requirements that maintain its bloc, loses its hegemony.

### *Hegel and ethical hegemony versus hegemony based on fraud*

We can use Gramsci's distinction between a 'philosophical' and a 'functional sociological' approach (first introduced in Part I when we discussed his understanding of ideology) to illustrate the how insights from Hegel's political philosophy further clarified Gramsci's understanding of hegemony. Gramsci praised Hegel not only because of his great influences on Marx,[31] but also because, 'Hegelianism ... attempted to go beyond the traditional conceptions of idealism and materialism in a new synthesis ... which represents a world-historical moment of philosophical inquiry.'[32] Gramsci's interest in Hegel's work was not confined to Marx's and Labriola's references, Gramsci was directly influenced by Hegel's analysis of the state, and, in the context 'hegemony,' especially by Hegel's view of the 'ethical state.'

Gramsci concludes that the, 'ethical content of the State,' is represented by the, 'political and cultural hegemony of a group in society as a whole.'[33] According to Gramsci, hegemony can be ethical insofar as a social group rules with the 'voluntarily given' consent of the ruled,[34] and as long as the hegemonic group performs an, 'educative and formative role' in respect to the subaltern groups and the popular masses,[35] both indirectly through the state, and directly though private organizations in civil society. This role manifests itself in a 'relationship between teacher and pupil [which] is active and reciprocal so that every teacher is always a pupil and every pupil a teacher.'[36] Thus, the leading social group performs its duty in an ethical way when it heeds the needs of the subaltern groups and establishes a dialogue with them in which it also has the chance of learning. Hegemony can be ethical when its goal is to elevate subordinate groups to the level of the dominant group, in both economic and cutural terms, and to eliminate the gap between leaders and led; 'the social group [exercising hegemony] puts the end of the State and of itself as the goal to be achieved.'[37] It made sense for Hegel to propose the concept of the ethical state, according to Gramsci, because at the time it appeared that the bourgeoisie might be able to absorb society as a whole, making all humankind bourgeois. Similarly, in Gramsci's view, the hegemony exercised by northern on southern Italy after the country's unification would have been ethical had it been temporary and, particularly, had it set itself the goal of developing the economically more backward part to the level of the more advanced part.[38]

When these expectations were not fulfilled—when society remained split between ruler and ruled, capitalist and worker, rich north and poor south—it meant that the ruling classes did not feel bound to carry out their ethical role. They pursued their own petty economic-corporative interests, using ideology as a weapon and exploiting popular aspirations and beliefs. When ideology becomes a tool of domination and leaders have no interest in learning from the masses, the role of ideas in society simply becomes 'functional' rather than philosophical and hegemony loses its ethical nature and becomes a 'fraud' at the expense of the subaltern classes, a 'deceit' by which they are victimized.

Gramsci offers several examples of fraud and deception used to maintain hegemony: Francesco Crispi, Prime Minister of the Kingdom of Italy from 1887 to 1891 and 1893 to 1896, began Italy's colonial policy in Eritrea. He understood the southern peasants' aspirations to own the land they worked, but, because he was unwilling or unable to expropriate large landowners he, 'conjured up the mirage of colonial lands to be exploited,' and, 'was popular for having created the "myth" of easy land.'[39] Similarly, Croce, the great liberal idealist, when appointed Minister of Education did not introduce the, 'world outlook of freedom,' into the curriculum, as he had always advocated, 'but [rather] the teaching of confessional religion,'[40] thereby adhering to the, 'old principle that religion is necessary for the people.'[41] Under the same rubric of hegemony secured by fraud or deceit, Gramsci places all the ways in which ruling classes co-opt the leaders, including the intellectuals, of potentially-antagonistic classes, relating this tactic to what Marx called the 'beheading' the working class, 'so as to throw the enemy ranks into disorder and disarray.'[42]

Thus, Gramsci took from Hegel a way to identify how hegemonies can vary. They can be more or less ethical, more or less free of fraud. All forms of hegemonic rule are characterized by the consent of many of the governed, but hegemonies can be distinguished by the degree to which they develop the critical understanding of the ruled or, contrastingly, the degree to which they exploit the ruled's unreflective common sense.

In fact, few ruling classes can maintain their dominance solely on the basis of the consent of the governed, even if that consent has been gained by fraud. That is why Gramsci's concept of hegemony reflects only one part, albeit an important one, of his analysis of political power. After introducing his analysis of hegemony, we can turn to the family of political relationships of which hegemony is only one member.

## Gramsci on supremacy

In Gramsci's terminology 'supremacy' means 'consolidated power.' If at times Gramsci uses 'hegemony' to refer to the broader concept, it is only because he holds that the active consent of the great mass of people must be a central goal of those seeking to exercise power and that, in fact, some degree of consent, active or passive, is, in the majority of cases, the precondition of a stable society. The society without hegemony is, after all, a society experiencing a 'crisis of authority.' Of course, Gramsci does not value stability in the abstract any more than he values hegemony in the abstract, as his distinction between ethical hegemony and hegemony based on fraud makes clear.

Gramsci concludes that a social group acquires power over society through the creation of a polity ('the state,' broadly understood) which subsumes and molds other, more specific, social and political organizations into an organic social whole. The national polities which came into being in Europe after the French Revolution are states created by a bourgeoisie with the energy and resources to prevail over older feudal forms of organization. The bourgeoisie has molded social organization to its needs. State functions have grown and expanded in different western societies in response to similar emerging bourgeois needs; a superficial diversity of organization forms and the specific political aims adopted in different circumstances mask a deeper similarity.

Gramsci's understanding of the state, thus, is a functional sociological one. He develops his concept of supremacy by contrasting his sociological view of the state to three philosophical views: that of liberal political theory (whose language he often uses), that of Giovanni Gentile's 'actualism' (the idealist philosophy that provided the philosophical justification for the organization of power in Mussolini's state), and an ideal Marxist model of regulated society.

None of these philosophical conceptions corresponds to reality, although, according to Gramsci, the Marxist vision is worth pursuing.

*Domination and hegemony, force and consensus*

Gramsci's functional sociology of power begins with some simple ideas he borrows from Machiavelli whose political insights, Gramsci argues, remain applicable today. 'Machiavelli,' Gramsci writes, 'is hated because he, "revealed the skeleton in the closet" in the art of government,'[43] exposing the instruments used by the ruling class. These instruments may ultimately be reduced to two:

corresponding to the dual nature of Machiavelli's Centaur—half-animal and half-human. They are the levels of force and consensus, authority and hegemony, violence and civilization, of the individual moment and the universal moment ('Church' [threatening hell] and 'State' [encouraging allegiance]), of agitation and of propaganda, of tactics and of strategy, etc.[44]

According to Machiavelli, rule may be based either on force or consensus or some combination of both.[45] Gramsci discovers the same distinction between force and consensus, in various guises, in other Italian Renaissance thinkers. For example, Gramsci says that according to Guicciardini, 'two things are absolutely necessary for the life of a State; arms and religion.' Gramsci notes, 'Guicciardini's formula can be translated by various other, less drastic formulae: force and consensus, coercion and persuasion . . .'[46]

Gramsci puts this distinction in his own terms by contrasting two ideal types of supremacy, 'domination,' the exercise of power without the critical, reflective consent of the governed, and ethical hegemony, i.e., intellectual and moral leadership:

. . . the supremacy of a social group manifests itself in two ways, as 'domination' and as 'intellectual and moral leadership.' A social group dominates antagonistic groups, which it tends to 'liquidate,' or to subjugate perhaps even by armed force; it leads kindred and allied groups.[47]

A class can consolidate power by acting as an ethical hegemon toward allied social groups, while dominating adversaries, even with force.

Note that Gramsci does not make the two pairs of concepts equivalent. The use of 'force' is not quite the same as 'domination' even though 'consensus' always characterizes 'hegemony.' We have already seen that hegemony may be based upon fraud and deception. When it does, Gramsci considers it a form of domination, although not domination achieved by force *per se*.

Gramsci considers the slightly different distinction between force and consensus to be important because elements of both must combine in inverse proportions in the exercise of supremacy. The broader the consensus, the less necessary the use of force. This does not mean that the state based on the broadest consensus will always be where the least force is used. The people exercising power may be guided by an ideology that glorifies force, ideas left over from an era when the use of force was more essential.

Gramsci notes further ways in which these ideal types combine in the real world, something that the philosophers have trouble understanding. Idealist philosophy, whether of the right or the left, sees a radical separation between force and consensus, but in the real world these two forms of rule are mutually supportive and often combine in ambiguous ways. Force rarely appears as brute force, nor do the representatives of power justify its use by invoking the interests of the dominant social group or dominant social alliance, even though that must always be the ultimate reason why force is used in the place of rule by consensus. To mask the lack of consensus, the representatives of power always proclaim grand moral principles to justify the use of force. In parliamentary democracies, Gramsci notes, mobilization of the 'organs of public opinion' always accompanies the use of force in order to assure wide approval of that choice, even if such consent can only be gained by fraud.[48] In the majority of actual cases a class maintains its supremacy by both force and consensus. Carrots and sticks reinforce each other.

One of the concrete examples that Gramsci uses to illustrate this point is the history of American industrial unions. In Gramsci's day the most radical of them (the Knights of Labor and the International Workers of the World) had been destroyed through a combination of the use of force with policies designed to gain the consent of much of the American working class to the dominant social order. Consensus was established both by the unusual economic concessions given to labor and through propaganda that played upon certain archaic themes in American common sense—racism, 'Americanism,' etc.—while lying about the activities of the industrial unions (a policy of 'domination' through consensus).[49]

The distinction between force and consensus may completely disappear, in the real world, if people consent only because they fear the use of force. Gentile's actualism elevates this real-world situation into a philosophical principle. In actualism, 'hegemony and dictatorship are indistinguishable; force and consensus are simply equivalent.'[50] Gramsci points out that the central flaw in this approach is its assumption that, ultimately, society is held together by force, that 'force' is the *sine qua non* of 'the state,' broadly understood.[51] The philosophical ideal of the 'regulated society' that Gramsci believes we should pursue is completely the opposite of Gentile's, as its aim is the realization of a society based upon the free and critically conscious consent of the people, either totally eliminating force or confining it to a completely marginal role.

Nevertheless, in the real world, where political action aimed at actualizing philosophical aspirations must take place, supremacy is achieved and maintained both by mobilizing consent and by using force. The practical political question of what is likely to happen when one or the other is chosen can only be answered by considering the different arenas, the different social realms, in which power must be consolidated.

*Civil society, political society, and the state*

Gramsci discusses the consolidation of power within three levels of society, the 'economic structure,' and the two superstructural levels, 'civil society' and 'political society' (the 'state,' narrowly conceived). We need to clarify these distinctions before illustrating how Gramsci used them in his analysis of supremacy.

This is how he conceives of the two superstructural levels:

> What we can do, for the moment, is to fix two major superstructural 'levels:' the one that can be called 'civil society,' that is the ensemble of organisms commonly called 'private,' and that of 'political society' or 'the State.' These two levels correspond on the one hand to the function of 'hegemony' which the dominant group exercises throughout society and on the other hand to that of 'direct domination' or command exercised through the State and 'juridical' government.[52]

In amplifying his conception of civil society Gramsci refers to Hegel's views. He maintains that Hegel advanced beyond liberal constitutionalist theories of society identifying, 'parties and associations as the "private" woof of the [Parliamentary] State.' But Hegel was unable to distinguish between the truly political goals such associations may have (when they are concerned with the remaking of the polity) and the economic nature of associations (their concern with the corporate interests of their members), simply because Hegel was only familiar with private associations that had a predominantly corporate character.[53]

By emphasizing this difference between politics and economics, and by emphasizing that 'economic' interest groups can develop political goals, Gramsci develops a conception of civil society which differs from Hegel's. For Hegel, civil society includes the economic structure of production and distribution. It is a realm of society located between the family and the State. For Gramsci, civil society excludes the economic structure, the 'limits of the possible' (to use Fernand Braudel's language) which are implied by a society's means of production. Gramsci's 'civil society' consists of the various forms of voluntary association and it constitutes the moment of transition from economic structure to political society, the social realm in which mere corporate interests (defined by a group's position in the mode of production) can be transformed into broader, more universal, political aspirations. For Gramsci, civil society is a primary political realm, a realm in which all of the dynamics of ideology, the activities of intellectuals, and the construction of hegemony takes place.

The differences between Hegel's and Gramsci's definitions of civil society lead to different evaluations of its role and ethical content. Hegel sees civil society as the sphere of universal egoism, where each person uses other people's needs to advance his or her own goals; it is the social realm from which liberal political philosophy and economic theory take their assumptions about human motivation. For Gramsci, civil society is the context in which one becomes conscious and first engages in political action. Civil society is where the aggregation of interests takes place, where narrow interests are transformed into more universal views as ideologies are adopted or amended and alliances formed. In contrast to Hegel, Gramsci sees civil society as a realm in which people can change society and make history.[54]

Gramsci locates 'political society,' the institutions regulating society, above civil society. In the liberal bourgeois states established after the American and French revolution, Gramsci says, three of the key institutions of political society correspond to the liberal notion of the 'separation of powers' into those of the legislature or parliament, the judiciary, and the executive. However, Gramsci maintains that liberal political philosophy does not recognize and understand a fourth institution that is just as essential to the bourgeois state, the bureaucracy, this, 'crystallisation of the leading personnel—which exercises coercive power, and at a certain point it becomes a caste.'[55]

With this one addition, what Gramsci calls 'political society' is the same as what liberal political philosophy understands as the 'state' or sometimes even just as 'government.' Gramsci considers important to differentiate between this conception, corresponding to what he calls the 'State proper,' and the 'State in the organic, wider sense,' what contemporary political theorists often call the 'polity.'[56] By 'State in the organic sense' Gramsci means the overall way in which the human community organizes itself and people relate to one another in a specific historical period. Thus, he writes about the 'ancient State,' the 'medieval State,' and 'modern State' as ideal types. The difference between the two archaic forms and the modern one, he says, is that in the ancient and medieval world:

> ... centralisation, whether political-territorial or social (and the one is merely a function of the other) was minimal. The State was, in a certain sense, a mechanical bloc of social groups, often of different race: within the circle of political-military compression, which was only exercised harshly at certain moments, the subaltern groups had a life of their own, institutions of their own, etc., and sometimes these institutions had state functions which made of the State a federation of social groups with disparate functions not subordinated in any way ... The modern State substitutes for the mechanical bloc of social groups their subordination to the active hegemony of the directive and dominant group, hence abolishes certain autonomies, which nevertheless are reborn in other forms as parties, trade unions, cultural associations.[57]

'State in the organic sense,' thus, implies the overall 'structure of the superstructure,' which includes institutions essential to the political life of the community even though they appear to be of a merely private nature, as is the case in contemporary civil society. Thus understood, the state is neither the external expression of society (merely an 'actor' in international relations), nor is it located above society; the state is a characteristic of society. In the modern world, the state is constituted by the articulation of political and civil society.

### *The spheres of force and consensus*

This brief description of Gramsci's conception of the superstructure allows us to examine the spheres in which for him force and consensus are used. Here, too, Gramsci continues his distinction between the philosophical and the functional sociological approach, developing his own philosophical approach through criticism of liberalism and actualism.

Gramsci argues that liberals maintain a sharp separation between political society and civil society, paralleled by a clear-cut functional specialization: force is exercised by the state proper or political society; consensus is constructed in civil society. In the latter a confrontation of ideas elaborated by private organizations to achieve hegemony takes place. In contrast, Gentile's actualism makes no distinction between the two levels, nor does it identify any functional specialization. In fact, it presents the state as an extended political society which absorbs civil society in itself. The absence of separation between political society and civil society mirrors the lack of differentiation between force and consensus; force takes on a pervasive role, turning itself into consent for fear of its use.[58]

Gramsci's philosophical approach thoroughly questions the model of actualism. On an ethical level, Gramsci disagrees with the paramount role attributed to force. He also believes that actualism's failure to distinguish between political society and civil society leads to the theoretical absurdity of equating the individual with the state and the state with the individual.[59] Approaching the liberal model, Gramsci notes that force is mainly exercised within political society while consensus is achieved above all in civil society.[60]

In locating force and, therefore, the main source of domination in political society, the state proper, Gramsci holds to Marx's conception that the state is, 'society's concentrated and organized violence,' and to Weber's view that the modern state should be defined, 'sociologically in terms of the specific terms peculiar to it . . ., namely the use of physical force.[61] Yet, unlike either Marx or Weber, Gramsci repeatedly asserts that the hegemony of a particular social group must be attained within civil society through the achievement of consciousness by its members, through organization, the spread of ideas, ideological struggle, and the formation of alliances with other social groups; in order to fundamentally change society, a social group must attain political and moral leadership in civil society.

To Gramsci, then, political society, or the state proper, becomes the ultimate arena of domination and civil society that of hegemony. This interpretation is confirmed by Gramsci's notion of the 'regulated society,' the model society identified by his political philosophy. Gramsci's regulated society involves the traditional Marxist 'withering away of the state,' the end of domination. Social organization must be based upon active and conscious consent. In that way political society is reabsorbed into civil society.[62]

Gramsci distinguishes his position from liberalism by criticizing the sharp separation it postulates between political society and civil society. It is a sociological fact, Gramsci asserts, that in illiberal societies (such as fascist Italy under the influence of actualism), 'civil society merges with political society,'[63] while in liberal-democratic societies the two remain separate. But we should never forget that the two components always make up an historical dialectical totality in the unity of the state in its broadest sense.[64] According to Gramsci, the ongoing connection between political society and civil society is ensured by the social group which exercises supremacy, that is, by the social group which, exercising an essential role in the economic structure, has achieved hegemony in civil society and domination in political society. When this does not occur, when different, non-allied social groups exercise these functions in conflict with one another, a gap ensues between political society and civil society, the unity of the state is no longer organic, and society experiences a 'crisis of authority.'[65]

Not only do liberals fail to recognize the ways in which civil society and political society are linked, they do not have a concept of polity, of the state in its broadest sense. Liberalism restricts the concept of the state to political society, the state proper. This inadequate understanding, or deliberate mystification, of the state in the organic sense by liberal theorists often leads them to suggest that programs of economic *laissez-faire* represent the elimination or reduction of the presence of the state in society and the end of domination and supremacy. To this approach Gramsci counters:

> ... *laissez-faire* too is a form of State 'regulation,' introduced and maintained by legislative and coercive means. It is a deliberate policy, conscious of its own ends, and not the spontaneous, automatic expression of economic facts. Consequently, *laissez-faire* liberalism is a political programme, designed to change—in so far as it is victorious—a State's leading personnel, and to change the economic programme of the State itself—in other words the distribution of the national income.[66]

The only way in which a reduction of the presence of the state proper in society can really be achieved is by the absorption of political society into civil society.[67] That means the creation of new historical type of polity based solely on consensus and the popular interiorization of the value system and norms of behavior which will make the use of force unnecessary.

Gramsci summarizes his philosophical approach in the formula: 'State = political society + civil society, in other words, hegemony protected by the armour of coercion,'[68] or, similarly, 'dictatorship + hegemony,'[69] which constructs the two levels of superstructure in the organic unity of the state and locates the use of force in political society and that of hegemony in civil society. This philosophical model gives Gramsci ideal types to use in his sociological analysis of existing societies.

Gramsci notes that in liberal-democratic systems the state proper (political society) has become more than just the depository of force. It has also become the site of the maintenance of hegemony. While the executive, with its army and police, and the judiciary may be considered repressive instruments, this does not hold for Parliament, which is, by definition, nearer to civil society because it contains the electoral expression of the social forces organized in political parties. Moreover, the executive itself has taken on an educational function. (In some countries this happened under the influence of Hegel's conception of the ethical state.) The executive provides schools, libraries, and much of the whole range of institutions which constitute the 'material structure' of the ideology of the dominant group.[70] Gramsci considers this development generally positive because it tends to replace the use of force with the rule by consensus and it may be seen as helping civil society adapt to changes in economic structure.[71] Clearly, Gramsci's evaluation becomes negative when, rather than pursuing these ends, state educational functionaries aim to preserve popular archaic beliefs in order to protect the interests of the dominant group, which, for example, is what he considers to be the role of denominational religious instruction in Italian schools.

Not only has liberal-democratic political society developed such hegemonic functions, but the distinction between the spheres of force and consensus are also blurred in the real world of class-divided societies because force is ubiquitous; it inheres in the economic relationships that define antagonistic classes. Force appears at the center of industrial capitalism in the expropriation of surplus value when, 'a specific commodity (labour) is devaluated from the very start, put in a position of competitive inferiority.'[72]

At the same time, consensus can be built by actions at the level of the economic structure. Changing the 'limits of the possible' faced by members of the working class through a general rise in wages (a reduction in exploitation) can encourage labor's cooperation in the maintenance of the social *status quo*, as Gramsci notes in his analysis of the demise of the first American industrial unions.

To further complicate matters, in the real world, civil society is not just a domain of consensus. Force can also be important. Gramsci notes that capitalist societies have witnessed the:

> ... formation of vast State and 'private' bureaucracies (i.e., politico-private, belonging to parties and trade unions); and after the transformations which took place in the organisation of the forces of order in the wide sense—i.e., not only the public service designed for the repression of crime, but the totality of forces organised by the State and by private individuals to safeguard the political and economic domination of the ruling

classes. In this sense, entire 'political' parties and other organizations—economic or otherwise—must be considered as organs of political order, of an investigational and repressive character.[73]

Gramsci's observations on the transformation of civil society in a repressive direction refers to more than the specifically Italian phenomena of the 1920s, when violent fascist paramilitary groups appeared. Gramsci makes the same observations about other societies, including the United States, where vigilantes have often played a role in destroying progressive movements.[74] Generally, force appears in civil society during crises of authority and when the ruling class's domination can no longer be justified by historical economic limits. Then social groups will use both legal force (the force of political society, the state proper) and illegal force (the force of private associations, of civil society) in combination.[75]

Thus, Gramsci's functional sociology of power recognizes the possibility of either force or policies designed to encourage consensus being used in all social realms from the economic structure, to civil society, to political society. But different deviations from the expectations of Gramsci's philosophical model have different origins and implications that his ideal types help illuminate.

## Toward applying Gramsci's concepts

In the balance of the book we look at how the United States applied both force and measures designed to gain consensus at both the level of the global economic structure and global civil society in order to rebuild its challenged supremacy. Gramsci's concepts let us ask and answer central questions about the reconstruction of American supremacy: Has it worked? Were the results achieved more by force or by consensus? And, can the result develop into a real, ethical form of hegemony, or has consensus masked domination because it has been achieved by fraud?

To answer all of these questions we must first look at the nature of the challenge to American supremacy that triggered US actions in the 1980s. The unusual origins of that challenge, in the policies of Third World nations, and the nature of the counter-hegemonic bloc that appeared possible in the 1970s are the subject of the next chapter.

## Notes

1. E.g. L. Gruppi, *Il concetto di egemonia in Gramsci* (Roma: Editori Riuniti, 1972); Federico Sanguineti, *Gramsci e Machiavelli* (Bari: Laterza, 1981).
2. See Giuseppe Tamburrano, 'Fasi di sviluppo del pensiero politico di Gramsci,' in *La città futura*, Alberto Caracciolo and Gianni Scalia, eds. (Milano: Feltrinelli, 1976). See also the interesting paper, 'Gramsci e la concezione della società civile,'

presented by Norberto Bobbio at the Convegno di studi gramsciani di Cagliari in 1967, in Antonio A. Santucci, ed. *Letture di Gramsci* (Roma: Editori Riuniti, 1987).

3. E.g. Louis Althusser, 'Ideology and Ideological State Apparatuses,' in *Lenin and Philosophy and Other Essays* (New York: Monthly Review Press, 1971), 127–86.
4. Other important influences included Marx, Sorel, and Labriola.
5. Antonio Gramsci, *Selections from Prison Notebooks* (*PN*), Quentin Hoare and Geoffrey Nowell Smith, ed. and trans. (London: Lawrence and Wishart, 1971), 56.
6. V. I. Lenin, 'Two Tactics of Social Democracy in the Democratic Revolution,' in *Selected Works* (Moscow: Progress Publishers, 1970), 459–563.
7. Ibid., 472.
8. Karl Marx, 'Theses on Feuerbach,' in *Marx—Engels Selected Works* (London: Lawrence and Wishart, 1968), 30.
9. *PN*, 365–6.
10. See Antonio Gramsci, *Quaderni del Carcere* (*QC*) (Torino: Einaudi, 1975), II, 1234–5 and *PN*, 55.
11. *QC*, II, 1237–8.
12. *PN*, 56.
13. *QC*, II, 1244.
14. Gramsci highlights the link between hegemony and Croce's 'ethical-political history' by claiming: 'It can be stated not only that the philosophy of praxis does not exclude ethico-political history, but indeed that the most recent phase of development thereof consists precisely in claiming the moment of hegemony as essential in its State conception and in its "enhancing" of the cultural fact, of cultural activity, of a cultural front as necessary alongside those merely economic and merely political ones' (*QC*, II, 1224).
15. *QC*, II, 1231.
16. Leonardo Paggi, 'Il problema Machiavelli,' in *Le strategie del potere in Gramsci* (Roma: Editori Riuniti, 1984), 387. See also, Sanguineti.
17. *PN*, 249.
18. *QC*, II, 724.
19. *QC*, III, 1691.
20. In this sense, Gramsci accepts the interpretation of the historian and critic of Italian literature Francesco De Sanctis that the most important and distinctive aspect of Machiavelli's work is the line he draws between ethics and politics.
21. *PN*, 161.
22. *PN*, 333.
23. *PN*, 77.
24. *QC*, III, 1612.
25. *PN*, 161.
26. *QC*, II, 1084.
27. *QC*, I, 134.
28. *PN*, 403.
29. *QC*, I, 58.
30. *QC*, III, 1637.
31. *PN*, 399.
32. *PN*, 465.

33. *QC*, II, 703.
34. *QC*, III, 1636.
35. *PN*, 242.
36. *PN*, 350.
37. *QC*, II, 1050.
38. *QC*, I, 131.
39. *PN*, 67–8.
40. *QC*, II, 1231–32.
41. *QC*, II, 1295.
42. See *QC*, III, 1638. Gramsci gives as an example the Italian political process of 'trasformismo.' In history books this term is generally used to describe the process of dissolution of the traditional political parties and of the 'programatic convergence' of many members of the right and left such as occurred during the Depretis government between 1881 and 1887. Gramsci says 'trasformismo' is a more general process in Italian history after 1860 involving a constant switching of left-wing opposition leaders to moderate conservative groups (*QC*, III, 2011).
43. *QC*, III, 1690.
44. *PN*, 169–70. We have changed the translators' word 'consent' to 'consensus.' In Italian only one word, 'consenso,' covers both meanings. Hoare and Smith always translate it as 'consent' although there are times where, in context, 'consensus' might be more accurate. We have used either word, depending on context.
45. The erroneous impression that Machiavelli only considered force, Gramsci argues, can be corrected by giving as much attention to the *Discourses* as to the *Prince* (*QC*, II, 1315).
46. *PN*, 170.
47. *PN*, 57.
48. *QC*, III, 1638.
49. *PN*, 285.
50. *PN*, 271.
51. Although we are unable to elaborate the matter here, it seems useful to point out the similarities between Gentile's philosophical concept and the philosophical foundations of the 'realist doctrine' in international relations.
52. *PN*, 12.
53. *PN*, 259–60.
54. On Gramsci's views, see Bobbio, op. cit. On the Hegelian concept of civil society as the seat of universal egoism, see Shlomo Avineri, *Hegel's Theory of the Modern State* (Cambridge: Cambridge University Press, 1972).
55. *PN*, 246. On this point Gramsci's analysis diverges substantially from that of Hegel, who saw bureaucracy as a universal class, the location of the general interests of society.
56. *PN*, 170. Not having perceived the difference between the state proper and the state in the organic sense, Perry Anderson is unable to distinguish the use of the two concepts in the various passages in Gramsci. He therefore believes he has discovered certain ambiguities in Gramsci. 'The Antinomies of Antonio Gramsci,' *New Left Review*, 100 (1976–77), 5–78.
57. *PN*, 54.

58. *PN*, 271.
59. *QC*, II, 1245.
60. *PN*, 12.
61. Quoted in Robert Bocock, *Hegemony* (London: Tavistock, 1986), 85.
62. See Bobbio.
63. *QC*, II, 734.
64. *PN*, 262–3. As Gramsci says (*PN*, 160.) the distinction between political society and civil society is 'methodic' not 'organic' because to Gramsci both constitute a unitary ensemble within the framework of the organic unity of the state.
65. Gramsci develops this concept in various places, identifying it with the loss of hegemony by the social group enjoying domination within the state proper. See in particular, *PN*, 210 and 275–6.
66. *PN*, 160.
67. *PN*, 260.
68. *PN*, 263.
69. *PN*, 239.
70. This is the basis of Althusser's argument. For a more general discussion of Gramsci on the expansion of the state see Christine Buci-Glucksmann, *Gramsci et l'Etat* (Paris: Fayard, 1975).
71. *QC*, II, 1253–4.
72. *QC*, II, 1258.
73. *PN*, 221.
74. *QC*, III, 1666–7.
75. See *QC*, II, 912–13 on the use of legal and illegal force.

# 7 The Third World and the challenge to American supremacy

The crisis in American supremacy in the 1970s threatened an American dream. For more than a century the country's expansion had followed the script written in the early days of the republic. It grew from its isolated infancy along the eastern seaboard to maturity as a global power after the world wars. Along the way foreign policy changed to reflect new capabilities. The isolationist republic, protective of its special virtues but conscious of its weakness, turned into the great power promulgating its unique vision of the world and crusading against alternatives. At the beginning of what was to be 'the American century' Truman and Eisenhower presided over the construction of an almost global political and economic system, a truly unprecedented 'hegemony,' both in Gramsci's sense as well as that of the realists. This empire was held together more by the rapidly growing world capitalist economy—by economic development that extended American hegemony well beyond the original historical bloc it served—than by force and the asymmetrical military alliances that the US forged with dependent nations. By 1961, when the relatively young and visionary Kennedy took office, the era of reconstruction and empire-building was at an end. American supremacy in the non-communist world was established. The US appeared at the height of its confidence and power, ready to convert the rest of the world to the American way, the task that Kennedy proposed in his inaugural address in phrases that Gramsci would have recognized as implying the creation of a true, ethical hegemony.

Yet, only a decade later the United States already become an old crusader: wounded, weak, cynical, and a bit blind. An analyst could conclude an important collection on American foreign policy at the time, 'The day when America could speak, as John Adams did, of producing a grand design that would illuminate the future of all mankind is gone.'[1]

The founding fathers of American foreign policy would not have been surprised that the glory of empire for which they had struggled and planned was so short-lived. All of them—from Benjamin Franklin, to George Washington, John Adams, and Alexander Hamilton, to John Quincy Adams—were worldly sons of a Protestant culture that made them wary of pride because they knew how hard the proud can fall. They would not have been surprised that one aspect of America's decline was the rise of the industrialized nations that the US had aided the most, and the most-selflessly, as it created its historical bloc. Yet, these worldly liberals probably never would have predicted the source of the only real challenge to American hegemony, the only stirrings of a counter-hegemonic bloc. It did not develop around another equally proud and powerful capitalist empire, nor even in a struggle with a more powerful evil, but among the kind of nations that the American policy-makers since John Quincy Adams's time have usually considered weak, unimportant, and populated by people of a definitely cruder sort than those in power in America, people the founders would have considered of 'lower races' although contemporary policy-makers would just call them 'developing.'

## America's historical bloc

To understand the source of the challenge to American hegemony in the 1970s it is important to understand the constitution of the historical bloc at the center of 'America's' post-war supremacy. In Gramsci's terms, the class at the center of the international system of dominance constructed in the capitalist world after the world wars is the American bourgeoisie. Scholars who have delved into the details of the social constitution of Franklin D. Roosevelt's administration make even finer distinctions that are less-relevant to our purposes, discussing the conflict pitting capitalists involved in older industries of the early nineteenth century against the owners and managers of newer, mass-production industries—those most-likely to benefit from global markets and most-influenced by the philosophy of systematic management. Each side had its own allies in American financial markets.[2] Intellectuals allied to this class fraction developed and articulated the ideological face of the historical bloc through new private institutions (institutions of civil society) that brought together businesspeople, government officials, scholars, and journalists. The Council on Foreign Relations is perhaps the most well-known of these institutions, although its influence often may be overstated. More significant was the development of the whole new 'American' science of international relations.[3]

The bloc that became the basis for American hegemony extended overseas, gaining the allegiance of government officials and, eventually, much of the bourgeoisie of Europe and Japan through the American post-war assistance policies and the successful establishment of a climate in which highly-profitable capitalist economic growth could be expected.[4] This development, too, had its ideological as well as material side. Intergovernmental institutions encouraging and monitoring government-to-government cooperation among developed market states—including the OECD, the Bank for International Settlements, the GATT, and the Bretton Woods institutions—helped develop shared economic expectations among the US and its allies. These institutions can be thought of as a special part of international 'civil society,' even though they have some 'governmental' powers, especially in relation to their Third World members. The intergovernmental organizations are 'private' to the extent that they are membership organizations and are not subject to the dominance exercised in a (nonexistent) global 'political society.' At the same time the limitation of their membership to national governments makes them more 'public' than other institutions which also served to develop consensus about American dominance in the post-war western alliance, for example, Harvard University's Center for International Affairs whose major mission is to build understanding and long-term cooperation among scholars and policy-makers throughout the alliance.[5]

In the post-war era the hegemony of the American bourgeoisie was extended inside the United States to much of the working class. Scholars disagree about the success of this extension and we have no reason to enter into a debate about whether or not some American industrial workers are truly 'part' of the hegemonic bloc at the center of the American system of dominance,[6] but we do want to recall the more generally-accepted observation that the two most important means for securing cooperation among American business leaders, labor, and government in all areas of post-war foreign policy (including foreign economic policy) have been, on the one hand, *anti-communism*, an ideology that the post-war American labor movement embraces and helped develop, and, on the other hand, the so-called 'politics of productivity,' the more-or-less explicit class compromise that helped create social harmony in the United States from the 1940s through the 1970s.[7] The later was more than just the promise of economic development that wise hegemons always make to subordinate and potentially-antagonistic classes, it involved an implicit pledge that the United States government would not use public policy in a way that had a predictable negative impact on any specific sector of the US economy and the workers within it.

In other developed market countries slightly different social compacts assured peace between the local bourgeoisie (including those most directly involved in the American historical bloc) and the local working class, although, overall, in the post-war world there developed what John Ruggie has called a system of 'imbedded liberalism,'[8] a liberal international economic order (which inherently benefits those with a great deal of liquid capital as well as the owners and workers in industries that can gain from exploiting new economies of scale by opening new markets, usually newer industries)[9] imbedded within similar local welfare states that guarantee certain minimum benefits to members of subordinate classes. While Ruggie's description is accurate, the phrase 'imbedded welfarism' or 'imbedded Keynesianism' might be a better summary of this state of affairs. International liberalism, the promotion of free trade and investment, has been at the center of the hegemonic system, part of the historical bloc that has linked the economic base of the capitalist world-economy with its superstructure under American dominance. The welfare states that have aided the world's industrial workers are less central; they have been imbedded within the historically more significant system. The welfare states have been more like the chocolate jimmies on a Boston ice cream cone, giving the surface some color and flavor, but not changing the essential cold structure.

Whichever way the metaphor, the post-war American hegemony involved few active attempts by the American bourgeoisie or the American national government to extend the *domestic* 'politics of productivity' to help insure industrial peace worldwide. Nor did workers outside the US become convinced of the validity and morality of the post-war world order.[10] Moreover, the anti-communist ideology which became such a significant source of social co-operation inside the United States was never replicated in any of America's major industrial allies. In some—France and Italy in particular—the Communist Party retained much of the allegiance of the working class and ultimately, became, itself, one of the institutions of the local governing consensus.

Equally peripherally-connected to the American hegemonic bloc were members of the ruling classes in the Third World, people in what Irving L. Markovitz and his students call the 'organizational bourgeoisie,' men and women who dominate society by dominating organizational positions in government and private industry.[11] The American world system gave this class advantages: decolonization and economic development were policies that had the effect of (and, in some cases, were designed to) encourage their acceptance of the historical bloc. But, much as the European and Japanese working class did, the Third World organizational bourgeoisie retained allegiance to economic and political theories that differed radically from those that provided the ideological face of America's historical bloc.[12]

## The significance of the economic growth of Europe and Japan

Much of the standard 'neorealist' discussion of the decline of American power in the 1970s completely ignores the ideological side of America's supremacy. For the neorealists it is enough that the material capabilities of America's major allies—western Europe and Japan—grew to the point that the United States no longer enjoyed the overwhelming material predominance it had at the end of the wars simply because the use of force against American territory had been so minimal. America's allies, as a result, have developed a greater economic capacity for establishing stronger military forces. Moreover, the allies' growth may reflect another 'long-term' problem for the US, a secular decline in the relative productivity of American industry due to the advantages the reconstructed industrial powers gained from developing brand new factories in all industries to replace those destroyed in the war. The neorealists admit that certain short-term, 'reversible' factors also contributed to US decline—the American public's reluctance to use force in the Third World after Vietnam and the increase in Soviet military capabilities in the 1970s—but nothing can change the overall trend.[13]

Critics of the neorealists who see no real evidence of US decline, including Bruce Russett[14] and Stephen Gill[15] note that despite its allies' growing material capabilities America's preponderance within its alliance has not been challenged. As Gill points out in his Gramscian analysis, the neorealists misunderstand the role that ideology plays in America's 'hegemony.' Japan's government and America's European allies agree with the system of liberalized trade established at the end of the war and they have developed little reason to challenge it.

The neorealist's argument assumes that supremacy, and international order, are a function only of the threat or use of force, which, as Gill points out, is simply not the case. This is especially true in America's relations with its industrialized allies. The wide systems of consultations the US employed at the end of the war in setting up the institutions of the post-war world, the continuing consultations in NATO, the OECD, at annual summits of the seven major industrial powers, as well as many other forums, and the real burden the US undertook in the reconstruction of Europe and Japan, indicate that American supremacy, in the alliance, has been more a matter of ethical hegemony than domination by force.

Moreover, as 'traditional' or 'classical' realists, like George Kennan, would argue, the temporary economic devastation of western Europe, Japan, and the Soviet Union at the end of the second world war was hardly a sensible measure of their capacity to use force in international relations. Reconstruction of these societies could be aided or impeded by the United States, but it could not be stopped.[16] It would have been foolish to try to build America's historical bloc simply on the basis of a temporary military preponderance. Moral and intellectual leadership and the will to take into consideration the allies' interests in economic development was essential.

The first real signs of the weakening of America's supremacy appeared when the US could no longer ensure its moral and intellectual leadership and guarantee the unity of the bloc, something that, despite Russett and Gill, did actually occur. In fact, the neorealists understand one of the proximate causes of this development—the new material demands that the United States placed on its industrialized allies at the beginning of the 1970s.

## The Third World and the new US demands on its allies

The neorealists have an unnecessarily moralistic model of these new demands, a model which sees the US as a victim beset by 'free rider problems' of ungrateful allies unwilling to accept their 'fair share' of the burden of maintaining 'collective goods' including 'security' (allied military expenditures) and stability of the monetary system. This aspect of their analysis may simply reflect the implicit political program of much the 'American' science of international relations; it should not distract us from the truths they uncover.

To see those truths clearly we need to look at more than just relations between the US and its allies. The American government made new demands on its allies due to failures in policies toward groups that were usually external to America's historical bloc, including the governing classes of the Third World.

Marshall Goldman, a liberal economist whose analytical framework resembles that of many neorealists predicted the sort of problem the US would face. In an early study of Soviet aid policy[17] he urged the US to not compete with the Soviet Union in this arena. The financial burden did not worry him; aid to the Third World cost little. But aid could lead to costly political commitments. Goldman feared the consequences of the evangelism that characterized Kennedy's policy in the Third World.

Lyndon Johnson paid the price of Kennedy's evangelism. He felt his 'Great Society' programs to quell unrest among America's poor were essential to the country's future.[18] Johnson needed Kennedy's backers to legitimate the comprehensive domestic agenda. To gain that support Johnson felt more compelled to complete Kennedy's crusades in the Third World than Kennedy, himself, probably would have, had he lived.

Fred Block correctly identifies Johnson's personal tragedy in the much greater, national, tragedy of the Vietnam war: his noble refusal to sacrifice his relatively-unpopular expansion of the welfare state in order to have the funds to fight what, in its early years, was a relatively popular war against Third World revolutionaries in Vietnam.[19] Johnson tried to pay for both without raising taxes. Nixon, as a result, inherited, what Triffin calls the unprecedented problem of 'infession,' economic stagnation caused by the inflationary pressure of the Johnson policies.[20] More popularly, we know the problem as 'stagflation.' Triffin's word is preferable only because it gets the historical order of the elements right.

A key characteristic of the early 'infessionary' period was an overvalued dollar and it was in this context that the United States began to make its new demands upon its allies. In the summer of 1971, when the Nixon administration began contemplating a boost for the American economy (not coincidentally, in time for Nixon's 1972 reelection campaign) its strategy had to involve finding a way to encourage both Americans and those abroad to buy US rather than foreign goods. The unique position of the US dollar in the post-war trading system meant that the American government could not devalue the dollar unilaterally; the states that pegged the price of their currencies to the dollar would have to change their value. In August, 1971 the Nixon administration announced a policy that led to devaluation of the dollar and successfully shifted some of the burden of US economic problems abroad. The US stopped trading gold for dollars and imposed temporary duties to discourage imports. The policy encouraged other states to let their currencies 'float,' find a market value against the dollar, resulting in the dollar's devaluation. Even though this new economic policy achieved most of the goals the Nixon administration set for it, it did mark a critical juncture. If nothing else, in exchange for putting part of the world's economic burden on its allies, the US was also forced to recognize their power in any future discussions about reform of the international economic system as a whole.

Moreover, while the neorealists may be wrong when they claim that Nixon's 1971 policies *responded* to a change in power *vis-à-vis* its industrialized allies, Gill and Russett probably overemphasize the degree to which things stayed the same. American supremacy may not have changed, but the glue that held its foreign allies into its historical bloc changed. The US no longer resembled the ethical hegemon *vis-à-vis* its allies, leading by an enlightened policy willing to sacrifice the immediate economic-corporate national interest in order to maintain a hegemonic position. Nixon's policy amounted to the use of force in the sphere of the economy; it changed the limits of what was possible for both governments and people in western Europe and Japan. Domination, not ethical hegemony, began to characterize American supremacy.

In the subsequent discussions about restructuring the international monetary system and returning to something like the Bretton Wood's system of fixed exchange rates pegged to the dollar, the United States government failed to articulate a long-term vision and even failed to convince its allies that the short-term measures it preferred would be the best for everyone. Members of the European Community responded by developing the beginnings of their own, regional monetary system. And the US played nowhere near as central a role in the tardy 'legalization' of the floating rate system in a revision of the International Monetary Fund Charter as it had in the writing of the charter in the first place[21]

Nixon and Ford administration officials recognized these events as a change in US power *vis-à-vis* other industrialized, capitalist states. Yet, the administration's analysis implicated US–Third World relations as well. After all, it was the American crusade in Vietnam, and Johnson's reluctance to give up the Great Society in order to carry it out, which had helped trigger the change in the relations within the industrial world. One of the lessons of Vietnam to Henry Kissinger was that such deep involvement in Third World conflicts was counterproductive, a view that fit with Kissinger's general desire to de-emphasize the Third World.

At the time, many commentators, especially in the Third World itself, argued that this new policy was simply a consequence of the American-Soviet detente. If the superpowers could cooperate, they no longer needed to test each other's will in the Third World. But the Nixon administration's desire to ignore the Third World was as much a cause of its interest in detente as it was a consequence. The administration had learned the lesson about the wastefulness of US-Soviet competition in the Third World that Goldman, among many others, had tried to teach. Beyond that, Kissinger's realism told him that the US needed very few friends in the Third World: Third World states were just not powerful enough to affect American interests except when they were aided by other great powers, as had been the case in Vietnam.[22]

## America's inability to shield allies from the oil shocks

International events throughout the Nixon and Ford years seemed to prove Kissinger wrong. The OPEC oil producers did affect American interests. Of course, some scholars argue that Kissinger gave more than tacit support to many of the oil price hikes of the early 1970s as a way to secure one of what he considered America's few important allies in the Third World, the Shah of Iran, whose country provided the United States with important intelligence on the Soviet Union and acted as a powerful regional barrier to Soviet 'advances.' Be that as it may, it is certainly the case that the Republican administrations neither engineered nor approved oil price increases as sharp and rapid as those that took place in 1973–74 and Kissinger tried to obtain alliance-wide and even global agreement to keep prices from rising further.

The American attempt to gain alliance-wide agreement was, perhaps, more successful than Kissinger's bid to get the less-industrialized countries to oppose OPEC, but even the industrialized alliance was reluctant to follow the American lead.[23] Most of America's most powerful allies were much more dependent on internationally-traded oil even though one, the United Kingdom, had just become much less dependent. All the industrialized allies had developed much more stringent public policies to reduce oil consumption than the United States had. Because the US was slow to adopt any conservation measures, it looked to some in France, West Germany, Italy, and Japan like the United States, the new glutton of a consumer in the oil market, was as responsible as the OPEC nations.

Conceivably, the United States could have been a more effective leader if at the first signs of the oil crisis it had found a way to flood its allies' markets with cheap oil. That probably was not possible from domestic production and stocks, given the growing dependence of the US on foreign oil. It may have been possible had the United States chosen to use its military might to break the OPEC cartel, for example, by engineering and supporting a coup in Libya similar to the one that kept the Shah in control in Iran in 1953.[24] For whatever reason—fear that the post-Vietnam war American public would not support the use of force in the Third World, the distractions of the Watergate affair, Kissinger's own hopes for resolving the Arab-Israeli conflict—the US apparently did not choose to do so.

## America's failure to respond to the New International Economic Order

Ironically, Kissinger's general policy of neglect of the Third World helped doom his effort to build solidarity against the oil producing states. His attempt to get Third World states to oppose the price increases was particularly ill-timed. In 1974, 'realism' suggested that the majority of Third World states would unite against the oil producers. After all, hardships imposed by higher oil prices in the poor nations of Africa or even the oil-dependent newly industrializing nations were likely to be much greater than they would be in the developed OECD states, even Japan, Italy, West Germany, and France. But the Third World was not on America's side because Nixon-era neglect had revitalized the Third World alliance which the oil producers then adroitly turned to their own advantage.[25]

In 1969, when Nixon came to power, the Third World was fragmented. Even its largely symbolic cooperation in the General Assembly was at a low ebb. But Nixon-era reductions in American foreign assistance and the impact of the new American economic policy of 1971 changed that. Nixon's across-the-board tariff increases imposed what Asia, African, and Latin America governments perceived as an unfair burden on them when other options, more directly aimed at America's developed trading partners, could have been tried. More significantly, by declaring some of the rules of the Bretton Woods system null and void, the Nixon administration opened the political space for negotiations over the transformation of international economic institutions.

Between 1971 and 1973 Third World governments patched-up the differences between the 'least-developed' and richest Third World countries and between recent colonies (who had tended to advocate a 'back-payments' view of aid) and those states that had long been independent. As Arab producers forced oil prices up, the renewed alliance heralded the event as reflecting the new power achieved through unity. The Third World responded to the oil crisis by calling for a radically-restructured 'New International Economic Order' (NIEO) at a 1974 UN special session originally called to discuss the crisis but whose agenda had been widened by the combined effort of oil-producing and non-oil producing Third World nations.

The American government's immediate reaction to the Third World demands was negative and sharp but moderated to a willingness to discuss some of Third World proposals in Kissinger's last few months in office and throughout the Carter administration. Essentially, the United States's positive response came down to a willingness to discuss linked commodity agreements which might serve to stabilize the foreign exchange earnings of some Third World raw material producers. The power of the United States assured that this one area of stated (but, ultimately, not substantive) flexibility became the basis for much of the NIEO discussion in the late 1970s.[26] This narrowing of the NIEO agenda ignored all the more substantive proposals for creating more automatic means for assuring the transfer of development funds, increasing Third World influence in the intergovernmental organizations that manage the world economy, and moving toward a system of global planning to prepare for and encourage the shift of industry to the Third World as comparative advantage shifts.

The immediate reason why the United States, unlike other developed market countries,[27] failed to respond more positively to the NIEO demands was simply ideological. The simplistic economic liberalism that has always been an important guide to American foreign policy simply could not accept the global Keynesianism underlying the Third World's demands; American policy makers could not accept the idea that government needed to intervene in the world economy because large investors, left to their own devices, fail to make the most profitable international investments possible, and thus systematically underprivileged the non-industrialized world.

But there is a deeper reason that explains why this ideological opposition to global Keynesianism was not challenged in the United States: the domestic social compact worked out during the Roosevelt years. The American governmental planning that would be needed in a global Keynesian world would contradict the domestic 'politics of productivity,' the unwritten promise that the core of the American historical bloc has made to American labor that governmental policy would not actively hurt any industry. Preparing the ground for the movement of some American industry to the Third World would be doing just that.[28] As Gramsci would predict, the aspirations of those more peripherally connected to American supremacy—the Third World organizational bourgeoisie and their NIEO program—would be sacrificed to the interests and aspirations of those more central to that supremacy—American industrialists and workers. For western Europe and Japan, where operating social compacts involve active planning for industrial change and greater compensation for displaced workers rather than faith in the fairness of the market, coming up with more positive responses to the NIEO was much easier.

### The failure to quiet the Third World with economic development or force

The conventional wisdom among American students of the NIEO is that all the Third World 'really' wanted in its demands of the 1970s was a bit more money. One scholar who has listened to Third World demands a bit more closely, Stephen D. Krasner, says no. The NIEO demands are really demands for increasing the state power of Third World states.[29] We do not fully agree. The ideologies underlying the NIEO are organic to the organizational bourgeoisie of the Third World. Because the power of that class, as Markovitz defines its, rests in the control of bureaucratic hierarchies (both public and private) within Third World states, and because so many members of the class hold both public and private roles (e.g. as high-level civil servant and international trader) improving the chances for the reproduction of that class's dominant roles either in government or in the private economy is likely to be 'acceptable.' Thus, high rates of simple economic growth—as long as it is not tied to policies that threaten the social status quo—might give supporters of the NIEO reason to reconsider their positions. Economic growth strengthens state institutions in the Third World simply by expanding the tax base as it strengthens the private economy, much of which is controlled by members of the same class.

Despite its opposition to the NIEO in the 1970s the US did not (and perhaps was not able to) pursue a policy of assuring economic growth in the Third World in order to deflect the demands. As we have seen in chapter 4, despite the temporary increases in America's aid allocations under Carter, the general trend was toward a less and less significant foreign assistance program. Moreover, as the United States continued into the 'infessionary' decade, the domestic pressure to slow consumption of foreign products grew, and the greatest victims of that pressure were newly industrializing Third World states, those societies that potentially could experience such rapid economic growth that the NIEO demands would quickly become less relevant to them.

Finally, and perhaps the most significantly, the US was unable to use a policy of deflecting the NIEO by encouraging growth in the Third World simply because American development theory of the 1970s did not ignore the social status quo in the Third World. The 'direct attack on poverty' developed in AID and championed by the World Bank meant allowing economic development to strengthen the least-advantaged within the Third World; it did not mean turning resources over to the organizational bourgeoisie in its private roles nor did it involve strengthening Third World states. Jimmy Carter's human rights evangelism further contributed to this tendency for American policy to challenge the ruling classes in much of the Third World. The moral foundation of these policies was admirable, but, in the short run, they exacerbated the crisis of America's supremacy and contributed to the Reaganite backlash.

The global economic adjustments needed in the immediate wake of the oil crisis were not even carried out by the intergovernmental institutions of global civil society or any other agencies in which the US government played a major role. Rather, the newly-rich oil states exchanged some of their wealth for the other currency of international power, arms, mostly from western firms, and they relied upon large private western banks to find profitable outlets for their funds. A significant proportion of the new wealth went to loans to a few large, seemingly highly-successful developing nations, including Brazil, Argentina, and Mexico. Many analysts have pointed to the ways in which these private, *ad hoc* mechanisms that let the world economy adjust to the new changes in oil prices also assured the severity of later wars in Lebanon and the Gulf and set the stage for the Third World debt crisis of the 1980s.[30] For our purposes here, what is more significant is that a leadership role in the world economy—essential to continuing economic stability let alone higher levels of growth—that in the 1940s, 1950s, or 1960s would almost surely have been played by the United States, was played in this instance, in the 1970s, by Third World oil producers and private western banks. This was a clear sign of the real diminution of American supremacy.

If the United States could not, or would not, use economic growth to extend its supremacy to the Third World groups that challenged it, the same was true of force. Neither Carter nor the Republicans who preceded him were willing to use America's military might to destroy the OPEC alliance. In large part this was a response to real Congressional pressure against military intervention in the Third World in the wake of the disaster in Vietnam. The strongest manifestation of this pressure occurred soon after the oil crisis when Congress stopped the US's 'covert' war in Angola.

The Nixon administration's 'failure' in Angola was linked to its earlier assumption that the revolutions taking place in white-dominated Africa could not succeed. But the defeat of the Portuguese army in Guinea-Bissau in the fall of 1973, at virtually the same time as the first oil crisis[31] led to the Lisbon coup staged by returning forces and the democratization of the metropole. The new government rapidly negotiated with revolutionary movements in Guinea, Cape Verde, São Tomé, Mozambique, and Angola. In all but the last, negotiations led to uncontested transfers of power to the independence movement. In Angola, where the independence movement was deeply divided, it did not. The American administration hoped to stop 'Soviet' advances in Angola by supporting minority factions that the Soviets did not support, but Congress repeated the administration's own logic back to them: If these areas of the world are only of secondary or tertiary importance to American interests, why should we be fighting wars there, even secret ones?[32] Congress's reluctance to let the United States use force in the Third World remained an important constraint until Reagan's victory. The removal of the ban on covert war in Angola was a signal of the new era of intervention.

## The failure of the alternative bloc's leadership

Because the United States became reluctant to use force in the Third World in the 1970s and, at the same time, was unable to take the lead in global macroeconomic policy, the decade presented an ideal opportunity for the consolidation of a new historical bloc, which is exactly what the Third World movement, centered on the OPEC oil producers, attempted to do. For almost the entire decade after the oil crisis of 1973, OPEC producers held a key position in the world economy, a position from which it was not unreasonable to attempt to consolidate a center of power to counter America's supremacy. Although, as we will see in the next chapter, OPEC only stopped being a significant factor in global power politics during the first Reagan administration, when OPEC lost its central position in the world economy, its inadequacies as a leader of the alternative bloc were already apparent in the late 1970s.

OPEC members did not use their resources as part of a complete strategy for consolidating power throughout the world economy. Rather than selectively and judiciously investing their wealth in ways that would bind new allies to the bloc, most of the OPEC members relied upon private institutions that shared the core interests of the old historical bloc, international banks. Of course, most of the OPEC states had very few other choices. The oil windfall was unexpected when it arrived and OPEC members simply had not developed the institutional structures needed to manage their new wealth by themselves.

Yet, even those policies of OPEC members that did take into account the interests of other bloc members, in particular the vast foreign assistance programs rapidly established by the Arab OPEC states, were not designed to uniformly support OPEC's allies throughout the Third World. Non-oil producing Arab states, other Islamic states, and Islamic minorities in other parts of the Third World were the primary beneficiaries of Arab OPEC largesse. This focused aid strategy was particularly unfortunate for Third World unity given the fact that rapidly-climbing oil prices—the foundation of OPEC power—ran counter to the interests of non-oil producers in all parts of the Third World.

Still, OPEC was able to keep the Third World bloc together, even after the second oil crisis of 1979 sent prices even higher. OPEC did so not by taking into account the economic interests of its Third World allies but by supporting their aspirations, the broad NIEO program for restructuring international economic institutions. The OPEC threat kept the developed market countries, even the United States, at the NIEO bargaining table throughout the decade and the north moved toward the south's position by consolidating the generalized system of trade preferences for developing nations and agreeing in principle to an integrated system of raw material pricing arrangements. Moreover, by the end of the 1970s there was agreement among all states except the US and a few very close allies on a general strategy for negotiating reforms in all of the international economic institutions established since the world wars.

But even OPEC's support of Third World aspirations could have gone further, had the oil producers been able to capitalize upon the conflict over the NIEO that split the United States from its industrialized allies. The oil producers failed to give western Europe and Japan material incentives to split with the United States completely and take a lead in resolving the north–south conflict. OPEC gave the more forthcoming northern states no special concessions on the issues of oil price and supply.

Perhaps the contradictions inside the oil producers' alliance were too great for it to become the leader of a hegemonic system, responding to its allies' economic interests as well as their aspirations and using economic incentives to break America's historical bloc. OPEC contained both states, such as Algeria, with a clear vision of the alliance's role as the center of an alternative historical bloc, and states that simply wanted to improve their own position in the existing system. Moreover, the poorest of the OPEC members were in no position to sacrifice part of their immediate windfall in the interests of longer-term bloc goals.

Nevertheless, despite the failures of the alternative bloc that were already apparent in the 1970s, it is important to remember that as the decade closed, these appeared only to be failures of strategy and tactics, failures of leadership. The foundation of the alternative bloc's power remained. The second oil price shock after the Iranian revolution demonstrated that the new bloc's challenge to American supremacy was still very real.

## Notes

1. Henry Owen, *The Next Phase in Foreign Policy* (Washington: Brookings, 1973), 309.
2. See Thomas Ferguson, 'From Normalcy to New Deal: Industrial Structure, Party Competition, and American Public Policy in the Great Depression,' *International Organization*, 38 (1984): 41–94.
3. This ironic identification is Stanley Hoffmann's. On the ideological significance of the field in the development of American hegemony see Steve Smith, 'The Development of International Relations as a Social Science,' *Millennium*, 16 (1987): 189–206; and on the links between the ruling class, private foundations, and the development of the new 'science' see Barry D. Karl and Stanley N. Katz, 'Foundations and Ruling Class Elites,' *Daedalus*, 116 (1987): 1–40, and Robert A. McCaughey, *International Studies and Academic Enterprise: A Chapter in the Enclosure of American Learning* (New York: Columbia University Press, 1984).
4. See Kees Van der Pijl, *The Making of an Atlantic Ruling Class* (London: Verso, 1984).
5. Despite our criticism of US policy, the present book might be considered only a slightly-flawed example of this institution's success.
6. Part of the debate takes the form of arguments about the privileges enjoyed by a 'labor aristocracy' that may benefit from 'imperialism,' understood as both the exploitation of peripheral economies and the militarization of the US economy. None of the empirical studies of these phenomena are very sophisticated, but the one with by far the most convincing design identifies no significant 'rents' of imperialism gained by any segment of American industrial workers. See Albert Szymanski, *The Logic of Imperialism* (New York: Praeger, 1981), 465–91.
7. The term is Charles Maier's, from 'The Politics of Productivity: Foundations of American International Economic Policy After World War Two,' *International Organization*, 31 (1977): 607–33.
8. 'International Regimes, Transactions, and Change: Embedded Liberalism in the Post-War Economic Order.' *International Organization*, 36 (1982): 379–415.
9. This could serve as a brief summary of the characteristic those industries in the US that Ferguson, op. cit., identifies as at the center of the Roosevelt hegemony, or that Van der Pijl, op. cit., places within the core an emerging Atlantic ruling class. As a statement about economic interests and their role in the political economy of the western system this view is not necessarily 'Marxist.' It could be found in a standard 'bourgeois' text on international economics; cf. Paul R. Krugman and Maurice Obstfeld, *International Economics: Theory and Practice* (Glenview, IL: Scott, Foresman and Company: 1988), 60–1.
10. Robert W. Cox, in the article that first introduced Gramsci's ideas to the 'American' science of international relations, even claims that within the International Labor

Organization, an institution of global civil society whose tripartite system of representation (government, management, and labor) would make it the ideal arena for extending hegemony by encouraging global consensus on labor–management relations, the US, on the contrary, has consistently used what in Gramsci's terms would be called 'domination' to influence agency action. 'Labor and Hegemony,' *International Organization*, 31 (1977): 183–224.

11. A class somewhat similar to the managerial class in the developed market countries and even more similar to the 'new class' of governmental and industrial managers in eastern Europe. Irving L. Markovitz, *Power and Class in Africa* (Englewood Cliffs, NJ: Prentice-Hall, 1977); Irving L. Markovitz, ed., *Studies in Power and Class in Africa* (New York: Oxford University Press, 1987).
12. This is the central point make in Murphy's, *The Emergence of NIEO Ideology* (Boulder, CO: Westview Press, 1984). The Third World elite's alternative ideology has always combined faith in a wide variety of ways of organizing *domestic* economies with a global *Keynesian* liberalism in contrast to the pre-Keynesian liberalism of the global economy promoted by the United States after the wars.
13. We summarize Joseph S. Nye, Jr's arguments in 'U.S. Power and Reagan Policy,' *Orbis*, 26 (1982): 391–412. William P. Avery and David Rapkin, eds, *America in a Changing World Political Economy* (London: Longman, 1982) is an excellent introduction to structural analyses of America's decline.
14. 'The Mysterious Case of Vanishing Hegemony; Or, is Mark Twain Really Dead?' *International Organization*, 39 (1982): 207–31.
15. 'U.S. Hegemony: Its Limits and Prospects in the Reagan Era,' *Millennium*, 15 (1986): 311–36.
16. A point classical realist, F. S. Hinsley, makes when discussing the continuing 'great power' status of Britain and France, *Power and the Pursuit of Peace* (Cambridge: Cambridge University Press, 1963), 354.
17. *Soviet Foreign Aid* (New York: Praeger, 1967).
18. Gramsci's analysis would agree: successful great powers always must solve the problem of extending hegemony to subordinate social groups before taking on the world.
19. *The Origins of International Economic Disorder: A Study of United States Monetary Policy from World War II to the Present* (Berkeley: University of California Press, 1977).
20. Robert Triffin, 'Reshaping the International Monetary Order,' in Anthony J. Dolman and Jan van Ettinger, eds, *Partners in Tomorrow* (New York: E. P. Dutton, 1978), 245–56.
21. The most comprehensive history of the period is Margaret Garritsen de Vries's three volume *The International Monetary Fund, 1972–1978: Cooperation on Trial* (Washington: International Monetary Fund, 1985).
22. See George Liska, 'The Third World: Regional Systems and Global Order,' in Robert E. Osgood et al. *Retreat from Empire* (Baltimore: Johns Hopkins University Press, 1973), 279–343. Kissinger had a bit more interest in the Third World earlier in his career, when that was the rage during the Kennedy administration, see Stephen R. Graubard, *Kissinger: Portrait of a Mind* (New York: W. W. Norton, 1977), 170. Osgood argues in *Retreat from Empire* that the Nixon strategy of downgrading

the Third World could be disrupted only by being drawn into another war in the Third World or by Third World 'harassing and importuning' to direct western energies toward economic development. (pp. 19–20.)

23. See Robert O. Keohane, *After Hegemony* (Princeton: Princeton University Press, 1984), 217–40; Linda B. Miller, 'America, Europe, and the Energy Security Dilemma,' in Derek Leebaert, *European Security Prospects for the 1980s* Lexington, MA: D.C. Heath, 1979), 63–78; and Miller, 'Energy and Alliance Politics: Lessons of a Decade,' *The World Today*, 39 (1983): 477–82. Keohane sees the weak institutions for inter-alliance energy policy adopted after the first crisis as representing, in part, a cooperative, power-sharing solution. Miller reflects more on the degree to which the US refused to deal directly with the European Community, as its allies desired, and sees the resulting agreements more as a function of domination; what we would call a further diminution of the consensual basis of America's historical bloc and a further move away from hegemony as the mode of America's supremacy.
24. See Fouad Ajami, 'Global Logic of the Neoconservatives,' *World Politics*, 30 (1978): 450–68. On the 1953 coup see Mark J. Gaisorowski, 'The 1953 *Coup d'Etat* in Iran,' *International Journal of Middle East Studies*, 19 (1987): 261–86.
25. Murphy, 96–105.
26. For a different analysis of this development emphasizing the role of the UNCTAD secretariat see Robert L. Rothstein, *Global Bargaining: UNCTAD and the Quest for a New International Economic Order* (Princeton: Princeton University Press, 1979).
27. See Jeffrey A. Hart, *The New International Economic Order* (London: St. Martin's Press, 1984), 103–42.
28. Craig N. Murphy, 'Why There Can Be No North-South Bargain,' *Polity*, 16 (1984): 529–46.
29. *Structural Conflict: The Third World Against Global Liberalism* (Berkeley: University of California Press, 1985).
30. Anthony Sampson explored both aspects. *The Arms Bazaar* (New York: Bantam, 1978); *The Money Lenders* (New York: Viking, 1981).
31. The country declared its independence in September and was recognized by the United Nations. At the time, the independence movement did not yet hold the capital, but the defeat of the Portuguese and their withdrawal was already assured.
32. On the Angola policy as a whole see Jonathan Kwitny, *Endless Enemies* (New York: Congdon and Weed, 1984), 126–51.

# 8 Force and consensus in the world economy

The reconstruction of American world supremacy in the 1980s took place in the international economy and was primarily the result of the effective use of economic instruments. As we will see in chapter 9, Reagan and his supporters disparaged the traditional superstructures of world economy, international civil society, and often disregarded them. Moreover, the US was in no position to use military force to secure its domination; ever since the Soviet Union acquired nuclear weapons and public opinion began to constrain the use of American forces abroad, large or prolonged military actions had become too risky. But America's political supremacy could be reconsolidated by exploiting the economic primacy the US had enjoyed since the second world war.

Some neorealist scholars still consider Reagan's military policy the key to the effective reassertion of American power in the 1980s, but this is only because they have misunderstood the real challenge to US supremacy in the 1970s. America's challenger was not a newly-assertive Soviet Union, but an alternative economic-political historic bloc emerging in the Third World. The Soviet Union was never as much of a fundamental threat to the post-war western system as OPEC was from 1973 through 1983. Despite the military threat the Soviet Union poses to the west, the socialist bloc plays no fundamental role in the capitalist world economy. The Soviet Union lacks the capacity to aggregate new allied states around itself, as the history of its relations with the Third World has shown. In the 1970s the Soviet Union even faced growing difficulties keeping its supremacy inside its own, relatively small, bloc.[1] And, finally, the Soviet Union's recourse to military force has never been a sign of strength but of a lack of power to change what is economically possible throughout the world.

Of course many of Reagan's partisans see the Soviet Union as the motive force behind the Third World alliance. But, Reagan's real policy appears to have been guided by a more accurate understanding. The policies used to reconstruct American supremacy did not target the Soviet bloc directly; Reagan applied economic pressure to the real sources of the challenge to American supremacy.

The US could use economic instruments so effectively because it still played essential roles in the world economy when Reagan entered office in January 1981; the US still fulfilled Gramsci's precondition for supremacy. It might no longer have the central place in the world oil market and its productivity gains might not match those of its industrialized allies, but, in spite of the growing importance of the Japanese and German currencies in world financial markets, the dollar was still the world's key currency. Moreover, although America's commercial presence had been shrinking, the US still accounted for 23 per cent of world trade. Finance and trade, thus, were levers the United States could use on its industrialized allies and the Third World.

The Reagan administration understood the central economic roles the US played and had a vision of America's global responsibility. Reagan and his supporters had that self-awareness that Gramsci identifies as a necessary requirement of hegemony. In the first year of his presidency, Reagan stated:

> No American contribution can do more for development than a growing, prosperous US economy. ... And as the world's largest single market, a prosperous, growing U.S. economy will mean increased trading opportunities for other nations. Lower U.S. inflation and interest rates will translate into increased availability of financial resources at affordable rates.[2]

His formulation reflects the assumption typical of every hegemonic power: What is good for the hegemon is good for the world. Reagan policy makers believed that renewed American leadership would benefit both western allies and the Third World.

Still, it is difficult to say how premeditated the Reagan administration's strategy for reconstructing American supremacy was. It is difficult to say if at the time Reagan became president his advisors' awareness of US economic power was associated with a clear image of how that power could be put to use. We are inclined to think the result was a mixture of luck and planning. Certainly Reagan's constantly stated faith in the 'magic of the market place' had very little to do with the substance of the reconstruction of American supremacy and his administration's actions aimed at 'freeing' world markets often amounted to nothing more than a way to make Third World countries submit to a new and harsher domination. Yet, some of his advisors seem to have had a very clear idea of how to use US economic power to reconstruct supremacy. In 1984, Henry R. Nau, a former member of Reagan's National Security council argued that the US could pursue the reconstruction of the international economic system on the basis of low inflation, market incentives and free trade without getting into lengthy negotiations with other countries, and that the administration did so because its power over the market was stronger than its power at the negotiating table.[3] When Martin Feldstein chaired Reagan's Council of Economic Advisors he said much the same thing but focused on other sources of US power. In June 1983 he maintained that the US could afford to endure considerable budget deficits over long periods because, contrary to what occurs in other countries, high interest rates in the US attract foreign capital, which would neutralize the deficit and support the dollar.[4] Still, even both of these highly accurate statements about how the US used force in the world economy cannot tell us how premeditated the administration's actions were because the statements were made after the fact, after Reagan's policies were already working to secure American supremacy.

## Reagan's domestic economic policy mix

The American policies that applied force in the world economy were initially conceived of and justified as domestic policies, albeit, as Reagan argued, as ones that would indirectly help the whole world. One month after entering office Reagan announced a long-term program to reinvigorate the American economy by reducing inflation and triggering growth.[5] The program had four key elements: 1) reducing the rate of growth in federal spending, 2) cutting taxes on personal income and business investment, 3) reducing economic regulations, and 4) reducing the growth of the money supply.

### *Theory*

This program, inspired by classical liberal economics, was, more precisely, based on a mix of monetarism and supply-side theory. The 1982 *Economic Report of the President* states, 'What some people have referred to as "monetarism" and "supply-side economics" should be seen as two sides of the same coin—compatible and necessary measures to both reduce inflation and increase economic growth.'[6]

Despite this claim, the theories actually are quite distinct and potentially contradictory. The monetarists' most-respected spokesman, the University of Chicago's Milton Friedman, is one of the most celebrated liberal economists of this century, styled by his supporters as the leader of a 'counterrevolution' against Keynesianism. Friedman criticizes both orthodox Keynesians and those economists who claim to have developed a 'neoclassical synthesis.' He sees a direct relationship between inflation and growth in the money supply as measured by simple monetary aggregates; monetarists deny that wage levels or external shocks (oil-related ones, for example) contribute to the phenomenon. Friedman questions the validity of the Keynesian analysis of the underemployment of factors of production (as a regular consequence of conservative, sub-optimal investment strategies) and holds that recessions are best managed by automatic mechanisms of the market.

Friedman's policy recommendations concentrate on the need to eliminate the budget deficits of sovereign governments that print new money to finance them. This can be done either by reducing governmental activity or imposing new taxes. Monetarists always say inflation must be fought by reducing monetary aggregates. Friedman, focusing his attention on the long-term instead of the Keynesian short term, maintains that even though Keynes was right to argue that new money acts as a stimulus to production, any attempt to overcome the 'natural rate of unemployment' in the short run will be paid for later with higher inflation and unemployment. Nonetheless, monetarists do see the need for regular increases in the money supply proportional to expected increases in production. This can eliminate the incentives that governments may have to interfere in the functioning of the market.

Supply-side economics does not enjoy the same prestige as monetarism; the principal supply-side theorists are not respected economists but professional writers who address the American business community. The economic analysis of Reagan's first chief economic advisor, Harvard's Martin Feldstein, is often presented by supply-siders as contributing to their own views, although Feldstein does not adopt the 'supply-sider' label himself. While they base their ideas upon classical political economy, supply-siders draw inspiration from Jean-Baptiste Say rather than Adam Smith. They believe there is no need to take Keynesian measures due to Say's Law: supply creates its own demand. According to the supply-sider's, Keynesian measures are counterproductive because they reduce incentives. When supply-siders argue for the elimination of government interference in the economy they put special emphasis on how taxes can reduce incentives to work, save, and invest. Thus, the supply-siders argue, lowering tax rates frees resources to expand the economy and may even result in higher governmental revenues, as government takes a sharper wedge out of a larger pie. This is the thesis that Arthur Laffer attempts to demonstrate with his extraordinarily simple formal model, the 'Laffer Curve.'[7]

Monetarism had already been applied in the US well over a year before Reagan's election by Paul Volcker, the man Carter had appointed to head the Federal Reserve.[8] What was fundamentally new in Reagan's policy was the mix of monetarism and supply-side economics. Previously, monetary and fiscal policy had functioned anti-cyclically. Western governments had always used *both* monetary and fiscal policies (lower interest rates and tax reductions) to expand the economy during a recession and to clamp down on the economy in expansionary phases when full employment of resources was reached and inflation generated. The Reagan administration proposed to clamp down on the money supply to try to stop inflation at the same time that it reduced taxes to prod a stagnant economy. The declared aim of this new approach was precisely to avoid the stop-and-go economic policy of the 1970s.

### *Results*

It is ironic that the supposed inadequacy of Keynesian economics is the one thing on which supply-siders and monetarists can agree because, leaving aside the folklore of official explanations, the clearest analysis of what happened following the joint application of monetarist and supply-side measures in the US comes from Keynesian theory. From the Keynesian point of view, Reagan's policies were based on two questionable assumptions which determined most of what followed.

First, as we have seen, monetarists believe governmental deficits financed by printing new money produce inflation. In Keynesian terms this happens when the new money generates such additional effective demand that the productive structure is saturated and cannot respond with sufficient output of new goods, then prices rise. This generates 'demand–pull' inflation, the type of inflation that the United States experienced in the Johnson years, the inflation that began the 'infession' that Nixon had attacked with his new economic policy of 1971.

But, unlike in 1970 or 1971, most of the inflation the United States experienced after the first oil shock was what Keynesians would call 'cost–push' inflation generated by the enormous increase in oil prices.[9] Keynesians accept that a tight money policy can help remove demand–pull inflation without pushing the economy into a recession. But the same policies will assuredly create a recession when they are used to attempt to correct cost–push inflation. This is what happened in the US when monetarist measures were applied at the beginning of the Reagan years.

The second questionable assumption underlying the Reagan policy mix lies at the core of supply-side economics: the conviction that lower taxes would speed up economic activity to such an extent that governmental revenues would remain as high as before the tax cut. Reagan's supporters knew that if Laffer were proved wrong they would either have to make massive cuts in the federal budget or else saddle the US with an unprecedented budget deficit.

Like the supply siders, but for different reasons, Keynesians see tax cuts as one of the possible means to encourage economic activity when production falls below full capacity. Unlike the supply-siders, Keynesians recognize that (other things being equal) the government that cuts taxes to encourage full production will go into debt if for no other reason because there is a time lag between government expenditure and revenue. This, again, is what happened in the US. The federal deficit grew following the tax cuts and it later reached record levels due to an independent increase in military expenditure not matched by reductions in expenditure in other sectors. But the growing budget deficits stimulated and sustained economic activity, eventually pulling the US out of the recession caused by the earlier application of Volcker's monetarist policies.

The sequencing of monetarist and supply-side measures was important. The monetarist brake was already in force when Reagan took office. Volcker, in charge of the extremely independent agency that acts as the United States's central bank, turned the monetary screws down first in late 1979 and again in October, 1980, after relaxing them in the summer. He thus gave Reagan the monetarist policy he wanted before he entered office. (And, parenthetically, despite the summertime relaxations, the downturn caused by Volcker's earlier monetarist brake and the rise in interest rates right before the election gave Carter little help in his reelection campaign.) In contrast, the tax cuts could not become policy until long after their architect became president. Congress had to be convinced. The first 5 per cent cut in personal income tax was applied in October 1981, although few expected it to have a marked effect on spending until after the April 1982 tax-filing date. The two more significant 10 per cent cuts were put in place in July 1982 and July 1983, with their impact on spending starting in 1983 and 1984. (Parenthetically, these tax cuts were perfectly timed to give Reagan an economic boost during his 1984 reelection year.) The different timing in the implementation of the two contradictory theories led first to a sharp recession and then to a strong expansion of the American economy.

On the effects of the monetary brake Reagan's Council of Economic Advisors themselves recognized that in 1981, 'decelerations in monetary growth led to a sharp decline in real output in the final quarter of the year.'[10] Recovery had begun under the Carter administration in the second half of 1980, after a brief relaxation of monetary restraints. It continued in the first quarter of 1981 with growth in real output of 8.6 per cent. But, in reaction to Volcker's new round of monetary restrictions, real GNP declined in the last quarter of 1981 at an annual rate of 5.2 per cent, business investment fell 10.9 per cent, and the unemployment rate rose sharply to 8.8 per cent in December 1981 while inflation declined modestly from 12.6 per cent to 9.6 per cent in 1981.

The tight money policy continued in the first half of 1982[11] and deepened the recession in the US. Real GNP fell by 2 per cent, going back to its 1979 level. Unemployment reached 10.8 per cent, with over 12 million people out of work, the highest figure since the Great Depression. The only positive effect of the two years of monetary squeeze was a reduction in the rate of inflation. The consumer price index fell to 6 per cent, reflecting the recession.

Finally, in 1983 and 1984, the tax cut accelerator of economic activity—accompanied by a new, accommodative monetary policy[12]—made its effects felt. As the *Economic Report of the President* recognized:

> The tax cuts in 1982 and 1983 raised after-tax incomes and therefore contributed to the rise in consumer spending that has been responsible for so much of the recovery ... Increases in consumption expenditures were widespread across various product categories.[13]

In particular, car sales increased substantially in the last quarter of 1982 and throughout 1983. Furniture and household equipment grew by 11.5 per cent in the same year. But, contrary to supply-side predictions that cutting the taxes paid by the rich would increase saving, 'the personal saving rate fell over the course of the year. The average rate for the year, 4.8 per cent, was below the 5.8 per cent rate in 1982 and substantially below the 6.9 per cent average for the 1950–80 period.'[14] As for investments, apart from an increase in residential housing construction starting in the last quarter of 1982 (due to lower than average mortgage rates), business fixed investments and inventory investments only picked up, as Keynesian theory would expect, in the last two quarters of 1983, pushed by consumer spending and by the new tax law's 'accelerated cost recovery system' that allowed businesses to depreciate their fixed investments more rapidly. The result was an economic recovery, with real GNP rising 3.6 per cent during 1983. The recovery strengthened during 1984 with real GNP growing at 6.4 per cent and unemployment declining from 8.1 to 7.1 per cent.

However, the inflation which Keynesians might have expected this growth to generate did not occur. The consumer price index fell to 3.8 per cent in 1983 and only grew to 4.0 per cent in 1984. But the immediate cause of this happy coincidence was external to the US domestic economy, although, as we will see in the next section, it was a complicated, indirect consequence of the earlier monetarist measures. Inflation moderated thanks to falling international commodity prices and to a massive influx of cheap imports which caused a growing current account deficit. Furthermore, contrary to supply-side expectations, the US federal budget deficit grew from around $60 billion in 1980 and 1981, to $111 billion in 1982, and then to around $200 billion in 1983 and 1984.[15]

The results of this peculiar combination of monetarism and supply-side economics pursued by the US from 1980 to 1984 include much more than the cycle of recession and boom at home. These policies have had the consequence, probably unforeseen at that time, of assuring American global supremacy. Both theories, of course, preach reliance on the free-market, but the reconstruction of American supremacy had very little to do with economic liberalization and deregulation. It had to do with the external consequences, both financial and commercial, of Reagan's sequential combination of monetarism and supply-side economics. American economic policy managed first to destroy the precarious unity of the alternative economic-political historical bloc which had grown during the 1970s. Then American policy served to reinforce US hegemony in the western bloc and to spread American domination to the rest of the world. This response, like the monetarist and supply-side mix upon which it was based, took place in two distinct phases, one in 1981 and 1982 and the other in 1983 and 1984. By the end of Reagan's first term his domestic economic policy mix had assured his country's reasserted position.

## Force in the world economy

Many people still assume that the world economic crisis which began in 1980 and lasted until the end of 1982 was caused by the 1979 oil shock, and thus, that it was ultimately triggered by the revolution which deposed the Shah of Iran. Yet even the World Bank, while giving ample justification and intellectual support to industrialized countries' new monetarist policies of the 1980s, recognizes that monetary policy played a significant role in the crisis:

> The contrast between the recovery of the mid-1970s and the continuing recession of the early 1980s has its roots in the policies adopted by the governments of the largest

> industrial countries. In the 1970s these governments reflated their economies out of recession by a conventional combination of fiscal and monetary expansion. By the end of the decade they were dissatisfied with the results. Inflation, though below its 1974 peak, remained stubbornly high. Interest rates had shown a secular tendency to rise. . . . Labor markets had grown increasingly rigid. . . . All these factors, combined with the second surge in oil prices in 1979–80, prompted most governments to change their policies . . . government policies in the industrial countries marked a definite break with the past. In particular, their monetary stance became more restrictive.[16]

Even these remarks, while they recognize the role of monetary policy in sharpening and prolonging the recession, confuse the issue because they refer to a single 1980–82 crisis, instead of two separate ones: one in 1980 and one in 1981–82. This is euphemistically recognized by supporters of the monetarist policies who declare that the recession of 1980–82 was 'W-shaped,' contrary to the oil-induced recession of 1973–75 which was 'V-shaped.'[17] In fact, the industrialized countries quickly pulled out of the recession which followed the oil shock of 1979; recovery began before the end of 1980. But a second recession began in the second quarter of 1981 and lasted until the end of 1982. This was neither due to an increase in oil prices, nor was it a cyclical downturn in economic activity. It was a recession induced by the American monetary policy. The squeeze on the money supply which led to a sharp decline in domestic economic activity in the last quarter of 1981 also cut-short the recovery overseas and started a deeper international recession.

Given the size of the American economy and its linkage to the rest of the world, American domestic economic policy is actually global economic policy.[18] The effects of Volcker's monetary policy were transmitted worldwide by trade and finance. America's trading partners saw their export market shrink. On the financial side, every squeeze on the dollar restricts the growth of the supply of money needed in international transactions; the American monetary policy provoked a liquidity shortage which resulted in a sharp increase in the value of the dollar and a general rise in interest rates. Of course the negative impact of these two effects differed from one part of the world to the next, depending on local economic conditions and the position of a region in the overall world economy. The effects were the most marked in the Third World.

### *Neutralizing OPEC*

The first effect of the American economic crisis was to destroy the leadership of the alternative historical economic-political bloc that had emerged during the 1970s by undercutting OPEC's power.

This result can be considered an implicit aim of America's monetarist policy. Still, OPEC's oil price increases could not be a specific, explicit target of monetarist policies because monetarists deny the separate status of 'cost–push' inflation. They believe that increases in input costs (even increases in salaries above gains in productivity) will not cause inflation as long as the governments tightly control the supply of money. At the micro-level, such tight money policies force managers to reduce input costs or close the factories. At the macro-level, the monetarist medicine for high prices requires accepting recessions as prolonged as necessary to force prices down. OPEC power over the price of oil thus could be an indirect target of monetarist policy. If the global recession were long enough, the price of oil would come down or, at least, its tendency to rise would be contained.

Earlier the US had tried to minimize OPEC's leverage by forming a consumers' cartel and reducing western dependence on OPEC oil. Neither policy worked as well as the deep monetarist recession. Reflecting on his failures, in an interview in *Business Week* in January 1975, Henry Kissinger had even raised the possibility of 'massive political warfare' against some oil producing countries as the only alternative to consumer cooperation to bring oil prices down. Because Europe and Japan feared what an *economic* war against OPEC would do to their economies (dependent on oil, respectively, for 60 per cent and 73 per cent of their energy) the American plan for a consumers' cartel was never implemented. The allies compromised by creating the International Energy Agency (IEA) with its very weak emergency oil-sharing regime and stated aim to reduce western dependence on oil through conservation, more efficient use of alternative supplies of energy, and development of new sources.

The IEA's impact was slight. In the mid-1970s conservation efforts and the development of new energy sources were not carried out with particular zeal because western governments were reassured by the fact that, thanks to global inflation and the primacy of moderate Saudi Arabia in OPEC, after the initial 1973–74 shock, real oil prices decreased by about 15 per cent between 1974 and 1978. While it is true that demand for oil in the western world in 1977 remained at 1973's level while supply was growing, this was mainly due to the recession of 1974–75 and not IEA conservation measures. According to 1977 OECD estimates,[19] barring unexpected policy changes, energy demand would have grown by one third by 1985. The second oil shock, triggered in 1978 by the Iranian revolution and sustained after 1980 by the Iran–Iraq war, found the western world completely unprepared and still dependent on OPEC supplies. While Saudi oil, at official OPEC prices, had only increased to $18.00 per barrel by June 1979, the price on the spot market which reflected the relation between supply and demand had risen to $35.40. After further pressure on the spot market, official prices were fixed by OPEC members at $41.00 per barrel in December, 1980.

The successful increase of oil prices by OPEC members in 1979 and 1980 only lasted until October, 1981 when official oil prices were reduced to $34.00, the first sign of the eventual loss of OPEC's potential for leadership in world affairs. Paul Volcker's tight money policy, at work since October 1979, was responsible. The short recession of 1980 and the longer recession of 1981–82 did what conservation policies and the promotion of new energy sources had failed to do in the 1970s. Between 1979 and 1982, American oil consumption was reduced from nearly 20 million barrels per day to only a little over 16 million. The OECD as a whole reduced its consumption from 40 to 33 million barrels per day. Certainly the huge increase in price in 1979 and 1980 eventually induced some conservation and substitution to reduce oil consumption, but the main factor in the reduction of demand was the world recession. According to an EEC study, 50 per cent of the reduction in oil consumption was due to the recession, 15 per cent to short-term fluctuations in response to the increase in price, 20 per cent to the de-industrialization of some of the oil-dependent regions (permanent plant closings triggered, in great part, by tight money), and only 15 per cent to, 'permanent reductions of energy intensity per GDP unit,' real conservation.[20]

Of course, factors other than the recession played against OPEC. Other sources of energy had become more important and high prices quickly made some non-OPEC sources of oil (Mexico, Alaska, and the North Sea) very significant. From 1979 to 1983 the contribution of oil to total energy consumption fell from 45 to 40 per cent and non-OPEC oil producers increased their total production from about 20 million barrels per day in 1979 to nearly 23 million barrels per day in 1983. Mexico alone increased from 1.6 million barrels a day in 1979 to 3.0 million in 1983. Moreover, after 1979 the oil spot market, an alternative to long-term OPEC contracts, had become increasingly important, thus reducing OPEC's ability to fix and maintain official prices.

But these complementary factors would have had a minor influence in the absences of the recession that the US's monetarist policies induced. OPEC could have resumed its control of prices at the end of 1982 if shrinking demand had not curtailed its members' potential income and made it difficult for them to agree on production cuts. Oil income for OPEC countries as a whole, which had reached $479 billion in 1980, fell to $202 billion in 1982. Given quite rigid international financial commitments and national plans of investment for economic development, the reduction in oil income meant a deterioration in the current account balances of all the OPEC countries. According to similar estimates made by the IMF, OECD and the Bank of International Settlements, OPEC's current account showed a positive balance of more than $110 billion in 1980, but by 1982 it showed a deficit of between $13 and $16 billion.[21] Saudi Arabia and Kuwait, with large financial assets and small populations could stand the blow, but the situation was different for others like Nigeria, Venezuela, and Indonesia. They had large debts and had to face the needs of growing populations. It was politically impossible for those OPEC members to cut production; they were forced to pump more oil to restore falling income to previous levels.

As a result, OPEC's March 1982 decision to defend its price structure by fixing a ceiling for oil production and allocating quotas to member countries could not be enforced. The weakest among OPEC countries could not comply with the agreement and started to produce more than their quota. They began by discounting their oil, saying that a reduction in price would stimulate demand and compensate the initial loss of revenue.

Increased production, price reductions, and falling OPEC income have since gone hand in hand. OPEC reduced its official oil price to $29.00 a barrel in March 1983, but OPEC's current account deficit still increased an additional $24 to $31 billion that year. The very development of the spot market was the result of this overproduction spiral which created an oil glut in the mid-1980s. When this happened OPEC lost its ability to control prices and, therefore, its political leverage. In the last instance OPEC lost its essential function in the world of production—the precondition Gramsci sets for every hegemony—because oil became a commodity in world trade just like any other.

### *The defeat of the Third World*

While OPEC's power was being destroyed by the global recession, few Third World governments realized that a struggle for world supremacy was taking place. Those that did, could do nothing to reverse the outcome and some may not have been eager to if they could have. After all, Third World countries had accepted OPEC leadership despite the drain increasing oil prices had put on their national economies, in the hope of changing the structure of the world economy through implementation of the NIEO. Yet, for its part, OPEC still remained only partly aware of its leadership role and continued to fail to make the economic-corporate sacrifices needed to attain hegemony, even after the second round of price increases. While it is true that OPEC's aid fund was transformed into an international development agency in 1980, by 1984 it was only extending aid to 3 countries in Latin America, 5 in Asia, and 20 in Africa, less than half of the Third World states with major economic problems caused by high oil prices. And even though, compared to OECD states, OPEC states gave unusually high percentages of their national income in aid at the beginning of the decade, the level of foreign assistance accorded was still not adequate to shield Third World countries from the consequences of booming energy prices. Once OPEC's potential for leadership was disrupted by the recession, other Third World countries received even less help and protection.

Force was applied against OPEC mainly through the lever of trade, as the market for oil in depressed industrial economies shrank, but its allies were pressured by a combination of trade and financial measures. As the World Bank recognizes, 'Even those developing countries with excellent growth records had to struggle for modest gains in the face of depressed export markets and high debt servicing costs.'[22]

The rest of the Third World experienced the same trade problems suffered by OPEC. The monetarist recession made the export market for Third World production shrink, reducing the regular growth in international trade, which was 8.5 per cent per year from 1965 to 1975 and still 5.0 per cent a year from 1973 to 1979, to 1.5 per cent in 1980. In 1981 world trade stagnated. In 1982 it fell by 2 per cent.[23] The decrease in Third World exports was accompanied by a parallel decrease in the price of their products. 'The decline in non-fuel commodity prices of importance to developing countries, which began at the end of 1980, continued into 1982. . . . At their lowest point, nominal prices of these commodities had fallen to their 1978 level.'[24] Reagan's economic advisors summarized the situation well:

> The rapid export growth of the 1970s came to an abrupt end in the early 1980s. Exports of the non-oil developing countries actually fell by 7.5 per cent from the first half of 1981 to the first half of 1982. Exporters of primary products were hit particularly hard: real commodity prices fell by 25 per cent from the forth quarter of 1980 to the second quarter of 1982.[25]

As a consequence, developing countries', 'export earnings fell [in 1982] for the second consecutive year . . . the result of declining dollar prices of exports and stagnant volumes.'[26] At the same time, since prices of developed countries' industrial products were not falling, the terms of trade of low-income African countries fell by 13.8 per cent between 1979 and 1982. The decrease for middle-income oil importers was 10.7 per cent. This meant that, 'in real terms—after adjusting for the rise in prices of manufactures imported by developing countries—commodity prices in US dollars were lower in 1982 than at any time since World War II.'[27] The global recession engineered by the US made the Third World less-powerful in the world trading system than it had ever been before in the entire history of American supremacy within the world economy

Trade measures alone were probably enough to bring most Third World countries to their knees. However, monetarism did not just induce an international economic recession, it also reduced international liquidity. The scarcity of the dollar led to an increase of its value and to rising interest rates. From 1979 to 1982 the dollar appreciated against most of the worlds' currencies by between 35 and 40 per cent.[28]

The Third World as a whole could be ambivalent about the dollar's rise. On the one hand it had positive implications for the newly industrializing countries (NICs); by making American products less competitive it facilitated the export of NIC manufactures. On the other it had negative consequences for all Third World debtors (and the most indebted states were the NICs) in that it increased the burden of foreign debts by the same amount of the revaluation.

As for interest rates, the six-month Libor (London Interbank Offer Rate), which determines interest payments on debt for private bank loans, was around 6 per cent in nominal terms during the 1970s, but it had been very low or negative in real terms for most of the decade due to the high rate of inflation. It stood at 16.6 per cent in 1981 and stayed high, in nominal terms, in 1982 at 13.5 per cent.[29] In real terms it *grew* steadily due to the falling rate of inflation. William R. Cline calculates that the difference between the average real interest rate for the period 1961–80 and the real interest rate for 1981 was 5.8 percentage points and 9.3 percentage points for 1982.[30] The Third World had no reason to be ambivalent about these increasing rates. They made borrowing capital—the productive factor which has always been the scarcest in the Third World—much more expensive. They made holding of stocks of commodities for which there was a reduced demand on the world market more costly. And, most of all, they increased the amount of interest indebted countries had to pay at regular maturities enormously. The Third World's annual interest payments doubled between 1979 and 1982 from $24 billion to around $50 billion.

Together, these trade and financial measures disrupted almost every Third World economy. As the World Bank recognizes, most developing countries suffered:

> import reductions because of stagnant or declining foreign exchange earnings, reduced inflows of external capital, and rising debt service requirements; falling government revenues due to declining economic activity . . . ; cutbacks in investment plans and the slowdown of ongoing projects . . . ; [and] shortages of funds to finance the operation and maintenance of existing facilities.[31]

Even if the direct effect of these measures had not been enough to damage the Third World movement, the fact that the negative effects of America's monetarist policies were felt in different degrees in different parts of the Third World, by itself, would have placed an unbearable strain on Third World unity.

The Latin American countries that had borrowed huge amounts to finance their development needs in the 1970s at very low or negative real interest rates suffered the most from the 1980s rising interest rates:

> more than 50 per cent of this debt was at variable interest rates compared with 21 per cent for all other developing countries. By 1982 their debt service burden had risen to 53 per cent of exports compared with 8.6 per cent for East Asian oil importers. To service their debt, they therefore had to reduce their imports, and thus their growth, considerably.[32]

Moreover, considering that Latin American economic policies during the 1970s were oriented toward import substitution, their exports consisted mainly of commodities which suffered a sharp fall in international demand and price. This is why their export earnings declined more dramatically than they did for other developing countries. As a result, with the sole exception of Mexico, the oil exporting country whose expanding production in the face of high debt-servicing demands was contributing to the ultimate defeat of OPEC, Latin American GDP declined by 2 per cent per year in 1981 and 1982.

Sub-Saharan Africa was relatively safe from the impact of increases in interest rates as most of its debt was to official sources at concessional and fixed rates and some of its earnings from the export of primary products were protected by international stabilization agreements, especially the European Community's STABEX scheme. Nevertheless Africa was badly hit by its declining terms of trade. As the World Bank reported in 1983:

> In 1981 and 1982, GDP in Sub-Saharan Africa, excluding Nigeria, grew at an average annual rate of 1.2 per cent and 1.6 per cent. Nigeria [with at least one-quarter of the region's population] experienced negative GDP growth rates in both years (−5.2 per cent in 1981 and −2.4 per cent in 1982) which means that for Sub-Saharan Africa as a whole GDP virtually remained unchanged. Consequently, income per capita declined again. Stagnation in GDP has been accompanied by a marked weakening of the fiscal and balance of payments situation. The burden of debt service payments has become oppressively heavy in a large number of countries, arrears have accumulated, and foreign exchange reserves have dwindled. . . . A situation in which output is persistently growing markedly less rapidly than the estimated 2.7 per cent rate of growth of population clearly cannot be permitted to continue.[33]

To have a more precise idea of the consequences of the international recession on Africa consider that the report prepared by Elliot Berg for the World Bank in 1981[34] had lamented the slowness of African growth in the 1970s. However, during that decade GDP had grown in the continent at an average of 3.6 per cent a year and per capita GNP at 1.6 per cent a year, while in the first two years of the 1980s GDP stagnated and per capita GNP fell.

Asian countries were generally less exposed to the international economic repercussions of American domestic policy than other parts of the Third World. Since Asia as a whole had a considerably smaller external debt than Latin America, the rise in interest rates was less devastating, especially to the Asian NICs. On the trade side, the large countries (especially China and India) were relatively insulated from the international market and their prospects for growth depended more on internal economic measures than on the dynamics of the external world. Asian NICs, while themselves hit by the fall in commodity prices, were in a better position than African and Latin American countries since a large part of their exports to the west are manufactured goods which became cheaper relative to US goods due to the rise in the value of the dollar. Nevertheless, the Asian NICs' brilliant economic success of the 1960 and 1970s was replaced by a period of uncertainty in the early Reagan era. These countries, while growing at a rate of 4 per cent, only grew at half their previous rate and were forced to borrow at very high interest rates on the international market to fill the gap in their trade and payments deficits. Their debt jumped from $94 billion in 1979 to $154 billion at the end of 1982.

Although Third World countries in Africa, Asia and Latin America suffered the consequences of the American-engineered international economic crisis in different ways and to different degrees, the defeat of the Third World as a political entity was total. This defeat was not determined by their diminishing growth rates during the period 1979–82, but rather by their increased dependency on western financial leverage. This dependency had always existed, up to a point, and, indeed, the New International Economic Order program, especially its proposals for linking increases in international liquidity to expanded multilateral development assistance and increasing the Third World role in governing the International Monetary Fund, World Bank, and debt-renegotiation regimes was aimed precisely at overcoming this problem. But, at the end of 1982 external financial constraints had reached a level which prevented any possibility of autonomous national economic policy-making for most Third World governments. Available financial resources had dried up. While Third World countries faced a decline in private lending by banks—alarmed by the debt crisis—and reduced export earnings, they had to comply with increased debt service obligations on a foreign debt which had jumped from $469 billion in 1979 to $751 billion in 1982.

Western economists euphemistically described the Third World's situation as indicating a need for 'structural adjustments' in their domestic economies to adapt to the changed external economic environment. The International Monetary Fund and World Bank proposed solutions that could have been derived from American common sense: Third World governments should force their economies to be more open to the world, allocating all their available resources to increasing exports in order to balance payments as international prices for their products fall, and allowing free capital movements across their frontiers partially in the hope that foreign financiers will invest but also in order to subject themselves to the discipline of local investors whose capital would fly from the country if the government increased its intervention in the economy. Given their capital needs, Third World governments were not even in a position to decide how national revenue was to be distributed among different sectors and social strata. The big international lenders demanded that they re-equilibrate their national budgets and correct what was defined as the 'price distortions' in their economies, policies usually derived from the same Keynesian economic roots and with the same political function of binding together a domestic hegemony as the similar 'social welfare' policies that Reaganism attacked in the developed world.

This attack on government involvement in the economy was much more successful in the Third World than in the developed countries, where subsidies to producers and consumers, government-sanctioned monopolies and whole industries dependent on government contracts, and monumental budget deficits remained. But the NIEO dream of moving toward a more global welfare state was dead. Western suggestions and direction had to be followed in the shaping of Third World economic policy. Third world governments entered a savage competition for survival—a classical liberal's nightmare world, or a Social Darwinist's dream world, of all against all—running the gauntlet of IMF 'structural adjustment' programs to meet the conditions for securing much needed Northern assistance.

### *Crisis in the western bloc*

The force that the US used in the world economy from 1980 to 1982 put stress on the western bloc. This could not be avoided. While a well worked-out plan to reconstruct supremacy should have been oriented toward protecting the allies from the negative consequences of the use of force, America's monetarist policy could not be selective in its effects. During the deep recession even the United States suffered growing unemployment, deindustrialization, farm foreclosures, the bankruptcy of major firms, and bank closings. Reagan was able to at least retain the illusion of the lack of selectivity implied by the old Roosevelt 'politics of productivity' even while the recession engineered by the Federal Reserve contradicted the core of the old social pact by failing to use government to encourage growth.

Europe was particularly affected by the world economic crisis. It came at a moment when Europe's lack of trust in the American ability to shield its allies from oil shocks had been growing. Indeed, the distrust and tension which arose in the first Reagan years were not entirely new, nor did they have only economic causes. Used to living next door to the Soviet Union, the Europeans had always had trouble understanding America's Manichean approach to its adversary; even America's closest European allies were not willing to caricature the Soviet Union as the 'Evil Empire.' Moreover, having progressively expanded their own welfare systems, European governments were more inclined to at least consider Third World requests for a more equitable distribution of the world's wealth. Finally, the fact that the Reagan administration tried to replace the lack of coordination in the western bloc during the 1970s with American leadership based more on force than on consensus was recognized by European governments as demonstrating a lack of sensitivity toward them.[35]

American monetarist policies had a major role in aggravating these tensions. Some European countries, especially the United Kingdom and the Federal Republic of Germany, also adopted stringent monetary measures and were willing to suffer a drop in economic activity to control inflation. But even they did not anticipate or desire the full cumulative results of the external shock derived from US economic policy. There can be an unfortunate snowball effect in the uncoordinated adoption of tight money policies to curb inflation. After the major economic power implements such policies, it becomes rational for the leaders of the next rank of economic powers to do so as well, as a way to avoid an unfortunate disequilibrium in the current account. As the second tier of states adopt such policies the smaller economies linked to them have the same incentive. Inevitably, a pattern of sequential, uncoordinated monetarist policies will have a massive deflationary effect on the world economy; the sum of such policies is likely to be much more than is needed to stop any demand–pull inflation in the world economy. Even though, individually, decisions to start monetarist policies may be rational, overall this is a recipe for a deep worldwide recession.[36] Perhaps recognizing the cumulative effects of snowballing monetarism, some European governments, such as France, tried to follow a different path, reflating their economies, but they were unable to bear the external constraint to their balance of payments. The negative effects all European countries suffered had both financial and commercial causes, as was the case with the Third World.

On the financial side, the high external value of the dollar and high interest rates were a blow to the European economy. While European countries were trying to neutralize the effects of the second oil shock's price increases, which sent inflation soaring, the increasing value of the dollar aggravated the cost–push inflation because oil is priced in dollars. The high American interest rates forced European countries to follow the same path in an attempt to stop the flow of European savings to the American investment market and the risk of a fall in the external value of European currencies, increasing inflationary pressures. High interest rates discouraged productive investments and worsened the European recession. At the Ottawa and Versailles economic summits of the major western economic powers of 1981 and 1982, European governments complained about the strength of the dollar and the high US interest rates, but could not find a common stance to propose to the American government.[37]

On the trade side, European economies were hit by the shrinking of the international market for their exports. In the 1970s they had survived the first oil shock and had even found that the recycling of petrodollars could open new trade opportunities in those expanding Third World economies. Europe therefore tried to find a way to reproduce that situation after the second oil shock. They were happy to enter into trade dialogue with OPEC and the Third World, but the effects of the US monetarist policy made that approach impossible. The growing external deficits of the oil producers forced them to use their available financial resources to keep their economies afloat, while other Third World countries were cutting imports to face the liquidity crisis created by the fall in export earnings and the increase in debt servicing costs. The American market itself, which should have offered new opportunities to European exporters due to the rising dollar, was, in fact, also shrinking under the effect of the recession.

These economic problems corroded one of the pillars of Euro-American solidarity. To make things worse, the new US government, with its reassertion of the cold war, decided to fight the Soviet Union on the economic battlefield and to make Europe join the fight. The US demanded that its European allies support its trade warfare with the Soviet bloc by cutting technological exports and by restricting their export credits. Western Europe needed these eastern European export markets to keep up their production, especially since the recession had destroyed the alternative markets in the OPEC states, Latin American NICs, and the rest of the Third World. The US-European conflict exploded when the American government extended its sanctions against the Soviet Union to cover US subsidiaries and licensees in order to prevent the construction of a gas pipeline between the Soviet Union and western Europe. European governments reacted angrily to the decision. The British Minister of Trade, from the European government that most shared Reagan's liberal economic ideology and his anti-Sovietism, typified the European reaction when he called the American move, 'an attempt to export unemployment from the United States to Europe.'[38]

American and European relations with the third party in the bloc, Japan, were also under stress. Highly competitive Japanese goods were invading the still-depressed American and European markets and industries in the United States and Europe were demanding protective measures. While the American government attributed the huge Japanese commercial surplus to trade restrictions, and, therefore, attempted to force the Japanese to open their markets to imports of goods and services, the European Community studied different forms of protecting their own industry, including a total ban on Japanese imports.[39]

The tensions and conflicts in the western bloc were exemplified by the failure of the 1982 Versailles summit. A commentary in the *Financial Times* read, 'The components of the Western Alliance are coming apart.'[40] The fact is that before 1983 the Reagan administration had not yet come to understand an essential Gramscian lesson: Supremacy can only be maintained by leading a bloc of allies, and, such a bloc can only be maintained by hegemony, not by force.

## Hegemony and domination in the world economy

Beginning in 1983 the United States reconstructed its supremacy in accordance with Gramsci's formula of hegemony within the leadership bloc and domination of adversaries. Reunifying the bloc was less difficult than the deep ideological differences among the western industrialized countries and the troubled state of the world economy at the end of 1982 made it appear.

Commentators who predicted a growing gulf between the United States and Europe in the first two years of the Reagan administration failed to understand the nature of the relationships within the bloc.[41] Japan and Europe expect the United States to support their aspirations for a peaceful and stable world (which they see as enhanced by the normal presence of America's peacetime military forces) and allow it allies to pursue their interests in national economic growth.[42]

Reagan's government had trouble fulfilling both of these expectations during its first two years. America's allies generally felt that the anti-Soviet crusaderism of the right-wing movement of which he was a part put them at risk rather than strengthening their security, although they never challenged American hegemony in security matters.[43] On the economic side, American policies prevented any real possibility of growth.

Positive developments on the security side started to ease European and Japanese fears even before the economic situation improved. The replacement of Secretary of State Alexander Haig with George Schultz helped,[44] as did the November 1982 revocation of the sanctions the US placed on allies who had supported the Soviet gas pipeline. Both acts suggested Reagan was adopting a more pragmatic attitude toward the Soviet Union, an impression that was reinforced by the resumption of dialogue between the superpowers.[45] The changes in American personnel and attitudes were paralleled among the allies by the emergence in November 1982 of a new internationally-minded Japanese Prime Minister, Yasuhiro Nakasone, and by the replacement of Germany's Social-Democratic Chancellor, Helmut Schmidt, with the Christian Democrat, Kohl, after the March 1983 elections. Both new leaders were closer to Reagan on security matters than the men they replaced.

Despite this new conservative wave, some security-related problems remained in 1983 and 1984, particularly in connection with NATO's decision to deploy Pershing II and cruise missiles in western Europe. These political problems had more to do with the relations of European governments to their respective publics than with relations between members of the western bloc. European governments were only too aware that Europe's security depended on the nuclear umbrella provided by the United States; they had no intention of undermining American leadership in that field. On the contrary, their concern was triggered by America's unilateralist, if not isolationist tendencies—that had been present since the beginning of Reagan's presidency—and it was reinforced by the European feeling that America's growing economic ties across the Pacific established a deeper political interest there.[46]

Once the allies' fear that the United States would behave in an irresponsible manner in security matters was eliminated, the US, still had to address the consequences of its economic policies, a problem that 'solved itself' as the consequences of the earlier monetarist policies in the Third World began to be felt along with the effects of the supply-side policy. The fear of rocketing oil prices and of an energy crisis which had haunted Japan and Europe in the 1970s and early 1980s disappeared. Oil was available in large quantities on the spot market and oil prices were still falling. After the relaxation of the American tight money policy (partially as a result of the Mexican debt crisis of the summer of 1982) interest rates began to fall. At the Williamsburg summit in 1983, Europeans who were still complaining about the American budget deficit were told by the US Treasury Secretary that it supported American economic expansion and would eventually pull Europe out of the recession.[47] This claim, which seemed to be based on the weak theoretical grounds of supply-side economics and, therefore, appeared contradictory to those conservative European governments that had adopted the monetarist approach, was perfectly reasonable in Keynesian terms. In fact, the boom engineered by Reagan's unprecedented budget deficits provides most of the explanation of how American hegemony was reconstructed within the western bloc.

While generating growing budget deficits, Reagan's tax cuts promoted American economic recovery, which started in the second quarter of 1983, gathered steam in 1984, and continued in the following years. At the same time, even with the relaxation of the Federal Reserve's tight money policy, the need to finance the growing budget deficits kept interest rates high and, as a consequence, the dollar appreciated by a further 20 per cent from the end of 1982 through 1984, i.e. its relative value increased by 65 per cent over its level at the time of Reagan's election.[48] If America's allies were justified in complaining about American interest rates, which drained their savings and discouraged national investments,[49] they still had less reason to complain in 1983 and 1984 than they had in the first two years of the Reagan government. At that time they had also been suffering from rocketing oil prices and the shrinking of their traditional export markets in the Third World. Now they could count on cheap raw materials and a growing American market for their manufactured goods. The American trade deficit, which doubled from 1982 to 1983 and nearly doubled again in 1984, induced an export-led recovery within the bloc. Between 1982 and 1984, Canada, Japan, and Europe increased their exports toward the American market at annual rate of 19, 25, and 17 per cent respectively.

Of course, the deficit-financed American growth did not spur recovery equally in all parts of the bloc because different industrial market nations have different degrees of integration with the American market. The share of total export sales to the US was 70 per cent for Canada, 30 per cent for Japan, and only 16 per cent for the European Community.[50] The different geo-economic positions of bloc members were reflected in the uneven pace of recovery. Western Europe still suffered from the loss of its traditional export markets (OPEC, the Third World, and eastern Europe) and was not in a position to engineer expansion by itself, as the French attempt to hold back the monetarist wave had proven. The four major European economies grew at only one-third the rate of Canada and Japan in 1983, and at less than half the Canadian and Japanese rate in 1984.

Nevertheless, even Europe grew. When the export-led recovery of the American allies took place, the leadership of the United States within the western bloc was re-established. The reconstruction of American hegemony occurred in accordance with the Gramscian formula. The United States renounced some of the short-term gains that it could have acquired in order to accommodate the interests of its allies. While expanding at a very rapid pace, the

US was willing to suffer the problems associated with a massive increase in imports in order to stimulate economic activity in the bloc. And the resulting trade tensions among the US, Europe, and Japan could be overcome through negotiation more easily in the context of economic expansion. Inter-alliance trade talks had not been as easy throughout Reagan's first two years in office.

The flow of imports into the United States—determined, as we have seen, by the strong national economic expansion in a stagnating world economy coupled with the high value of the dollar—caused a transformation of the American economy. Traditional industries suffered[51] and resources concentrated in the high technology field and the services sector. This process allowed the United States to extend its hegemony not only to the industrialized countries in the bloc, but to the more-industrialized Third World states that were export-oriented and had established trade ties with the American market. This was the case with the Asian NICs: Hong Kong, Singapore, South Korea, and Taiwan. Their existing industrial structure, know-how, relatively cheap and disciplined labor force, and apparent political stability put these countries in an ideal position to take advantage of the growing American export market. They also attracted investment away from the increasingly less-competitive industrial sectors in the US. In South Korea, for instance, real export growth accelerated by over 10 per cent and GDP grew by 9 per cent in 1983–84.[52]

The rest of the Third World continued to suffer under the harsh economic domination which started at the beginning of the decade. In theory things should have been better as western economies expanded and offered new opportunities for export. But after two years of grave economic disruption Third World countries found themselves without foreign exchange and with heavy financial obligations to meet. Interest rates, which had slowly declined in the second half of 1982 and in early 1983, rose again in 1984. High interest rates not only discouraged investment, they also maintained a heavy burden on the indebted developing countries. Annual interest payments on the medium and long-term loans of all developing countries grew a further 14 per cent to $58 billion in 1984.[53] Given the stagnation in the flow of official foreign assistance, developing countries would have needed to run a current account surplus and keep the rate of growth of export earning above the rate of interest in order to meet these growing obligations. This was possible for only a few Third World states. The Third World's debt grew from the very high level of $751 billion it had reached in 1982 to $840 billion in 1984. Furthermore, while the Third World's terms of trade improved in 1984, many raw materials and commodities—which constitute the bulk of exports for most Third World countries—did not undergo the normal cyclical price rise in dollar terms.[54] To cope with this situation many developing countries were forced to cut imports and face sharp negative consequences at home.[55]

A report prepared by the World Bank at the beginning of 1985 provides an excellent summary of the effect of this domination on the Third World:

Growth has slowed in most developing countries. . . . Average per capita real incomes in Africa are no higher than they were in 1970; in much of Latin America they are back to the levels of the mid-1970s. Dozens of countries have lost a decade or more of development.[56]

These words not only attest to the validity of Gramsci's formula about domination outside the bloc, but also to his proposition that, '. . . *laissez-faire* liberalism is a political programme, designed to change—in so far as it is victorious— . . . the distribution of national [and we would add *international*] income.'[57]

## Notes

1. The task the Soviet Union faces in maintaining its bloc should be easier than the one faced by the US since the Soviet bloc is much smaller than the OECD and Third World states dependent upon it.
2. Quoted in Kenneth Oye, Robert Lieber and Donald Rothchild, eds., *Eagle Defiant* (Boston: Little Brown, 1983), 137.
3. *International Reaganomics* (Washington: Georgetown Center for Strategic and International Studies, 1984).
4. Quoted in Richard Feinberg and Valeriana Kallab, eds., *Adjustment Crisis in the Third World* (New Brunswick, NJ: Transaction Books, 1984), 131.
5. *Economic Report of the President 1982* (Washington: United States Government Printing Office), 23.
6. Ibid., 21.
7. See Bruce R. Bartlett, *Reaganomics—Supply-Side Economics in Action* (New York: Quill, 1982); Thomas J. Hailstones, *A Guide to Supply-Side Economics* (Reston, VA: Reston Publishing Company, 1982); and Paul Craig Roberts, *The Supply-Side Revolution* (Cambridge, MA: Harvard University Press, 1984).
8. For a synthetic account of monetary measures during the Carter years, see David P. Calleo, *The Imperious Economy* (Cambridge, MA: Harvard University Press, 1982), 144–50.
9. Monetarists deny the validity of the distinction between demand-pull inflation and cost-push inflation; for them inflation is only generated by an increase in money supply.
10. *Economic Report of the President 1982*, 194.
11. The *Economic Report of the President 1983* says: 'the Federal Reserve reduced the M1 target growth rate range from 3.5 to 6 percent in 1981 to 2.5 to 5.5 percent in 1982. . . . Starting in August, M1 growth began to speed up. By the fourth quarter of 1982, M1 had risen 8.5 percent above its level in the fourth quarter of 1981, well above the upper end of the 1982 target range.' (pp. 139–140.)
12. The *Economic Report of the President 1984* says: 'Growth in the monetary aggregates in the first half of 1983 was high. M1 grew at a 14.5 percent annual rate, up somewhat from the 11.2 percent annual rate over the last 6 months of 1982. . . . The high rates of money growth in the first half of the year were the result of an accommodative monetary policy stance.' (p. 193.)

13. Ibid., 39, 179.
14. Ibid., 180.
15. As Feldstein stated (no doubt much to the horror of his supply-side fans) in the *Economic Report of the President 1984*, economic growth can reduce the cyclical component of the budget deficit but not its structural component: 'a one percent increase in the current level of real GNP growth would reduce the budget deficit by only about $12 billion. It would require an increase of 40 percent in the projected growth rates over the next six years to eliminate the budget deficit by the end of the decade without a change in spending or tax rules.' (p. 36.)
16. *World Development Report 1983* (Oxford: Oxford University Press for the World Bank), 8.
17. Samuel Brittan, 'The World Economy,' in *Foreign Affairs*, 61 (1983): 542.
18. In his article, 'Linkage Effects,' in Sylvia Ann Hewlett, Henry Kaufman and Peter B. Kennen, eds., The Global Repercussions of U.S. Monetary and Fiscal Policy (Cambridge, MA: Ballinger, 1984), Richard Cooper writes: 'It used to be said that when the United States sneezes the rest of the world catches pneumonia. That is probably less true today than it was when Dennis Robinson uttered the phrase thirty years ago. The US share of the world economy has declined steadily over the last quarter century. But it is still true that when the United States sneezes the rest of the world catches cold.' (p. 29.)
19. OECD, *World Energy Outlook* (Paris: 1977).
20. These data are taken from Bichara Khader's presentation to the XI International Conference, 'Development—Interdependence—Cooperation,' organized in October, 1985 by the Pio Manzu Research Centre. The proceedings were published under the title *Oil for Peace* in *Strutture Ambientali*, 75, no.2 (1986).
21. Ibid., 64.
22. *World Development Report 1983*, 7.
23. Ibid., 9.
24. Ibid., 10.
25. *Economic Report of the President 1983*, 73–74.
26. *World Development Report 1983*, 19.
27. Ibid., 11.
28. There has been considerable discussion among economists and several theses have been put forward to explain the progressive revaluation of the dollar in the period 1983–84. Most economists recognize the limited explanatory power of the theory of 'purchasing power parity,' and have looked to other factors such as differences in interest rates (either real or nominal) from one industrialized country to the next, differences in national inflation rates, and the emotional attachment of investors to America as a 'safe haven' for money in a world of economic and political insecurity. In our opinion, all these factors are rooted in the US monetarist policy which made nominal and, more significantly, real interest rates rise. Further, the policy reduced inflation in the US earlier than in other countries and, thus, destabilized the world economy by getting the major industrial powers somewhat out of phase, creating greater uncertainties and risks for investors. We agree with Stephen Marris's conclusion in *Deficits and the Dollar: the World Economy at Risk* (Washington: Institute for International Economics, 1985) that for the later period, the years

1983–84: 'the key factor was that an unusually marked divergence had developed between a strong rise in investment relative to domestic savings in the United States—essentially due to the deterioration in the structural federal budget deficit—and weak investment relative to domestic savings in the rest of the world. Foreign savings were sucked into the United States through the financial markets faster than the U.S. economy's need for them to finance its growing current account deficit.' (pp. 30–1.) Marris's book provides a thorough analysis of the subject (see particularly pp. 16–36). See also the *Economic Report of the President 1983*, 61–6.

29. *World Development Report 1983*, 19.
30. *International Debt and the Stability of the World Economy* (Washington: Institute for International Economics, 1983), 23.
31. *World Development Report 1983*, 24.
32. Ibid., 25.
33. *Sub-Saharan Africa: Progress Report on Development Prospects and Programs* (Washington: World Bank, 1983), i–ii.
34. *Accelerated Development in Sub-Saharan Africa—An Agenda for Action* (Washington: World Bank, 1981).
35. In August 1982 vice-president Bush declared to the press: 'We've heard a lot of protests from our European allies ... I'm sorry. The U.S. is the leader of the free world, and under this Administration we are beginning once again to act like it.' (Quoted in Josef Joffe, 'Europe and America: The Politics of Resentment,' *Foreign Affairs*, 61 (1983): 575–6.)
36. See Michael Stewart, *The Age of Interdependence: Economic Policy in a Shrinking World* (Cambridge, MA: MIT Press, 1984), esp. 60–81.
37. See Robert D. Putnam and Nicholas Bayne, *Hanging Together* (Cambridge, MA: Harvard University Press, 1984), 151–2.
38. Quoted in Andre Gunder Frank, *The European Challenge* (Westport, CT: Lawrence Hill, 1984), 61.
39. Ibid., 41.
40. Quoted in Putnam and Bayne, 167.
41. See Gunder Frank, *The European Challenge*, and John Palmer, *Europe without America?* (Oxford: Oxford University Press, 1987).
42. In the case of the Europeans, speaking only of their aspirations for security and their interests in economic development means, in fact, reducing their political and economic needs to the essentials. Their aspirations were certainly higher and included the kind of desire to see their world outlook established internationally which has typified American foreign policy. However, since the second world war, European governments have clearly perceived that their political disunity would prevent them from attaining any kind of leadership. This impotence caused conflict and frustration inside the alliance, but did not appear to put the external unity of the bloc at stake.
43. This hegemony can never fail until Europe and Japan take responsibility for their own security.
44. On the role of Schultz see Putnam and Bayne, 179.
45. See Stanley Hoffmann, 'The U.S. and Western Europe: Wait and Worry,' *Foreign Affairs*, 63 (1985): 633–4.

46. Ibid., 651.
47. Putnam and Bayne, 187.
48. *Economic Report of the President 1985*, 103–04.
49. It has been calculated that between 1982 and 1984, 40 percent of American private investment, $90 billion, was financed by external capital inflow. Ibid., 101.
50. Ibid., 110.
51. Nigel Harris, *The End of the Third World: The Newly Industrializing Countries and the Decline of an Ideology* (Harmondsworth: Penguin, 1987), 40–4.
52. See *The World Development Report 1985*, 68.
53. Ibid., Table 2.2, p. 19.
54. As the *Economic Report of the President 1985* recognizes: 'Counties that depend heavily on exports of certain raw materials (such as copper, rubber, tin, and oil) have been set back by recent price declines. In general, price trends for exports of developing countries have not been favorable lately: the average dollar price of industrial raw materials (excluding oil) has fallen by almost 15 percent since the end of 1983.' (p. 108)
55. On this subject the *Economic Report of the President 1984* states: 'The increase in the debtors' trade balances have been achieved largely by cutting imports. Cutting imports is the only practical way of achieving a large increase in the trade balance in a short period of time. But, past a certain point, it is difficult to sustain. It means that a population's standard of living is falling, inventories of raw materials and spare parts have been exhausted, and investment is at a standstill. In some cases, inadequate supplies of imported inputs have forced firms to curtail production, even firms producing for export markets.' (p. 72.)
56. *World Development Report 1985*, 1.
57. Antonio Gramsci, *Selections from Prison Notebooks*, Quentin Hoare and Geoffrey Nowell Smith, ed. and trans. (London: Lawrence and Wishart, 1971), 160.

# 9 Force and consensus in international civil society

American policies both within and against international civil society supported the economic limits the US put on both its adversaries and allies in the early 1980s. By 'international civil society' we mean, following Gramsci, the realm in which politics first emerges from the international economy. The concept encompasses the concepts of 'world society,' proposed by John Burton,[1] 'international society,' employed by many British scholars,[2] and 'transnational relations,' advanced by Robert Keohane and Joseph Nye.[3]

While the traditional subjects of international relations are only nation-states, international civil society includes the private non-governmental institutions that reflect and reinforce the aggregation of economic interests and the articulation of the aspirations of those social groups that cross national boundaries. As the 'world society' scholars emphasize, transnational institutions have organized and articulated interests and aspirations for some time. The older, influential private associations include the International Chamber of Commerce, the various international labor federations, and the socialist, communist, and Christian democratic international parties, and even anti-internationalist transnational bodies concerned with promoting the primacy of national interests against those who would claim the priority of global interests. Newer groups of this sort were particularly important to the reconstruction of American supremacy in the 1980s.

Gramsci's theory helps us see that all of these private groups 'work through ideology,' they work by building consensus, not by using force. Therefore, as Gramsci would expect, intellectuals play a central role in these institutions, articulating new visions and defining new bases for consensus. Most of these institutions not only support their own intellectuals, they also attempt to convince intellectuals organically tied to antagonistic groups.

Work toward consensus also characterizes most traditional diplomacy. Those who have advanced the concept of an 'international society' of states point out that the 'anarchy' of international relations is held together by agreement upon some fundamental norms including the rule of equal sovereignty that makes it possible for governments to 'agree to disagree,'[4] as well as the rules of diplomacy, which provide a means for aggregating interests and sharing aspirations.[5]

At times diplomatic activity creates fundamentally new institutions within international civil society, alliances and intergovernmental agencies that have some characteristics of a nascent international political society and global polity.

Intergovernmental agencies involve more than state-to-state cooperation, as those who study transnational relations argue.

Because intergovernmental agencies often consult private associations within international civil society as well as state members, they allow a broader aggregation of interests than can be achieved either by traditional diplomacy or by private associations themselves. Furthermore, in their roles as facilitators of international cooperation, monitors of international agreements, triggers of sanctions used to enforce international agreements, and distributors of development assistance, intergovernmental agencies take on some functions like those of the modern welfare state proper.[6] Finally, intergovernmental agencies have been linked to attempts to form the beginnings of a international state in the wider sense, a world polity, at least among the market-economy states. The initial importance of the United Nations system to the American vision of the post-war world is widely recognized. Equally significant are the innovations in the system that took place when the notion of the responsibility of wealthier nations to aid poorer ones began to gain wide acceptance. Officials of the UN system have long attempted to establish a single worldview shared by all their members. As a result, the UN system itself has become a champion of the interests of those governing elites in the world-economy excluded from the American post-war historical bloc; the UN has become a sort of transnational interest group of the Third World.

Conceivably, one could also include the use of military force by one state against another under the heading of 'international civil society' if it was considered (as many internationalists do) a 'private' use of violence in the international system (one not sanctioned by political society) similar to the private violence in domestic civil society of the Ku Klux Klan in the United States or the fascist paramilitary groups in Italy in Gramsci's time. This interpretation has some very interesting implications, but we will not adopt it here simply because interstate violence remains much more legitimate than the organized private violence that occurs in domestic civil society where the state maintains the monopoly of legitimate violence.

## The rhetorical value of Reagan's use of military force

Nonetheless, interstate violence can be initiated as part of a strategy that focuses on civil society. This, we believe, was the case with the Reagan administration's deployment of military force in the Third World. The administration used the military to make a policy of coercive diplomacy in the Third World credible. To do so it took on battles that the United States was sure to win (Grenada), maintained arms-length military support but massive propaganda support for conservative opposition movements (Nicaragua, Angola, Afghanistan), and backed-away from serious fights against effective and well-armed adversaries (in Lebanon and Iran) that would have confronted the US with the dilemma it faced in Vietnam: losing a war or escalating violence to levels that the American public, and perhaps the Soviet Union, would not accept.

The major targets of this policy were in the core of America's historical bloc; the use of military force in the Third World was an issue of domestic politics in the United States and an issue of inter-alliance relations. A constant theme throughout Reagan's first campaign was the need to overcome the legacy of Vietnam. Reagan's military interventions have demonstrated that different groups affected by the 'Vietnam syndrome' will choose to stand behind the use of force in the Third World. What was achieved by this was not so much the immediate goals of the various military campaigns; they have generally been very insignificant. But each deployment of military force increases the legitimacy of that tool and enhances the credibility of the more significant *threats* to use force that characterize coercive diplomacy. Reagan's small deployments of force in the Third World enhanced the message of his simultaneous military buildup: The US might once again do everything it can to protect its interests anywhere.

Thus, the targets of the Grenada invasion included the American public at large (who were given a longed-for victory), America's allies in the Caribbean (who were required to invite US intervention), and the members of the Organization of American States (who risked significant economic hardships if they did not condone this reaffirmation of the United States's right to remove unfriendly governments in the hemisphere). In the same way, one major target of Reagan's low-level wars in Nicaragua, Angola, and elsewhere has been the Congress which had to be convinced to remove or ignore legislative impediments in order to increase the credibility of American coercive diplomacy. Similarly, the American 'retaliation' on Libya required America's European allies to support the use of NATO bases against the Third World, making the possibility of the international projection of American forces from its worldwide network seem much more real than it was in the late-Vietnam era when European displeasure with US policy in southeast Asia tended to restrict America's NATO forces and bases to NATO duty.

Reagan's use of military force has come under a great deal of scrutiny by journalists and the US Congress. In the final year of the Reagan administration public attention focused on the extent its low-level military conflicts with Third World states (in particular in Central America and the Gulf). Without telling Congress or the public, members of the Reagan administration made an inconsistent effort to reestablish the United States's role as the 'free' world's policeman, to act as if an international political society existed within the boundaries of American influence and as if American military and intelligence services were the agencies of this international state proper.[7]

Despite all the attention that the press and Congress have paid to them, the secret wars guided by the CIA and Reagan's National Security Council staff were far from the most significant policies his supporters pursued in their attempt to restructure the international superstructure to secure American supremacy. Although often maligned by administration rhetoric, private persuasion, traditional diplomacy, and policies aimed at intergovernmental institutions were all much more important to the quest for supremacy.

## Force in international civil society

Reagan and his supporters sometimes appear to deny the existence of international civil society. They always deny its necessity. And they seem to be of two minds about its significance. This attitude comes from the extension of the atomistic assumptions of liberalism to the international sphere. The most consistent version of the administration's position on international civil society recognizes its existence in order to claim that intergovernmental agencies play a primarily negative role in world affairs because they support the Third World alliance. Reagan and his supporters deny that international institutions have played any essential role in assuring the operation of a global market economy; they hold, alternatively, that state-like domination of the US has been needed to keep states cooperating through market mechanisms. As a result, the Reagan administration has looked for ways to use traditional diplomacy and the intergovernmental agencies to transmit and reinforce its economic priorities to Third World governments; at the same time it has sought to deny them the power of intergovernmental agencies.

### *With allies and intergovernmental agencies in policy dialogue*

Foreign assistance provided the Reagan administration with an important lever on the Third World. By the end of Reagan's first term the practice of using international development agencies and the coordinated aid of western donors to impose economic policies upon Third World states was secured by what the Reagan administration called 'policy dialogue,' one of the 'four pillars' of American aid policy, along with strengthening the private sector in the Third World, transferring American technology by having Third World countries make it highly profitable for American firms to invest there, and 'institution building,' meaning training Third World leaders (both public and private) in the United States.[8] The explanation of policy dialogue given to Congress by AID is worth quoting at length:

> *Policy Dialogue*: Domestic policies are the dominant influence on the development prospects of any country in the long run. Foreign assistance is relatively ineffective in developing countries with countervailing policies. Food pricing policies, for example, are vital to stimulating (or depressing) agricultural production, and increased production is crucial for food security as well as rural employment in many countries. Policy reforms are needed in many sectors, but desirable reforms are often locally contentious. Policy dialogues with recipient governments can initiate needed reforms, and our assistance can

smooth the path of such reforms in some countries. I wish to assure that we are concerned with equity as well as efficiency of the policy reforms that we underwrite via policy dialogue.[9]

Despite the very positive vision suggested here, policy dialogue became one of those forms of rule that lies on the continuum between force and consensus, between coercive diplomacy and unconstrained international cooperation. Due to the critical Third World needs for assistance in the wake of the worldwide recession in the early 1980s, there can be no question that at the time the Reagan administration first made policy dialogue a pillar of foreign assistance it was more a form of coercive diplomacy. This new policy direction meant that the United States demanded changes in Third World domestic economic policies in exchange for aid. At a micro level the US would look for 'institutional impediments' to the desired results of each project funded in part with US funds and demand their removal. Typically, in Africa, where the US came to support a number of land-reclamation and irrigation projects, AID would argue that government price controls on food would reduce the incentives of landowners to make the greatest possible use of the new resources a proposed project would provide; therefore, price controls would have to go if the US was to support the project.[10]

The US also demanded broader sector-level policy dialogue and macroeconomic policy dialogue, discussions in which an aid recipient's entire range of domestic economic policies could be scrutinized and American development administrators could select those that would have to be changed in exchange for broader foreign assistance, not just the funding of individual development projects, but the provision of broader 'structural adjustment' loans from the International Monetary Fund or the World Bank.[11] Invariably, the policy advice recommended throughout the Reagan years amounted to an export of Reaganomics to the Third World. Third World governments were asked to emphasize their local private sectors and to make their countries open to American investment (the two substantive 'pillars' of AID's policy under Reagan) and Third World governments were also asked to adopt the four domestic economic goals that Reagan had proposed for the United States in his first budget message: a smaller central government, lower taxes, less regulation, and tighter control of the money supply to reduce inflation.

For the moment we do not wish to consider whether or not these policy prescriptions were wise. We want to first consider the political question, the issue of force versus consensus. Even what might be, in the end, highly enlightened (albeit, paternal) policy changes achieved through this sort of dialogue represent the use of force in international civil society, force explicitly aimed at transforming the Third World alliance. Policy dialogue tried to remake aid-receiving governments in the image of the Reagan administration and its most conservative allies in the west.

Moreover, policy dialogue was never simply one of the Reagan administration's means of using force against the Third World alliance *within* international civil society, it has always been a policy aimed *against* institutions of international civil society, against the independent development of north–south economic diplomacy by other OECD states and against the independence of western-funded international financial institutions. Policy dialogue not only means dialogue between the United States and aid recipients, it also means dialogue among donors to assure that all of them are holding back aid commitments in order to assure the same type of policy changes. After all, as a tactic of influence, policy dialogue would hardly have worked if the only sanctions that the US could use were those provided by its small economic aid budget. American aid allocations grew under Reagan, but the part available to back policy dialogue actually shrank as a greater emphasis was placed on military aid and as American aid became more concentrated in a small group of countries with which the US had security ties. Coordination reduced the scope for independent judgment by the other major donors. It was an essential means of husbanding American aid resources by using the aid given by other donors in policy dialogue.

Ironically, the whole idea of 'policy dialogue' as negotiations that explicitly link the funding of aid projects to broad economic liberalization was originally an independently developed idea of the World Bank. The concept first appears in Elliot Berg's 1981 report, *Accelerated Development in Sub-Saharan Africa*.[12] It refers to a means for achieving the *laissez-faire* liberal north–south social pact that Berg recommends in lieu of the NIEO or the global Keynesian social pact suggested by the Brandt Commission or the basic needs theorists within the Bank. Instead, Berg offers more aid to Third World governments in exchange for domestic liberalizations.

'Policy dialogue' first appears in official American aid justifications in 1982. As it becomes progressively more prominent, its meaning changes. By 1983 'policy dialogue' meant making all aid contingent on liberalizing reforms; the idea of increasing flows of aid was lost.[13] By 1985, after policy dialogue had become on of the 'four pillars,' US aid policy makers had decided that such quasi-coercive diplomacy was the only way to get Third World countries to initiate liberalizing reforms as well as the only back-up system needed to find solutions to problems as reforms are instituted. Furthermore, they had decided that policy dialogue was no longer just for Africa. It would be required of every state, and, in fact, must be 'coordinated' with other donor states and intergovernmental agencies, as well, to keep them all focused on encouraging private enterprise and freeing markets.

Berg's report was the first of a number of international agency documents which helped convince many donor governments that less-industrialized nations have only themselves to blame for their economic woes. Therefore, most donors accepted that the best remedy for such ills was considered domestic policy reform. The idea of coordination among donor countries was generated by powerful intergovernmental agencies even earlier. The OECD began discussing technical aspects of aid coordination in the 1970s. Initially, coordination was designed to avoid overlapping foreign assistance commitments and all-out commercial competition among donor countries and to assure a more efficient allocation of resources through the complementarity of various types of development intervention. This remains the argument that most of America's allies advance in favor of broad coordination, the rules for which were formalized at the suggestion of the American delegation in a joint statement of the Development Assistance Committee in 1983,[14] but even such 'technical' coordination takes on a new valence in the new international context of reasserted American power and general inter-allied agreement on the need for Third World policy reforms.

Furthermore, in the wake of the global recession, the bilateral donors indirectly ended up coordinating their assistance around the US's economic vision due to the key roles played by the World Bank and International Monetary Fund in 'structural adjustment' assistance. What they, especially the Fund, demanded in exchange for absolutely critically-needed funds was exactly the sort of liberalizing domestic policy reforms that the conservative economists of the Reagan administration attempted to export. Deference to the Fund's analysis of macroeconomic policies which may influence balance of payments problems assures that when it denies 'structural adjustment' assistance because a Third World government has not agreed to sufficient policy reforms, funds from the World Bank and the bilateral donors dry-up as well. Contrastingly, when the Fund certifies a Third World government as engaging in significant policy reforms, funds from all sources start to flow.

### *Against intergovernmental agencies*

In the early 1980s, G. K. Helleiner, who advised Tanzania when that country put up unusual resistance to the IMF's structural adjustment demands, argued that the wave of structural adjustment discussions that the IMF would have to engage in the wake of Africa's depression and the financial problems of the large NIC debtors might have some positive outcomes. It might prove a learning experience for Fund economists, who might modify their monetarist orthodoxy and fear of inflation so organic to the agency's original, narrowly-conceived role as the protector of the value of its member's currencies.[15] Helleiner's argument makes sense. The bureaucratic imperative of actually accomplishing an institution's stated mission—in this case, actually assuring the kind of adjustments that would end cycles of indebtedness—provides policy-makers with one of the most powerful incentives to give up old ideas and try new ones. Yet, the Fund did not change its views, and not because its structural adjustment ideas actually worked; in fact, Helleiner's fears about the continuing debt and stagnation in Africa under a monetarist regime proved accurate. But he failed to see that Fund staffers were under even a more powerful bureaucratic pressure to become all the more committed to their orthodoxy, the fear that their institution might disappear altogether if they did not.

The fears of IMF or World Bank economists were magnified in the secretariats of most of the other UN agencies. From its beginning, the movement that brought Reagan to power in the United States had targeted international organizations. In particular, the influential Heritage Foundation argued for:

> ... American withdrawal from a UN system it could no longer dominate. The title of recent publications testify to the Foundation's hostility toward the UN: *The PLO's valuable Ally: The UN; The UN's Economic Credo: The Way the World does not Work; Spotlighting the UN's Anti-American Record; The Many Ways the UN Serves the USSR* and so on.[16]

The Reagan administration accepted much the Heritage Foundation's analysis, but did so almost exclusively as part of a strategy to change the way the intergovernmental organization system acted as in intermediary between the developed nations and the Third World. Reagan did not mount the concerted attack on the UN system that he could have. He fought international organizations only as a way to make them an instrument of US policy in its fight against the Third World.

In retrospect, the administration's most brilliant, if paradoxical and unconscious, tactic in this battle was to first threaten the two agencies involved in development where, in the past, the United States had been the most successful at thwarting Third World initiatives, the IMF and the World Bank. Policymakers in both agencies agree that one result of the major review of American involvement in international lending agencies initiated by the Reagan administration in its first days[17] was a reaffirmation by the IMF, World Bank, and regional development banks that the purpose of development aid was to foster open economies, a purpose that many American officials felt the banks had lost sight of in the 1970s under the influence of McNamara's direct assault on poverty. An even more important result was the fear of displeasing the United States that the review created among officials in agencies traditionally antagonistic to American views; if Reagan would threaten the IMF who knows what he would do to more pro-Third World institutions like UNIDO, the UNDP, or UNCTAD?

In fact, Reagan did very little. It would have been costly for the United States to have to find ways to accomplish all the many things that the United Nations specialized agencies do that powerful interests in the US consider important. Although the administration threatened to withdraw, Reagan did not pull out of the International Telecommunication Union, UNCTAD, or a host of other agencies. But he did make his threats to withdraw credible by withdrawing from one prominent agency that was a source of ideological opposition to his views,

UNESCO. This was not a very costly act. UNESCO's major operations involve creating autonomous international non-governmental organizations for cooperation in every field of science, education, and culture. That means that while there are many interest groups in the United States involved in international scientific and cultural cooperation that never would have existed without UNESCO, no large constituency in the US actually relies upon the agency at any given moment.

UNESCO even had enemies among those Americans least-likely to be in Reagan's camp. UNESCO was not popular among American intellectuals and journalists due to its proposals for a 'New International Communication Order,' which, for a brief time, seemed designed to assure growing state control of the press. Equally negative in many Americans' eyes were the agency's condemnations of Israel. Finally, to top things off, UNESCO has long been plagued with such bad management that even America's most knee-jerk internationalists had little good to say about it.

It is clear that in withdrawing from UNESCO the American government's concern with demonstrating the credibility of its general threat to undo the international organization system was more important than worries about restrictions on the press, the status of Israel, wasted funds, or even the Soviet Union's influence over the Third World. In the year required between the US's notification and its actual withdrawal almost all of its original complaints about the agency, especially the issues of internal management and the New International Communication Order, had been resolved.[18] The Reagan administration did not stay to secure those reforms. It left, making the Soviet Union the largest contributor to UNESCO and the major force in the agency, ironically, a more powerful force than it would have been before the reforms aimed at preventing US withdrawal had been enacted: the US had demanded greater accountability of the agency to those countries who paid most of its bills.

Reagan and his supporters continued to press for this kind of accountability throughout the United Nations system. Congress, pressed to find funds to pay for the unfathomable new budget deficits and always closer to the popular isolationist impulse than most presidents are, found Reagan's policy enticing. They supported an amendment to America's annual provision of funds to international agencies first proposed by Kansas Republican Nancy Kassebaum. The amendment holds back America's regular dues to intergovernmental agencies until they adopt some form of voting weighted by financial contribution. This would assure a level of American influence in the entire intergovernmental organization system as great as it had in the World Bank or International Monetary Fund.

Of course, given the complex forces that lead to different international agencies having different voting systems, the Kassebaum demand was never completely realistic. However, the administration used the Kassebaum amendment to keep all intergovernmental organizations on a short financial string.

Thus, it could explicitly use the power that has always been implicit in the US's role as the largest contributor to most agencies. The US cut the funds available for intergovernmental cooperation by going as far in arrears on its dues as possible without losing its vote, creating a massive financial crisis in the UN and encouraging the agencies to modify their views on north–south economic relations to try to please their delinquent contributor.

Even agencies which generally supported Reagan's views about the Third World such as the Inter-American Development Bank felt the push for proportional voting.[19] More significantly, the US even kept the powerful intergovernmental agencies in which it had a preponderant voice, the IMF and World Bank, on a short financial tether. At each point at which the question of increasing the resources for the multilateral agencies came up, the Reagan administration responded by demanding that any new finances only be given in exchange for the institutions' more strict adherence to American economic policy preferences in recipient states, and, in the end, in each case, despite new procedures or commitments to make the agencies better conduits of Reaganomics, only a small extension of resources was allowed.[20]

At the cost of only a small loss of power in UNESCO the Reagan administration successfully turned the intergovernmental agencies around in just a few years. By the end of Reagan's first term, no longer was the demand for a New International Economic Order or the need to meet basic human needs the central focus of their debates and policies.

### *Ending negotiations to reform international institutions*

The Reagan administration's attack on the New International Economic Order was at times a bit more direct. Under Reagan the US simply stopped negotiations aimed at reforming intergovernmental agencies along NIEO lines. In the long run probably the most significant case was Reagan's rejection of the Law of the Sea Treaty. The treaty established the principle that there were resources outside the control of national governments or private adventurers, resources that are a 'common heritage' of humankind. Even though it had been painstakingly negotiated for years, and, for the most part, under Republican presidents, Reagan refused to sign the treaty completed almost as he took office. The part of the treaty that the administration found the most objectionable would have set up the first system of global taxation from the proceeds of deep-seabed mining.

Despite the Reagan administration's quick rejection of the Law of the Sea Treaty, the illusion that the NIEO might come to pass persisted well into his first administration. When Reagan was elected most advocates of the NIEO had been focusing their attention on the problem of negotiating procedures. The Third World alliance proposed a series of 'global negotiations' on different topics in the different functional intergovernmental agencies—money issues in the IMF, aid issues in the UNDP and World Bank, trade issues in UNCTAD and the GATT, issues of the transfer of technology in UNIDO and the World Intellectual Property Organization, etc. All of these negotiations would be subject to some form of oversight from the General Assembly. Throughout the Carter administration the United States and a few of its most significant allies differed with the Third World only over whether the final venue for substantive negotiations would be the functional organizations (which the wealthy states control) or the General Assembly, where the Third World has an automatic majority. Of course, this seemingly 'minor' disagreement was fundamental.

The stalemate would have been permanent had it not been for the work of the private group of business-people, development professionals, and policy makers from both the First and Third World called together by former West German Chancellor and leader of the Socialist International, Willy Brandt. In their 1980 report,[21] the Brandt Commission proposed that a small meeting of key heads of government of first and Third World countries be called to try to overcome the impasse in global negotiations.

Austria and Mexico agreed to organize such a summit, but it was delayed because Carter decided that the new administration should be the one to decide if the United States should take part. Before Reagan took office Mexico's president, Lopez Portillo, raised the question of the summit. In a captivating series of events played-out before televisions audiences on both sides of the border Portillo presented Reagan a handsome white horse and Reagan announced that he would attend the summit, as long as it would really be nothing more than a general philosophical discussion of development, free from substantive negotiations and even without a final communique, and as long as Cuba was excluded.

Reagan used the summit in the Mexican resort of Cancun as an opportunity to lecture Third World leaders on Reaganomics and offer American technical assistance to Third World governments that wanted to emulate his domestic policies. He did not agree to launch global negotiations, but said that he was doing more than other presidents to aid the Third World just by giving the American economy its own dose of the Reagan medicine. When steady, non-inflationary growth was restored in the US, things would look up for the Third World.[22] Afterwards, the US simply refused to engage in global negotiations, forcing the north–south dialogue to a stall. Without the US, such negotiations seemed pointless.

## International civil society and attempts to extend hegemony to the Third World

Reagan's pronouncements were typical of the other side of American actions toward the Third World in international civil society throughout the 1980s. At times Reagan and his followers did more than apply force through coercive diplomacy and international agencies, they attempted to convince their adversaries in the Third World and intellectuals everywhere of the soundness of America's economic prescriptions, even though a few of Reagan's own economic advisors and economists working with the intergovernmental agencies most sympathetic to Reagan's policies understood many of the weaknesses of the programs the US advocated. If they had succeeded in convincing leaders throughout the Third World, the resulting hegemony just would have been another form of domination, one based on deception and fraud, the opposite of ethical hegemony.

Three things lead us to this conclusion. First, there is the evidence that many intellectuals in the movement of which Reagan was a part were not willing to treat their Third World adversaries as intellectual and moral equals, as people whose good judgment could be trusted to lead them to rational, ethical conclusions, a supposition of ethical hegemony. Second, there are all the inconsistencies in the Reaganomic analysis of Third World problems. Finally, there are the ways in which America's applications of force in international civil society have slowed criticism of these inconsistencies and made the formation of alternative visions more difficult.

We have chosen one example to illustrate the first point, a product of one of the newer private institutions established as part of America's 'right turn' in the 1970s when business began to take a more direct interest in both politics and intellectual life.[23] This Institute for Contemporary Studies volume[24] edited by W. Scott Thompson (whose landmark 1969 study of Kwame Nkrumah's foreign policy[25] was one of the first scholarly analyses of international relations in the Third World) exemplifies the authoritative way in which conservative groups tried to convince western audiences that the problem of the Third World had been given disproportionate emphasis in the 1970s. At the same time the volume betrays the movement's lack of interest in engaging in any real dialogue with the Third World alliance.

In that book we learn from Kenneth Adelman, who worked to stall global negotiations as a part of the US team at the UN and later became Reagan's director of the Arms Control and Disarmament Agency, that without the United Nations there would be no Third World.[26] That is, without the incentive to unite African, Asian, and Latin American elite opinion provided by the goal of development written into the UN Charter and without the quasi-Parliamentary structure of the intergovernmental agencies, the Third World political movement would never have formed. This statement might be convincing to many Third World officials, and it could easily provide the foundation for a convincing argument that many Third World governments should give up their support for an alliance that has come to contradict their interests. But this volume clearly was not directed toward Third World elites; its image of them is too demeaning. Richard E. Bissell amplifies Adelman's view by saying that the General Assembly's call for a New International Economic Order was an international attack on the entrepreneurial middle class, designed by Third World leaders to strengthen the state against this dynamic sector.[27] Of course, this analysis would probably be convincing to those members of the organizational bourgeoisie who rely upon positions in business more than in government. But even they would be insulted by Bissell's further conclusion that the demands for a New International Economic Order are the result of 'cultural backwardness' and the lack of the 'spirit' shared by the people who settled the United States. (Significantly, the business elites of Brazil and South Africa are excluded from this condemnation.)[28] And Thompson tells us that the ideology of Third Worldism informing the New International Economic Order program should not even be dignified by the term 'ideology.' It is too incoherent.[29] He later implies this is because many of its advocates, '. . . do not share the traditions of reason that long marked political development in the West.'[30] From across the Atlantic, Max Beloff makes the point more explicit, the NIEO merely reflects 'black racism,' an envious attack on the success of white-dominated societies.[31] As Thompson states at the beginning of the text, there is no Third World, just places that are not of the US camp and not of the Soviet camp.

Thompson's book may have provided a convincing and coherent analysis of problems of the Third World to those members of the new right wing coalitions in the United States, Britain, and even other parts of the western alliance whose views are dominated by the specter of Soviet communism; by quietly bringing up themes linked to the American tradition of elite racism, the analysts have helped explain away the problem of the Third World and reinforced the case for the American common sense solutions to development problems. But the book was not designed to convince the Third World.

Yet, extending America's reconstituted hegemony beyond the western bloc did mean convincing the Third World that no reasonable alternative to Reaganomics existed. Reagan certainly had many supporters who believed this and who could address officials from the Third World without denigrating them. Other supporters were able to repeat the theme that there was no alternative to conservative domestic economic policies with unusual conviction and forcefulness. But, as Gramsci suggests of the litanies repeated by even the most compassionate or eloquent of village priests, if you listen closely, the lessons still may not make sense.

Of course, very coherent, sophisticated, and convincing versions of the lessons Reagan offered in Cancun can be found. Even before Reagan's election conservative American and British economists played significant advisory roles in the Third World. University economic departments dominated by monetarists, especially Milton Friedman's at the University of Chicago, have a long history as institutions of international civil society, advising rightist governments in the Third World and training people who become officials, especially in treasury ministries, even in some of the more 'radical' Third World states. The 'Chicago Boys' offer a strong medicine of devaluations, limits to government, and (often) restricted domestic credit to their Third World clients. As with Reaganomics at home, the formula appeals to those entrepreneurs in advantageous positions in the Third World because it promises 'survival of the fittest.' As one advocate says about Chile's experience following Chicago advice:

Many of Chile's businesses needed high tariffs to survive. When forced to compete, a lot of them went under. But those that survived and learned to compete prospered.[32]

The significance of the more conservative international centers for training economists increased in the 1980s when intergovernmental development agencies, especially the World Bank, increasingly began to turn to them for innovative analyses of Third World economic stagnation. An agency's bureaucratic imperative to learn why it has failed at a core mission can lead to considering a wide variety of different solutions, from the direct attack on poverty popular in the Bank in the 1970s to the attack on Third World domestic policies that typified the 1980s. This was the organizational context of Elliot Berg's study of Africa for the Bank.

The report's basic recommendations about liberalizing international trade and moving toward market rates of exchange, using resources more efficiently in the public sector, improving agricultural policies to give more incentives to farmers, and doubling western aid to Africa in the 1980s contained much that was appealing to some entrepreneurial elites in the Third World as well as a wide spectrum of professionals involved in development. The report recast some of the more 'radical' themes in old development debates in a new, more 'tough-minded' language. It makes a powerfully persuasive case for significantly increasing aid to the continent as a necessary incentive to governments to undertake the policy liberalizations designed to trigger accelerated development. Even the report's call for increasing returns to African farmers was a position shared by domestic critics of African development policies from both the left and the right.[33] But this hardly means that a sound case could be made for adopting the *entire* Reaganomic package in all parts of the Third World.

Reagan's own policy advisors recognized that the main causes of the Third World's immediate economic problems were not state intervention and price distortion. The *Economic Report of the President 1984*, which is addressed to an American audience, and, therefore, need not repeat the litanies the administration read to the Third World as part of the ideological struggle, notes that faulty Third World domestic policies cannot even be blamed for the problems of the major debtors or the banks that loaned them vast sums in the 1970s. Prior to the recession at the beginning of the 1980s, the economic outlook for these countries was excellent.[34] After the recession, they faced the same problems faced by the rest of the Third World:

First, inflation rates fell and real interest rates rose in the United States and in other countries. ... Second came the 1980–82 world recession. ... A third factor that contributed to the debtors' loss of export revenue was the large appreciation of the dollar. . . . A fourth factor for some countries was the decline in oil prices after 1981. . . . It is worth noting that virtually all the major Latin American countries got into trouble, the oil exporters as well as the oil importers, those that followed monetarist and free market policies as well as those that increased the money growth rate and expanded the role of government in the economy.[35]

The adoption of Reaganomic policies does not even explain the success of the east Asian NICs after the American recovery. Third World states with rapidly growing economies can still have big central governments, high taxes, lots of regulation, protectionist trade policies, and relatively loose credit. What distinguished the east Asian 'Gang of Four' was the export orientation of their manufacturing sectors which allowed them to take advantage of the expanding market in the US.[36]

Not only have domestic policy suggestions offered by the US government to the Third World often been inconsistent with its own most authoritative economic analysis, they have been inconsistent with American practice. American authorities have never explained why growing US budget deficits are good for the world economy while Third World deficits must be cut through IMF 'structural adjustment' programs.

The stated American faith in 'structural adjustment,' in and of itself, often seems strange. But, then, the IMF and World Bank have never really looked at all the ways that Third World economies could be adjusted to the new external conditions. They have simply pushed for turning Third World economies toward exports and reducing state intervention in the economy. This has not led to successful 'adjustment' in the majority of cases in the Third World, at least if such success is to be indicated by a return to growth rates at least as high as those before the recession.

The inadequacy of this policy advice can be illustrated by the Berg report's optimistic forecasts for boosting the African economies through a series of measures, including liberalizing policy reforms. A follow-up report in 1984 continued to promote the same measures without noticing that, if anything, a degree of such liberalization had taken place in Africa since the earlier report, yet:

Gross domestic product (GDP) grew at an average of 3.6 percent a year between 1970 and 1980, but has fallen every year since then. With population rising at over 3 percent a year, income per capita in 1983 is estimated to be about 4 percent below its 1970 level. Agriculture per capita has continued to decline, so food imports have increased; they now provide about a fifth of the region's cereal requirements. Much industrial capacity stands idle . . . [37]

The World Bank refused to see the primary cause of Africa's economic decline in the years between the two reports as external financial and commercial constraints. Instead, they continued to blame Africa's low rate of return on private investment which they continued to see as the result of inappropriate economic policies, which still needed to be modified through policy reforms designed to eliminate state intervention.

The inadequacy of this advice was particularly marked for the least-advantaged parts of the world, as the Bank's own analysis indicated. American *laissez-faire* liberalism implied that growth would be the rule everywhere once free trade and domestic policy reforms were in place. Yet, this is not what the Bank's 1985 simulations suggest. The high simulation for 1985 through 1990 assumed not only the steady economic growth of industrialized countries, but successful policy reform in the Third World—reduced fiscal deficits, reductions in labor market rigidities, and a steady decline in trade protection. As the report concludes:

> The two simulations outline a continuing bleak outlook for many low-income African countries. In the High simulation, their average per capita income stagnates at present reduced levels; in the Low simulation, there is yet another period of falling per capita incomes.[38]

The promise Reaganomics offers to Africa is illusory.[39]

These World Bank simulations appear to recognize a simple fact explained by those Keynesian analysts from the Third World whose ideas informed the NIEO program. Expecting greater Third World growth as a result of forcing them to produce more for export assumes growing demand for the specific products in which the Third World has a comparative advantage, something that cannot simply be assumed. Demand for raw materials and tropical products often does not grow at the same pace as world demand, therefore their prices fall. Further, boosting export crop production often means making your country more dependent on imported food, which must be paid for with hard currency. Third World countries that rely upon manufactured exports often face growing northern barriers to their goods as their export success increases. In either case, concentrating the bulk of development resources in export promotion can be risky.

Sadly, the capacity that those of us interested in the Third World have to evaluate the fraudulent claims made on the behalf of Reaganomics as a development strategy has been sharply reduced at the same time that the power and authority behind those claims has grown. This has been a consequence, in great part, of the Reagan administration's attack on the links between the UN system and the Third World alliance. The realistic assessment that the World Bank made of Africa's growth prospects is quite the exception among the recent projections made by the Bank, the UNDP, and even UNCTAD. All have tended to paint a rosy picture of the short-term prospects for economic growth throughout the Third World, and all have tended to be wrong.

Sam Cole, the analyst of social forecasting techniques who first pointed out this pattern, cites a number of reasons for the very strong, optimistic bias. At the deepest level these include what he calls the 'institutional imperatives' of the international agencies to: 1) demonstrate that the recession of the early 1980s was not like the Great Depression (something which should no longer be possible, so the institutions' self-justification goes, because we now have forms of multilateral cooperation that prevent it ever happening again), 2) assume that the economies of the developed market countries will grow, and 3) assume that those countries can pull the Third World out of any recession.[40] The final two assumptions are ones that the Third World Keynesian advocate of the NIEO would be as likely to make as the World Bank economist who sees no reason to change the present system.

On top of these institutional imperatives Cole cites the pressure that the United States has exerted on the international organization system since 1981. Fear of displeasing Reagan helped convince even UNCTAD to present unrealistic rosy scenarios about the extended effects of US policies on the Third World similar to the ones about the effects of Reaganomics at home that Reagan's budget director, David Stockman, concocted, and for much the same reason.[41]

The UN system's growing inability to critique Reaganomic prescriptions for the Third World has been matched by the growing silence of scholars about alternatives. Although it is probably the case that few people in the Third World have become completely convinced of any of the questionable Reaganomic claims, few of the western intellectuals who at one time had supported versions of the Third World's NIEO program can be heard denying them. Reagan and his supporters dominated the ideological battle against the Third World within the western bloc. This is especially true in the United States. This victory was not so much the result of governmental policy, but of activities of new private institutions of international civil society.

As we pointed out in our discussion of Reagan's rise to power (chapter 5), the conservative wave of the 1980s was preceded by the increasingly explicit involvement of business-oriented and religiously-oriented groups in American political life. One form that this involvement took was the rise of privately-endowed US-based institutions concerned with supporting a right-wing international relations agenda in contrast to the liberal internationalist agenda of the foundations that had previously given the most financial support to analysts of international relations in all parts of America's post-war empire.

Because the 1970s was so self-evidently a critical period for the post-war system a whole spectrum of associations were formed within international civil society, all with the same purpose: to influence powerful elites to take one direction or another out of the crisis. The most-wide reaching groups, such as the Brandt Commission, tried to influence not only American business leaders and the broad middle class alliance in the United States, but also the European and Japanese bourgeoisie, labor leaders throughout the OECD, and both the entrepreneurial and governmental fractions of the Third World organizational bourgeoisie, and even the organizational elite of the eastern European socialist countries. Some of the wide-reaching and innovative new associations—e.g., the Club of Rome and the Trilateral Commission as well as the Brandt Commission—received immediate, but brief, scholarly and public attention. But it was groups that were the most narrowly Anglo-American and the least-likely to challenge traditional American common-sense solutions to international economic problems that ended up having the greatest impact in the 1980s, institutions like the American Enterprise Institute, the Institute for Contemporary Studies, the Georgetown Center for Strategic and International Studies, the Lehrman Institute, Stanford University's Hoover Institution, and, especially, the Heritage Foundation and its British counterpart, the Adam Smith Foundation.

Private agencies played a role in justifying the American use of force in the world economy, the 'domesticist' policy outlined in the last chapter. Henry Nau's Georgetown Center for Strategic Studies report is exemplary. His basic audience is economists and political scientists from the OECD countries who believe that the increasing interdependence of the world economy requires rational American policy makers to *negotiate* coordinated economic policy with its allies, the view shared (in slightly different ways) by supporters of the New International Economic Order, the Brandt Commission, the Trilateral Commission, the Carter administration, and a great deal of mainstream scholarship in the 1970s.[42] Nau's view that if every government adopted Reaganomic policies, the world economy's problems would solve themselves, never became the single consensus view of economists and political scientists even in the OECD nations. Reagan's years in office saw the development of powerful counterarguments demonstrating that the uncoordinated adoption of domestic monetarist policies will push the world economy as a whole toward stagnation.[43] Nevertheless, the greater power of the domesticist position assured that the counterarguments failed to become an OECD orthodoxy as well, in part, because they lost their private sponsors in international civil society.

What happened to the international economic policy agenda of the Council on Foreign Relations at the beginning of the 1980s is indicative of the trend. Throughout the Carter years the Council had supported an innovative and wide-reaching scholarly initiative, 'The 1980s Project,' aimed at setting the agenda for international economic policy for the thirty or forty years after the crisis of American power in the 1970s, in much the way that a similar Council project in the 1940s had influenced the policy agenda of the first thirty years of American supremacy. The new project's studies tended to emphasize conscious collaboration among national governments; the final study, which concentrated on the institutional structure of international economic collaboration, even proposed the kind of international Keynesian compromise suggested by the Brandt Commission and supported by those New International Economic Order advocates like Mahbub ul Haq who also supported the poverty-elimination and 'basic needs' development goals articulated in the

World Bank in the late 1970s.[44] Despite the impressive scholarly credentials of the project's authors and the innovativeness of some their proposals, the Council's effort did not become that influential in the 1980s. The loss of influence struck at the core purpose of the organization. In retrospect, as he left to become Reagan's ambassador to China, the Council's president, Winston Lord, called the 1970s a decade of 'ambivalence' when the organization did not know what to do about America's diminished power in the world, whereas the 1980s became a decade of 'renewal.'[45] It was also a decade in which the Council's support for intellectuals who advocated multilateral solutions to the world economic crises of the 1970s waned.

Other things contributed to the same trend. The late 1970s and early 1980s were also a period when many international relations scholars, especially in the United States, developed a certain admiration of formal economics, both for its rigor and for the new influence of some of its practitioners. This encouraged the adoption of formal models of international politics through which it was difficult to even frame the questions raised by the NIEO about changing the world-economy's superstructures.[46] Western intellectual attention was also diverted from the problems raised by the Third World because Reagan's election started some of the more moderate philanthropic foundations concerned with international relations (e.g., Carnegie, Ford, Rockefeller) to worry more about US-Soviet relations and the about peace movement, which had been revitalized by America's new bellicosity. Very few sponsors wanted to support the study of north–south cooperation and few even worried about ways to transform international institutions to respond to the global economic crisis. As a result, the Third World's agenda dropped off the agenda of many western scholars.

## Supremacy: summary and conclusion

Gramsci's theory of supremacy lets us understand the challenge the United States faced after 1973, and reasons that its response in the Reagan era was so successful. The first oil crisis gave the Third World an opportunity to change the way in which the international economic system was managed. Western dependence on oil forced the industrial countries to listen to Third World demands and OPEC's price policy revealed potential rifts in the western bloc.

Ultimately, the Third World wasted its brief opportunity. OPEC failed to understand its own potential as a world leader. Its refusal to keep the interests of the poorer, oil-dependent Third World nations in mind and its own internal contradictions undermined OPEC's ability to enforce a program of change based on the NIEO. Beyond playing a fundamental role in the world economy and recognizing the aspirations of its allies through its support of the NIEO, OPEC lacked all the other characteristics Gramsci identifies as essential for the construction of supremacy. When 1979 oil prices were raised to historically high levels, regardless of the consequences to OPEC's allies, the Third World coalition was shaken, but it continued to exist thanks to western disunity and to the illusion of the Third World's poorest countries that the NIEO would be established soon.

Given this internal weakness of the challenger to the western bloc, the policy of force that the US employed starting in 1979 quickly destroyed the economic foundation of the alternative bloc. Political and military force played only a psychological role, reinforcing the new verbal assertiveness of the Reagan administration. The force that really mattered was economic. Monetarism's combined effects of lower export earnings and high interest rates caused a crisis of liquidity which was catastrophic for the Third World. But, even more significantly, the monetarist recession in the industrialized countries and cash-short oil producing nations made oil abundant, thus depriving the Third World of the leverage which gave credibility to the demand for the New International Economic Order.

After the Third World bloc was defeated at the end of 1982, the US was free to apply itself to the task of reconstructing its hegemony within the western bloc, a task completed before the end of Reagan's first term. As Gramsci would expect, hegemony in the western bloc was accompanied by the domination of adversaries, the Third World. The United States not only dominated the Third World by restricting its options indirectly, through the application of force in the world economy, it also worked more directly through international civil society. The western bloc used the leverage of foreign assistance to try to remake third world economies in a *laissez-faire* image. The United States targeted the international institutions (which had been so important in formation of the NIEO consensus within the Third World) and succeeded in making the UN system a more effective conduit of western policy preferences.

The intergovernmental agencies became one of the few power centers in the reconstituted western bloc interested in transforming the policy of applying force to the Third World into one of building consensus. The intergovernmental agencies joined some private institutions in international civil society in the ideological struggle against the many versions of global Keynesianism. The anti-Keynesians used the economic success of a few developing countries under the new global regime as evidence in favor of global Reaganomics. In fact, the success of the east Asian NICs had more to do with their unusual position in the world economy than with any adherence to American common sense formulas for the relationship between business and government. Moreover, even the economic analysis of those agencies most concerned with promoting the program of structural adjustments and economic policy reform reveals that the least-advantaged regions and people within the world economy can expect little in a Reaganomic world. For much of the Third World the new global economic vision of the reconstituted bloc was simply a deception. But this was a fact that both the intergovernmental agencies and those western scholars who had been supportive of the Third World movement have been increasingly less likely to point out due to their defeat in the ideological struggle.

From 1984 through the end of the Reagan administration new economic problems put strains on the western bloc: the over-valuation of the dollar and its subsequent fall, the growing deficit of the US current account and the concomitant rapid increase in foreign ownership of productive assets in the United States, and the continuing instability of world financial markets. The new bases of consensus in the western bloc constantly had to be tended and secured. It is not the task of this book to determine if Reagan's foreign economic policy has secured a lasting hegemony inside the western bloc. In fact, it remains an open question whether the American economic policies used to re-establish its world supremacy have increased or undermined its capacity to maintain its hegemony inside the western bloc in the long run. Nevertheless, in the short run, this task was simplified because the Third World as an independent actor had disappeared from the world scene and it is uncertain if it will ever reappear as an actor whose interests and aspirations must be considered by any supreme power.

## Beyond American common sense

Given the defeat of the Third World and the reconstruction of American supremacy accomplished by the end of Reagan's first term, the American public may have reason to believe that its common sense has passed the test; it has proven to be an excellent guide for policy within the 'great commercial empire' that the United States finally succeeded in constructing after the second world war.

Or has it? It could be argued that Reagan failed to follow some common sense lessons in his reconstruction of American supremacy. In its relations with the Third World, his administration has become less concerned with, and less dependent upon, economic science, even (or, perhaps, especially) of the experimental, empirical kind. (The kind of economics that identifies policies that work in one place and not in others and tries to explain why.) And in relations with other industrialized countries the administration has relied less and less upon the religious sources of its original vision, retaining its view of America's special destiny, of course, but becoming quite a bit less of the crusader, quite a bit more willing to deal with the 'evil' Soviets and even quite accommodating to its 'decadent' allies. Liberalism, the traditional core ideology of America's ruling elite and traditional guide for the country's foreign policy has come to the fore again.

Does Reagan's success, therefore, imply that somehow his economic liberalism represents what Gramsci would call 'good sense,' the rational and ethical guide for social action that is supposed to come from the interaction between the popular masses and their organic intellectuals? On a global level, is Reagan the quintessence of the Gramscian intellectual?

We do not think so, and our reasons for rejecting this conclusion allow us to close by reemphasizing one of Gramsci's most important themes: We cannot measure the success of a political movement simply by its ability to dominate and we cannot measure the veracity of ideas simply by the success of those who advocate them. The ideas motivating action must be internally consistent and correspond to reality to be what Gramsci calls 'good sense.'

American common sense, like 'common sense' anywhere, cannot be 'good sense' simply because it is internally contradictory. Gramsci would expect, as we do, that those internal contradictions—for example, the contradiction between a faith in applied science that makes Americans want to anticipate and plan for their collective future and the liberal urge to minimize the institutions which would make that possible—will remain important; they will become fault lines along which the leadership of America's reconstituted historical bloc is likely to crack under new, perhaps not-yet-foreseeable, social pressures.

Similarly, global Reaganomics cannot be simply 'good sense' because of the internal contradictions in this (almost purely liberal) vision, the contradictions between its supply-side and monetarist bases. In addition, there is the contradiction between the advice it offers the Third World and the actual economic policies it sanctions in the US. Finally, there is the evidence that even economists sympathetic to Reagan have amassed which suggests that this policy mix will not work as a development strategy in much of the Third World. To argue that it is would be to perpetrate a fraud.

Ultimately, actual 'good sense' could not be a guide for domination based on fraud, although it would characterize ethical hegemony, supremacy based upon unconstrained consensus, leadership that takes into account the interests and fulfills the aspirations of the led. At the most, only America's reconstituted leadership of the western bloc can be characterized in this way; more broadly, American supremacy entails domination both of the Third World and of the disadvantaged within the developed market countries. The most simple indicators tell the story: the restoration of economic growth in the industrialized world in the 1980s has been accompanied by stagnation in the Third World and chronic unemployment at home. The quest for American supremacy may (for a time) be complete, but the quest for a world economy based on good sense remains.

## Notes

1. J. W. Burton, A. J. R. Groom, C. R. Mitchell, and A. V. S. De Rueck, *The Study of World Society: A London Perspective* (Pittsburgh: International Studies Association, 1974).
2. Hedley Bull, ed. *System of States* (Leicester: Leicester University Press, 1977).
3. *Transnational Relations in World Politics* (Cambridge, MA: Harvard University Press, 1972).

4. A theme developed by Terry Nardin, *Law, Morality, and the Relations of States* (Princeton: Princeton University Press, 1983).
5. On the importance of activating potential shared interests through cooperation see Robert O. Keohane, *After Hegemony* (Princeton: Princeton University Press, 1984), 50–5.
6. In many agencies there is little oversight of day-to-day activities by delegates of nation-state members. The agencies' activities can be both quasi-governmental and relatively autonomous.
7. Unfortunately for the backers of these policies, the domestic foundation for them did not exist. In fact, the public light shed upon the 'Iran-Contra affair' emboldened Congress in early 1988 to end their military backing of the administration's anti-government allies in Nicaragua even though the replacement of Nicaragua's government had been high administration priority throughout its tenure.See Linda B. Miller's analysis in, 'Innocence Abroad? Congress, the President, and Foreign Policy,' *The World Today*, 43 (1987): 62–5.
8. Gramsci might consider the last point simply a bold statement of a conscious policy of coopting the intellectuals of adversary social groups in the world economy.
9. *Congressional Presentation Fiscal Year 1985*, main volume (Washington: Agency for International Development), 4–5.
10. Enrico Augelli, 'Policy Dialogue in the American Conception' (Cambridge, MA: Harvard University Center for International Affairs, 1985), 2.
11. Ibid., 2–6.
12. *Accelerated Development in Sub-Saharan Africa* (Washington: World Bank, 1981).
13. Enrico Augelli, 'Il "dialogo sulle politche" secondo Washington,' *Politica Internationale* 14 (1986): 108–11.
14. OECD press release PRESS/A (83) 61, 29 November 1983.
15. 'The IMF and Africa in the 1980s,' *Canadian Journal of African Studies*, 17 (1983): 3–30.
16. Yves Beigbeder, *Management Problems in International Organizations: Reform or Decline?* (London: Frances Pinter, 1987), 12.
17. United States Department of Treasury, *United States Participation in the Multilateral Development Banks in the 1980s* (Washington: US Government Printing Office, 1982).
18. See the analysis in Roger A. Coate, *Reform Politics in UNESCO: Multilateralism at Bay?* (Boulder, CO: Lynne Reinner, forthcoming). Coate served on the staff of the commission set up to evaluate UNESCO's progress toward US goals.
19. Alexander Nicoll, 'IDB Board Seeks End to Deadlock Over Votes,' *Financial Times*, 23 June 1987, 4.
20. See the National Advisory Council on International Monetary and Financial Policies' special reports on, *The Proposed Increase in the Resources of the International Monetary Fund* (Washington: 1983), *The Proposed Replenishment of the Resources of the International Development Association* (Washington, 1984), and *The Selective Capital Increase of the International Bank for Reconstruction and Development* (Washington, 1985).
21. Independent Commission on International Development Issues, *North-South: A Programme for Survival* (Cambridge, MA: MIT Press, 1980).

22. Secretaria de Relationes Exteriores, *Cancun 1981: Framework, Debate, and Conclusions of the Meeting on International Cooperation and Development* (Mexico City: 1982).
23. On the new institutions see Thomas Byrne Edsall, *The New Politics of Inequality* (New York: W. W. Norton, 1984), 117–21.
24. W. Scott Thompson, *The Third World: Premises of U.S. Policy*, revised ed. (Los Angeles: Institute for Contemporary Studies, 1983).
25. *Ghana's Foreign Policy 1957–1966: Diplomacy, Ideology, and the New State* (Princeton: Princeton University Press, 1969).
26. 'Third World Voting Patterns at the U.N.,' in Thompson, 141.
27. 'The Political Origins of the NIEO,' in Thompson, 224–25.
28. Ibid., 229–30.
29. 'The Third World Revisited,'in Thompson, 9.
30. Ibid., 14.
31. 'The Third World and the Conflict of Ideologies,' in Thompson, 21.
32. Bruce R. Bartlett, *Reaganomics—Supply-Side Economics in Action* (New York: Quill, 1982), 198.
33. In the 1960s and 1970s most mainstream economists held that Africa's farming sector had to be the cash cow to fund industrial development. Critics on the left charged that this policy abused the rural poor. See, e.g. Peter Osei-Kwame and Craig N. Murphy, 'The Case for Increasing Cocoa Producer Prices in Ghana,' *The Legon Observer*, 8 (1973): 466–73.
34. *Economic Report of the President 1984*, 73.
35. Ibid., 74–5.
36. Ibid., 76. And see Nigel Harris, *The End of the Third World: The Newly Industrializing Countries and the Decline of an Ideology* (Harmondsworth: Penguin, 1987), esp. 145–69 on the expanding state in the NICs.
37. *Toward Sustained Development in Sub-Saharan Africa—A Joint Program of Action* (Washington: World Bank, 1984), 1.
38. *World Development Report 1985*, 10.
39. C.f., Sayre P. Schatz, 'Laissez-Faireism for Africa,' *Journal of Modern African Studies*, 25 (1987): 129–38.
40. 'World Economic Forecasts and the Intergovernmental Agencies,' *International Studies Quarterly*, 31 (1987): 379.
41. Ibid., 380.
42. *International Reaganomics: A Domesticist Approach to World Economy* (Washington: Georgetown Center for Strategic and International Studies, 1981).
43. See Michael Stewart, *The Age of Interdependence: Economic Policy in a Shrinking World* (Cambridge, MA: MIT Press, 1983).
44. Miriam Camps and Catherine Gwin, *Collective Management: The Reform of Global Economic Organizations* (New York: McGraw-Hill).
45. Council on Foreign Relations, *Annual Report 1984–85*, 16–17.
46. See Richard K. Ashley, 'The Poverty of Neorealism,' *International Organization* 38 (1984): 259–60.

# Index